THUCYDIDES

Also by Donald Kagan

The Peloponnesian War

The Heritage of World Civilizations
(with Albert M. Craig, William A. Graham,
Steven Ozment, and Frank M. Turner)

The Western Heritage
(with Steven Ozment and Frank M. Turner)

While America Sleeps
(with Frederick W. Kagan)

On the Origins of War and the Preservation of Peace

Pericles of Athens and the Birth of Democracy

The Fall of the Athenian Empire

The Peace of Nicias and the Sicilian Expedition

The End of the Roman Empire: Decline or Transformation? (ed.)

The Archidamian War

The Outbreak of the Peloponnesian War

Great Issues in Western Civilization, vols. I and II
(ed., with L. P. Williams and Brian Tiernery)

Problems in Ancient History, vols. I and II (ed.)

Sources in Greek Political Thought (ed.)

*The Great Dialogue: A History of Greek Political Thought
from Homer to Polybius*

THUCYDIDES

THE REINVENTION
OF HISTORY

DONALD KAGAN

VIKING

VIKING
Published by the Penguin Group
Penguin Group (USA) Inc., 375 Hudson Street,
New York, New York 10014, U.S.A.
Penguin Group (Canada), 90 Eglinton Avenue East, Suite 700, Toronto,
Ontario, Canada M4P 2Y3 (a division of Pearson Penguin Canada Inc.)
Penguin Books Ltd, 80 Strand, London WC2R 0RL, England
Penguin Ireland, 25 St. Stephen's Green, Dublin 2, Ireland
(a division of Penguin Books Ltd)
Penguin Books Australia Ltd, 250 Camberwell Road, Camberwell,
Victoria 3124, Australia (a division of Pearson Australia Group Pty Ltd)
Penguin Books India Pvt Ltd, 11 Community Centre,
Panchsheel Park, New Delhi–110 017, India
Penguin Group (NZ), 67 Apollo Drive, Rosedale, North Shore 0632,
New Zealand (a division of Pearson New Zealand Ltd)
Penguin Books (South Africa) (Pty) Ltd, 24 Sturdee Avenue,
Rosebank, Johannesburg 2196, South Africa

Penguin Books Ltd, Registered Offices: 80 Strand, London WC2R 0RL, England

First published in 2009 by Viking Penguin, a member of Penguin Group (USA) Inc.

1 3 5 7 9 10 8 6 4 2

Copyright © Donald Kagan, 2009
All rights reserved

Maps by Jeffrey L. Ward

LIBRARY OF CONGRESS CATALOGING IN PUBLICATION DATA
Kagan, Donald.
Thucydides : the reinvention of history / by Donald Kagan.
p. cm.
Includes bibliographical references and index.
ISBN 978-0-670-02129-1
1. Thucydides. History of the Peloponnesian War. 2. Greece—History—
Peloponnesian War, 431–404 B.C.—Historiography. 3. Greece—Intellectual
life—To 146 B.C. 4. Greece—Historiography. I. Title.
DF229.T6K28 2009
938'.05—dc22   2009008368

Printed in the United States of America
Set in Dante
Designed by Francesca Belanger

To the memory of Adam Parry,
a friend and a great Thucydidean scholar

CONTENTS

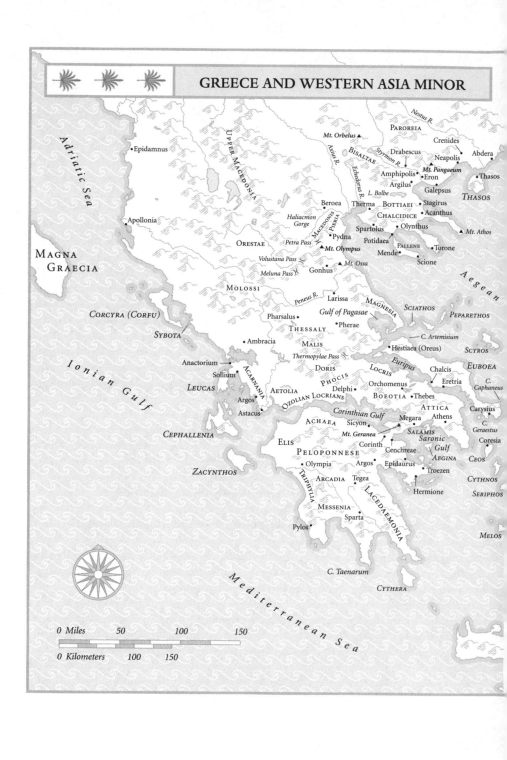

GREECE AND WESTERN ASIA MINOR

Adriatic Sea

Epidamnus

UPPER MACEDONIA

Nestus R.

PAROREIA

Mt. Orbelus ▲

Axios R.

Echedorus R.

BISALTAE

Strymon R.

Drabescus

Crenides

Neapolis

Abdera

Amphipolis

Mt. Pangaeum

Eion

Thasos

Argilus

Galepsus

THASOS

Apollonia

Beroea

Therma

L. Bolbe

BOTTIAEI

Stagirus

Haliacmon
Gorge

MACEDONIS

PIERIA

CHALCIDICE

Acanthus

MAGNA
GRAECIA

ORESTAE

Pydna

Petra Pass

Spartolus

Olynthus

Mt. Athos ▲

Potidaea

Mt. Olympus

PALLENE

Torone

Volustana Pass

Mende

Scione

MOLOSSI

Meluna Pass

Gonhus

▲ Mt. Ossa

Aegean

CORCYRA (CORFU)

Peneus R.

Larissa

MAGNESIA

SCIATHOS

PEPARETHOS

Pharsalus

Gulf of Pagasae

THESSALY

Pherae

SYBOTA

Ambracia

MALIS

C. Artemisium

Anactorium

Thermopylae Pass

DORIS

Hestiaea (Oreus)

SCYROS

Sollium

ACARNANIA

AETOLIA

PHOCIS

LOCRIS

Euripus

Chalcis

EUBOEA

LEUCAS

Delphi

Orchomenus

Eretria

C.
Caphaneus

Argos

OZOLIAN LOCRIANS

BOEOTIA

Thebes

Astacus

Corinthian Gulf

ATTICA

Carysius

CEPHALLENIA

ACHAEA

Sicyon

Megara

Athens

C.
Geraestus

Mt. Geranea

SALAMIS

Coresia

I o n i a n   G u l f

ELIS

Corinth

Cenchreae

*Saronic
Gulf*

AEGINA

CEOS

PELOPONNESE

Olympia

Argos

Epidaurus

Troezen

ZACYNTHOS

TRIPHYLIA

ARCADIA

Tegea

Hermione

CYTHNOS

LACEDAEMONIA

SERIPHOS

MESSENIA

Sparta

Pylos

MELOS

C. Taenarum

CYTHERA

0 Miles   50   100   150

0 Kilometers   100   150

M e d i t e r r a n e a n   S e a

Black Sea

Hebrus R.

T H R A C E

▲ *Mt. Rhodope*

Propontis

Maronea •
• Doriscus

Tyrodiza •

Aenus •

• Cyzicus

C. Sarpedon   Melas Bay   • Cardia

CHERSONESE   Lampascus •

SAMOTHRACE   Sestus •   • Abydus

IMBROS   Elaeus •

Sigeum • • Troy   *Scamander R.*

LEMNOS   • Colonae   Antandrus •

▲ *Mt. Ida*

• Adramyttium

Caicus R.

Mytilene •

LESBOS

Hermus R.

Phocaea •   • Sardis

Sea

Maeander R.

CHIOS   • Erythrae

• Teos   Lebedus •

Buthia •

Ephesus •

SAMOS   •— Magnesia

• Priene

ANDROS   Miletus •—   • Teichiussa

TENOS   CARIA

MYCONOS

DELOS   LEROS •   Pheselis •

PAROS •   LYCIA

• Naxos   Cos •

SIPHNOS •   *Chelidonian Is.*

THERA •   RHODES

CARPATHOS

Mediterranean Sea

CRETE

© 2003 Jeffrey L. Ward

Introduction

THE STUDY OF THUCYDIDES and his famous *History of the Peloponnesian War* has never been as intense, as widespread, or as influential as it is in our time. Thucydides claimed that his work was "a possession forever" that was meant to be useful to "such men as might wish to see clearly what has happened and what will happen again, in all human probability, in the same or a similar way" (1.22.4).[1] More than twenty-four hundred years later political leaders and students of politics approach it in just that manner.

A great wave of interest in Thucydides' work arose with the coming of the cold war, when people saw the long struggle between Athens and Sparta as strikingly similar to the contest between the United States and its NATO allies and the Soviet Union and its Warsaw Pact satellites. In 1947 the American Secretary of State George C. Marshall said: "I doubt seriously whether a man can think with full wisdom and with deep convictions regarding certain of the basic international issues today who has not at least reviewed in his mind the period of the Peloponnesian War and the Fall of Athens."[2] Ever since, Thucydides' *History* has had a strong and continuing influence on those who think about international relations and war.

The collapse of the Soviet Union and the end of its confrontation with the United States has not diminished the interest in Thucydides or the conviction that his work can illuminate our understanding of politics and foreign policy. Devotees of the "realist" or "neorealist" schools of international relations regard Thucydides as their founder. Thousands of college students read his work each year. His *History* is a staple at the military academies and the war colleges, and no course in foreign relations or the history of warfare is likely to be without it.

What Thucydides called "the war between the Peloponnesians and the Athenians" and we call the Peloponnesian War broke out in 431.[3] The Spartans were then the head of the Peloponnesian League and the leading power in Greece. The states that had joined in the Greek coalition to resist the Persian invasion of 480–479 had chosen them to command their forces on land and sea. Just before the Persian War, however, the Athenians had built a great new fleet, already the greatest in Greek history. That navy was the core and backbone of the Greek fleet that crushed the Persian fleet at the battle of Salamis in 480 and then again at Mycale in the following year. These victories had raised Athens to a level of prestige that challenged Sparta's hegemony even after the Spartans led the Greeks to victory in the decisive land battle at Plataea at the same time as Mycale.

When the Persians fled from Europe the Spartans showed no interest in liberating the Greek cities in and around the Aegean Sea still under Persian rule or in preserving the freedom of those who had rebelled. A voluntary alliance of Greek states accordingly invited Athens to take the lead in continuing the war of liberation and vengeance against Persia. "The Athenians and their allies" (modern scholars call this alliance the Delian League) gradually became an empire under Athenian command functioning chiefly for the advantage of Athens. Over the years almost all the members gave up their own fleets and chose to make a money payment into the common treasury instead of contributing their own ships and men. The Athenians used the money to increase the size of their own force, and to pay the rowers to stay at their oars for eight months each year, so that the Athenian navy became by far the biggest and best Greek fleet ever known. On the eve of the Peloponnesian War only two islands, Lesbos and Chios, of some 150 members of the league had their own fleets and enjoyed relative autonomy, although even they were unlikely to defy Athenian orders.

As the Delian League grew in size and power, some Spartans became jealous, suspicious, and fearful of the Athenian challenge to their supremacy. Quarrels in the 460s led to the First Peloponnesian War, which started about 460 and lasted, sporadically, until 445. It came to an end with the Thirty Years' Peace, in which each side recognized the hegemony of the other in its own sphere, and each side agreed to submit any future disagreements to binding arbitration.

The peace lasted for well over a decade, but a series of conflicts between Athens, on the one hand, and Sparta and several of its allies, on the other, ultimately led to the great war. In the winter of 432/1 Sparta's ally Thebes attacked Athens' ally Plataea. In the spring a large Peloponnesian army invaded Attica and cut down some of the Athenians' grain, grapevines, and olive trees, as well as destroying some of their farmhouses and country homes. This was the first of annual devastations carried on in the early years of the Ten Years' War, which the ancients called the Archidamian War after the Spartan king who led the first invasions.

Pericles, leader of Athens, had opted for a strategy of avoiding land battles, launching commando raids around the Peloponnesus, and waiting until the Spartans realized that they had no winning strategy of their own, a conclusion they would reach within a year, or two, or three, he thought. His most difficult job was to restrain the many Athenians who wanted to go out and fight. In 430, however, a terrible plague broke out, causing fearful physical, social, and psychological disasters. Pericles' political opponents convinced the Athenians to ask the Spartans for peace, and to remove Pericles from office and punish him with a heavy fine. But the enemy refused any acceptable terms, and the war went on. With peace no longer an option, the Athenians reelected Pericles and resumed his policy. He himself contracted the plague and, in the fall of 429, he died.

In 428 Athens' situation grew worse. The major city on the island of Lesbos, Mytilene, rebelled against the Athenians, raising the fear of a general revolt in the empire. The Athenians' treasury was by now nearly depleted, so for the first time they introduced a direct tax on the citizens to pay for the immediate cost of the war. It took until the following summer to crush the rebellion. In their panic and fury the Athenian assembly voted to kill all the men of Mytilene and sell its women and children into slavery. The Athenians changed their minds overnight and decided to kill only the men thought to be the instigators of the rebellion. These turned out to be about one thousand in number, perhaps a tenth of the male population. The Spartans soon followed suit for such atrocities by killing all that was left of the garrison at Plataea upon their surrender.

After Pericles' death, no dominant leader emerged to hold the Athenians to a consistent policy. Two factions vied for influence: one, led by Nicias, wanted to continue the defensive posture, while the other, led by Cleon, preferred a more aggressive strategy. In 425 the latter faction was able to win a victory at Pylos that changed the course of the war. Four hundred Spartans surrendered after the battle, and Sparta offered peace at once to get them back. The great victory and the prestige it brought Athens made it safe to raise the imperial tribute, without which Athens could not continue to fight. The Athenians, however, wanted to remain on the offensive, for the Spartan peace offer gave no adequate guarantee of Athenian security.

In 424 the Athenians adopted a more aggressive policy and sought to make Athens safe by conquering Megara and Boeotia. Both attempts failed, and defeat helped discredit the combative faction, leading to a truce in 423. Meanwhile, Sparta's ablest general, Brasidas, took a small army to Thrace and Macedonia and captured Amphipolis, the most important Athenian colony in the region. Thucydides was in charge of the Athenian fleet in those waters and was held responsible for the city's loss. He was exiled and was thereby given the time and opportunity to write his famous history of the Great Peloponnesian War. In 422 Cleon led an expedition to undo the work of Brasidas. At Amphipolis, both he and Brasidas died in battle. The removal of these two leaders of the aggressive factions in their respective cities paved the way for the Peace of Nicias, named for its chief negotiator, which was ratified in the spring of 421.

The peace, officially intended to last fifty years and, with a few exceptions, to guarantee the status quo, was in fact fragile. Neither side carried out all its commitments, and several of Sparta's allies refused ratification. In 415 Alcibiades persuaded the Athenians to attack Sicily to bring it under Athenian control. This ambitious and unnecessary undertaking ended in disaster in 413 when the entire expedition was destroyed. The Athenians lost some two hundred ships, about forty-five hundred of their own men, and almost ten times as many allies. The defeat undermined Athens' prestige, reduced its power, provoked rebellions, and brought the wealth and power of Persia into the war on Sparta's side. Remarkably, the Athenians continued fighting despite the disaster, surviving a brief oligarchic coup in 411 and winning several important victories at sea as the war shifted to the Aegean. As their allies rebelled, however, and Persia paid for fleets to sustain them, Athenian financial resources shrank and finally disappeared. When its fleet was caught napping and was destroyed at Aegospotami in 405 Athens could not build another. The Spartans, under Lysander, a clever and ambitious general who was responsible for obtaining the Persian support, cut off the food supply through the Hellespont and starved the Athenians into submission. In 404 they surrendered unconditionally; they dismantled the city walls, gave up their fleet, and lost their empire. Because Thucydides never finished his *History*, it was left chiefly to Xenophon to describe the last years of the war and the Athenian surrender: "Lysander sailed into Piraeus, the exiles returned, and the Peloponnesians with great enthusiasm began to tear down the walls to the music of flute girls, thinking that this day was the beginning of freedom for Greece."[4]

Thucydides was not the first to write history. The Greeks believed that Homer's epic poems, the *Iliad* and *Odyssey*, though composed in poetic meter and filled with divine and mythological characters, nevertheless reported real events and people of the distant past. Even the hard-headed Thucydides used them as evidence for the early history of the Greeks. In the sixth century, however, a new way of thinking arose among the Greek cities of Ionia on the western coast of Asia Minor and especially Miletus. It is not too much to say that the new approach substituted rational, even scientific thought for myth as a means of understanding and explaining the world and the universe.

This intellectual revolution took place between the time of the poet Hesiod, who described much of Greek mythology about 700, and that of Hecataeus of Miletus, about two centuries later. Hecataeus, unlike earlier Milesian inquirers who speculated about philosophical-scientific questions like the nature and composition of the universe, concerned himself with more tangible matters. He produced the first map of which we know, a "description of the earth." He also investigated the past experience of human beings in the form of *Genealogies,* in which he brought reason to bear on the heroic myths of the past. He applied critical judgment to the stories of noble families who claimed descent from the gods. He began his *Genealogies* with a challenge to tradition: "I Hecataeus will say what I think to be the truth; the stories of the Greeks are many and ridiculous." That did not lead to his either making up whatever story he liked or despairing of finding the truth, but rather to questioning and research and the reasoned quest for accurate knowledge and understanding—that is, toward history.

It is not Hecataeus, however, whom we call the father of history but Herodotus, born in Halicarnassus, a Greek city on the same Aegean shore of Asia Minor as Miletus, about 484, between the battle of Marathon in 490 and the great Persian invasion of 480. He died about 425, several years after the start of the Peloponnesian War. Herodotus did not write about his own times like Thucydides but relied chiefly on what he was told about earlier times. But while Hecataeus appears to have confined himself to the comparison and rational criticism of what was thought to be known, Herodotus, in his effort to preserve valuable memories of great deeds of the past, undertook new inquiries, even traveling to foreign countries to gather relevant evidence. His attempts both to preserve traditions and to discover new facts demanded a novel method that required not only the rational weighing of likelihoods but also the evaluation of the reliability of evidence.

Herodotus, nevertheless, did not enjoy a reputation for accuracy, truthfulness, and objectivity among ancient writers. They pointed to factual inaccuracies, with many calling him a liar outright, while Plutarch wrote an essay on his "malignity," charging him with a lack of patriotism and a prejudice in favor of Athens. The "father of history," in fact, is said to have read his work in public performances, like epic poetry, for the delight of his audiences. With his meandering style full of discursive side trips into the customs and habits of various peoples, and his serious consideration of the causal role of the gods in human affairs, he entertained his listeners, but he did not become the model for what was considered to be the best historical writing in the ancient world.

It was Thucydides, rather, who most influenced the leading ancient writers of history. He approached the subject in a thoroughly different manner. Without directly naming the historian of the Persian Wars, Thucydides corrected some of Herodotus' factual errors, dismissing him as one who wrote "a prize-essay to be heard for the moment" compared to his own more serious effort, which was meant to be a "possession for all time" (1.22.4).

Who was this Thucydides, and what was the nature of his work that continues to interest and influence us more than twenty-four hundred years after its creation? He was an Athenian aristocrat of the bluest blood and considerable wealth who came of age at the height of the greatness of Periclean Athens. Born between 460 and 455, he was only in his twenties when the great Peloponnesian War broke out, and he died not many years after the end of the war, his great work unfinished. His father, Olorus, bore not an Athenian but a Thracian name. It was the same name as the grandfather of Cimon, the great general and statesman who dominated Athenian public life in the two decades after the Persian invasion. Thucydides was almost surely related to Cimon and also to another Thucydides, the son of Melesias, who was the most dangerous political opponent of Pericles in the 440s. As one scholar has put it, "born in the anti-Pericles opposition, he followed Pericles with a convert's zeal."[5]

Thucydides is careful to let us know that he was old enough to appreciate the gravity of his task: "I lived through the whole war, being of an age to understand the events, and I applied my mind to them so as to see them accurately" (5.26.5). He was in Athens from the start of the war until his exile in 424 and, no doubt took part in some of the campaigns of those years and contracted the great plague that struck Athens between 430 and 427. He was lucky to survive, given that the contagion killed about a third of the population, and used his own experience to give a detailed account of its symptoms and its devastating effects, although precisely what disease it was remains a mystery. In 424 he was elected general, one of ten men who served as the foremost military and political leaders in Athens. He commanded the naval force in the Thracian area, whose chief city was the Athenian colony of Amphipolis, a place of great economic and strategic importance. He may have been given that assignment because of his connections in the area: he tells us that he controlled gold mines there and "had great influence among the leading men" of the region (4.105.1). When the brilliant Spartan general Brasidas took the city by surprise the Athenians held Thucydides responsible for its defeat and convicted him of treason, sending him off to exile for the twenty years that remained in the war. This great misfortune had its advantages, especially for us, his readers, because it allowed him "to know what was being done on both sides, especially the Peloponnesian, because of my exile, and this leisure permitted me to get a better understanding of the course of events" (5.26.5–6).

Grasping the ideas of Thucydides in *The Peloponnesian War* is not easy. He did not write a philosophical or political treatise in which he presented his views and the arguments for them, but rather a history, aiming at the highest possible objectivity, clinging assiduously to his subject, and avoiding tangents almost entirely. He does make important direct statements of his opinion, and these form the soundest basis for understanding his thought. Some of them deal with his method of inquiry, and others with his view of the general processes of political life.

In considering the ideas embodied in his work it is useful and interesting to compare Thucydides with his great predecessor Herodotus. The remarkable difference in the minds of the two historians is immediately striking. In contrast with Herodotus, whose rationalism does not challenge his traditional piety, Thucydides seems to have taken a spectacular leap into modernity. He neither accepted nor rationalized myths but ignored them or analyzed them with a cold eye. He did not seek explanations for human behavior in the will of the gods nor, sometimes, even in the will of individuals, but in a general analysis of the behavior of men in society. Thucydides, however, was not a sport who miraculously and inexplicably appeared on the scene. He represented the culmination of a growth of intellectual forces in the fifth century that came to exert an important influence on Greek life and which together are sometimes called "the Greek enlightenment."

Two elements of that enlightenment seem to have affected the thought of Thucydides with particular force: the Sophistic movement and the school of medical writers surrounding Hippocrates of Cos. In their different ways each of these was a branch of the tree of rational investigation of the universe that took root in the Greek cities of Asia Minor in the sixth century. Thales, Anaximander, Anaximenes, and their successors differed from previous speculators on the nature of the world and its origin in that their theories were entirely naturalistic. Thales, for instance, proposed an account of the origins of the earth in which everything developed naturally, without divine intervention, out of primeval water, in a process like the silting up of the Nile.

This tradition of naturalistic theorizing gave birth to both science and philosophy. These disciplines were indistinguishable in their early conceptions of the physical world, but by the fifth century speculation about the physical universe seemed to have come as far as it could. What remained alive and potent was the spirit of inquiry in the naturalistic vein, and the sense of the new age was that the proper study of man was man. The Sophists took a deep interest in the role of man in society; the Hippocratic school of medicine concerned itself with the investigation of his physical well-being. Both continued to avoid nonrational or supernatural explanations and to seek an understanding of man with reference only to his own nature.

It is in this respect that the various Sophists, otherwise very different from one another in doctrine and method, may be seen to form a unified point of view. They all had in common a skepticism towards tradition, whether it be religious, political, or social, and a desire to discover the ways of nature, particularly human nature. Their skepticism is the best-known element of their thought, and their agnostic approach to the gods was especially notorious to their contemporaries. Already in the sixth century Xenophanes of Colophon had expressed agnostic tendencies inherent in his Ionian predecessors when he pointed out that men think that the gods are born, have clothes, voices, and bodies like themselves; if oxen, horses, and lions had hands and could paint like men, he argued, they would likewise paint gods in their own image: the oxen would draw gods like oxen and the horses, like horses. Negroes believed in flat-nosed, black-faced gods, and the Thracians in gods with blue eyes and red hair.[6] A similar attitude was expressed more succinctly by Protagoras: "About the gods I can have no knowledge either that they are or that they are not or what is their nature. For many things prevent our knowing: the uncertainty of the matter and the fact that the life of man is short."[7] Protagoras does not deny the existence of the gods, but is clear that they are surrounded by such uncertainty as to make any explanation of events dependent upon them quite absurd.

This same skeptical rationalism is a basic component of the Hippocratic thought.[8] One of the Hippocratics, for instance, wrote of the mysterious disease epilepsy: "It seems to me that the disease is no more divine than any other. It has a natural cause, just as other diseases have. Men think it divine merely because they do not understand it. But if they called everything divine which they do not understand, why, there would be no end of divine things."[9] The Hippocratics, moreover, were feeling their way to a clearer conception of the scientific method. One writer, discussing the treatment of internal ailments, deals with the correct use of inference where the facts are not to be apprehended by the senses:

Without doubt no man who sees only with his eyes can know anything of what has been here described. It is for this reason that I have called these points obscure, even as they have been judged to be by the art. Their obscurity, however, does not mean that they are beyond our mastery but as far as is possible they have been mastered, possibility limited only by the capacity of the sick to be examined and of researchers to conduct research. More pains, in fact, and quite as much time, are required to know them as if they were seen by the eyes; for what escapes the eyesight is mastered by the eye of mind, and the sufferings of patients due to their not being quickly observed are the fault, not of the medical attendant, but of the nature of the patient and of the disease. *The attendant in fact, as he could neither see the trouble with his eyes nor learn it with his ears, tried to track it by reasoning.*[10]

The field of Thucydides' investigations was not the nature of the physical universe nor the physical nature of man, but the society of man living in the *polis*. Politics in the largest sense—the search for an understanding of the behavior of man in society—was his surpassing interest. In this he differed from physical theorists, Sophists, and Hippocratics, but their ideas influenced and helped shape his own thought. Like all of them he began with the observation of phenomena and proceeded to discern and describe the rational patterns that emerged from them. His data were the historical actions of men in the past, whether remote or very recent. When sufficiently repeated and properly grasped, these gave rise to general rules of human behavior that might prove useful to men in the future. The student of social behavior—that is, the historian—has a dual responsibility: first to seek out with diligence and accuracy the truth of what has taken place, and then to interpret the events with wisdom and understanding, in this way making a permanent contribution. To establish the facts (*ta erga*) was of vital importance but was ultimately subordinate to the formulation of interpretations (*logoi*) that emerged from them. To some it appears that these interpretations attempt for the study of human society what the Hippocratics were trying to do for medicine: just as in medicine certain formulations were needed if medical science was to escape from mere empiricism, a comparable system of such classifications would raise history from the level of mere chronicle, a form that was characteristic of the annalists. Assessing a set of symptoms to arrive at a general description of a malady and penetrating, if then possible, to its true classification is the procedure that Hippocrates advocates, which he designates by the words *semeiology* and *prognosis*. It was this very process that Thucydides sought to apply to history, which thus for him becomes the semeiology and prognosis of human life.[11]

Thucydides was both less and more than a scientist of any particular discipline, but no one reading the historian's account of the great plague in Athens that broke out in 430 can fail to acknowledge his debt to the Hippocratics. As he himself was infected with the disease, he gives a detailed and precise description of its symptoms and progress so that, "perhaps it may be recognized by the student, if it should break out again" (2.48.3). The clear implication is that an accurate account could be used in the future to help arrest the progress of the disease, or at least to prepare to deal with its symptoms.

But because Thucydides is a student of society, his description of the plague includes more than just its physical consequences. For him the effect of so great a shock on the morale of a society was of greater interest. As death and desperation weakened the moral fiber of the community, the normal religious and legal restraints on men's actions ceased to operate, and the Athenians yielded to a lawless hedonism that may have been as damaging as the physical suffering itself. A historical account of the plague is therefore not merely a useful and humane digression but a necessary component of the *erga* that will help account for the outcome of the war.

Thucydides assumes the role of diagnostician of the ills of society again in his account of the civil war that broke out at Corcyra in 428, an event that was an excellent paradigm of class warfare, encouraged by and intensified by wartime conditions. Oligarchs attempted to bring in the aid of the Peloponnesians; the reigning democrats used Athenian help to destroy their enemies and entrench themselves in power. Fear and hatred drove both sides to increasingly extreme measures, as considerations of party gave way to personal vendetta. Thucydides describes the events at Corcyra in careful detail because he means them to serve as a model for similar disturbances in the future: "Later on, one may say, the whole Hellenic world was convulsed; struggles being everywhere made by the popular chiefs to bring in the Athenians, and by the oligarchs to introduce the Lacedaemonians" (3.82.1).

But the careful description and analysis of the revolution at Corcyra does not illuminate only the future course of the Peloponnesian War. A proper understanding of these events can foster a better comprehension of all human history. The revolutions that disturbed Greece during the war brought with them terrible calamities, "such as have occurred and always will occur, as long as the nature of mankind remains the same; though in a severer or milder form, and varying in their symptoms, according to the variety of the particular cases" (3.82.2).

To this examination and analysis of politics that he had invented Thucydides brought the tools supplied by the Sophists as well as those of the Hippocratics. One of the characteristic ideas of the Sophistic movement was the distinction it drew between two elements that determine man's behavior in society: *physis* (nature) and *nomos* (custom or law). In the Sophists' view *physis* represents the innate inclination of man to satisfy his wants, while *nomos* is the artificial device by which society protects itself against the antisocial drives of man's *physis*. Greek society rested on the common acceptance of *nomos* as sacred, and the radicalism of the Sophists lay in large measure in their skeptical attitude towards it. Thucydides did not adopt the extreme iconoclasm of some Sophists, but he did find the distinction between *physis* and *nomos* a useful tool in his own thinking. How are we to understand the fearful atrocities that men commit in time of civil war? How can we explain the transformation of normally law-abiding citizens into ravening beasts carried away by uncontrollable passion? "In the confusion into which life was now thrown in the cities, human nature (*hê anthropeia physis*), always rebelling against the law and now its master, gladly showed itself ungoverned in passion, above respect for justice, and the enemy of all superiority" (3.84.2).

This passage is a splendid example of Thucydides' method. It assumes the essentially uniform nature of man—in this instance, his jealousy and suspicion of all distinction and superiority. Under normal conditions custom and law control it, but when circumstances—in this case, protracted warfare—permit, these artificial bonds dissolve and men revert to their natural state. Proper analytical diagnosis can foresee the emergence and development of such behavior in the same way that a physician acquainted with a particular set of symptoms can predict with great likelihood the progress of the associated disease, since he knows its general character and natural course.

The gods and other supernatural forces can play no part in such a view of human nature, and the *History* rigidly excludes all supernatural involement in human affairs. Although Thucydides does mention the growth of disbelief as a disruptive force in Greek society and praises the piety of Nicias, as John Finley pointed out, "He simply did not believe that the gods intervened in the working out of the political forces which he thought operative in history."[12]

Such austerity and so close an approximation to the methods of the natural sciences might seem to lay Thucydides open to the charge that he is too scientific and, thus, antihistorical. It is, however, wrong to suggest that Thucydides cared little for the power of particular events; his very adherence to the Hippocratic ideal requires a careful concern for the specific events that, as a whole, constitute the subject of his study. No one, moreover, who reads Thucydides' brilliant and touching account of the Sicilian campaign, from its buoyant planning stage to its tragic ending, can doubt his narrative genius or his historian's love for the vivid details of the events themselves. It is wrong, furthermore, to chide Thucydides for attempting to seek patterns in history. In his own way Herodotus did the same and thus earned the title "the father of history," for to concentrate fully and exclusively "on the events themselves" is not to be a historian but a chronicler. To be sure, the patterns Herodotus typically discerned were moral and religious, unlike the primarily social and political ones observed by Thucydides, but it is also misleading to view Thucydides' attempt to establish a rigorous empirical study of politics as a search for "some unchanging and eternal truth."[13] He sought only the degree of certainty and consistency possible in the study of events in human society, not of elements in nature.

Thucydides' own statements make it clear that his understanding of human events has nothing to do with laws like those of physics or the "absolute" truths of the philosophic sort. The Thucydidean view of political analysis involves no adamantine chain of determinism and in fact takes real cognizance of the unaccountable. At several crucial points in his *History* he explains important events by ascribing them to *tychê*, chance. It was chance that led to the Athenian fortification of Pylos, a vital turning point in the war (4.3.1), and chance that produced an eclipse that prevented the Athenian escape from Syracuse (7.50.4) and helped cause the terrible Sicilian disaster. Such cases are not, however, evidence of the historian's belief in the essential irrationality of the world. On the contrary, Thucydides believed the world to be subject to reasoned analysis, if not to absolute or scientific certainty, and that intelligent individuals with unusual gifts could, by careful and systematic study of human behavior, make good and useful estimates of the likely reaction of people, especially en masse.

Thucydides' conception of the study of political behavior differs in a still more fundamental way from the determinism that has been held to underlie the physical sciences. He lays great emphasis on the role of the individual in history and on his ability to change its course. The didactic aspect of his work—the attempt to identify underlying patterns—is intended to supply some perceptive individual with the insight (*gnômê*) with which to see the course of political events and to control them. And there were, in Thucydides' estimation, a number of such gifted political leaders. Themistocles, for instance, "was the best judge of what was about to happen and the wisest in foreseeing what would happen in the

distant future" and could "excellently foresee what was better or worse
that was hidden in the unseen future." As a consequence, "he surpassed
all others in the faculty of intuitively meeting an emergency" (1.138.3).

Even clearer is Thucydides' conviction that the course of the war was
affected by the unique talents of Pericles, which included foresight, patriotism, and incorruptibility (2.60.5): "For so long a time as he was at the
head of the state during the peace, he pursued a moderate and conservative policy and in his time its greatness was at its height" (2.65.5). He was,
tragically, succeeded by men who lacked his talents and deviated from
his wise policies. "And yet," says Thucydides,

> after losing most of their fleet and all their other forces in Sicily, with rev-
> olution already breaking out in Athens, they still held out for ten years
> against their original enemies, with the Sicilians now by their side and
> against their own allies, most of which had revolted, and against Cyrus,
> son of the King of Persia, who later joined the other side and provided
> the Peloponnesians with money for their fleet. And they did not give in
> until they had destroyed themselves by their own internal conflicts. So
> immensely great were the resources that Pericles counted on at the time
> through which he foresaw an easy victory for Athens over the Pelopon-
> nesians alone. (2.65.12–13)

There can be no clearer endorsement of the idea that wise men can
make accurate and well-founded plans for the future. At the same time,
Thucydides makes it plain that even the best plans may go astray when
confronted with unpredictable actions and events, which is a telling rebuttal to the charge of scientific determinism. These examples likewise
refute more recent interpretations suggesting that Thucydides did not
expect his work to have practical use or that he even intended it to show
the futility of such an effort.

It is precisely this expectation that remarkable men will find his account useful in the future that explains his extraordinary emphasis on accuracy in the work of the historian. Apart from the rare direct statements

that he quotes in *The Peloponnesian War*, Thucydides' own opinions may be sought in the speeches he puts into the mouths of his characters. As he explains: "It was in all cases difficult to carry them word for word in one's memory, so my habit has been to make the speakers say what was in my opinion demanded of them by the various occasions, of course adhering as closely as possible to the general sense of what they really said" (1.22.1).

But far from settling the question, Thucydides' account of his method has given rise to every conceivable interpretation. It seems to me that, whatever nuances may be intended by his complex statement, and whatever the ambiguity of the first clause and its relationship to the latter, the clarity of its intent cannot be ignored: "adhering as closely as possible to the general sense of what they really said." That represents a claim to reporting speeches that were actually spoken, not invented by the historian, and to the attempt to record them as accurately as possible. If Thucydides had another agenda—if he fabricated speeches or inserted his own ideas rather than trying to report the topics addressed by the speaker in the manner he expressed them—then he has lied to his readers. And if he cannot be trusted as to this statement, then he may be considered just as deceptive and unreliable in his reporting of other facts, for a speech delivered is no less a fact than a city attacked. His claim to the goal of accuracy in reporting speeches is no less binding than his claim to take the greatest pains in the discovery of the true character of the events he describes. Since few have doubted him in the latter case, there is no reason to doubt the former.

The assumption here is that Thucydides meant precisely what he most obviously said; therefore, those speeches that he is likely to have heard himself should be taken as reasonably accurate accounts of the speaker's ideas. Thus, all the speeches of Pericles are here taken to present reliably the ideas of the speaker, not the historian. Speeches Thucydides could not possibly have heard, or about which he is not even likely to have received a reliable report (if indeed there are any), may be taken to be expressions of his own ideas.[14] Speeches that the historian may or may not have heard or have received good accounts of are to be examined individually and tested against canons established by more reliable evidence.

The more important question regarding the speeches in Thucydides, however, is that of selection. Of the hundreds of speeches delivered of which Thucydides had knowledge, why did he choose to report some and not others? Any attempt to understand what function each speech serves in the *History* is likely to reveal much about Thucydides' ideas and purposes, quite apart from the vexed question of its authenticity.

After explaining his method of depicting the speeches he reports, Thucydides tells the reader of the great pains he took to ascertain the particulars of the war itself:

> But as to the facts of the events of the war, I have thought it right to write them down, not just as they happened to come my way, nor according to my own predispositions, but only after investigating each one with the greatest possible accuracy, concerning both the events at which I myself was present and of those about which I was informed by others. And the effort to discover the truth about these facts was very hard work, because those who were eyewitnesses of the events did not give the same reports about the same things, but each report differed because of partiality for one side or the other or because of faulty memory.
>
> And, perhaps, my account will seem less pleasing to those who hear it because of its lack of fabulous tales, but if it be judged useful by those who seek an exact knowledge of the past as an aid to the interpretation of the future, which in the course of human things must resemble if it does not reflect it, I shall be satisfied. It has been composed not as an entry in a competition to be heard for the moment but as a possession forever. (1.22.2–4)

Few have sufficiently noticed that the latter paragraph is closely tied to the preceding one and is its necessary complement. It explains *why* Thucydides has taken such great pains to present the facts of his history as accurately as possible. Only then can they serve his purpose as the material from which wise men of the future can study the patterns of human behavior, especially in such strained circumstances as war, learn from them, and thereby make better decisions. If the facts of his account are wrong, so will his interpretations be wrong, and neither will serve to foster political wisdom.

Typically, studies of Thucydides' thought, his purposes, intentions, or methods treat him almost as a disembodied mind, not as a living human being, part of his time and place and influenced by them and his own experience in them. To be sure, his was an extraordinary and original mind. Thucydides stood on the edge of philosophy. He was sufficiently a historian to feel compelled to establish the particulars, to present the data as accurately as he could, but he was no less concerned to convey the general truths he had discovered. But a satisfactory understanding of Thucydides demands a critical look at him, the man himself in the world of action, not merely of thought. We must remember that he was a contemporary of the events he describes and a participant in some of them. What was his relationship to the world in which he lived, and how did his understanding of events accord or disagree with that of his contemporaries? Where was he when he wrote? Among what sort of people did he live? To what degree were his views influenced, even shaped by such factors?

If more than any historian in antiquity, Thucydides put the highest value on accuracy and objectivity, we must not forget he had human feelings and foibles. In Greek his style is often very compressed and difficult to understand, so that any translation is necessarily an interpretation. When I began my study of Thucydides and his *History* so many years ago I came to realize that there could be no hope of understanding his thought and purposes merely by reading his work and pondering it carefully. That could be only the first step. The next required a painstaking comparison between what he said about the subject and what really happened. No historian, much less one removed from the events by more than twenty-four centuries, could hope to recover those events with certainty, but it would be a reasonable, if arduous and lengthy, undertaking to compare Thucydides' account and interpretation of events with the other ancient evidence and opinions available. Considerable resources exist for such opinions, which appear in contemporary inscriptions and plays, are preserved in the writings of later authors in antiquity, and are discussed by Thucydides himself.

For almost two decades I have worked on the project of establishing— to my own satisfaction, at least—how Thucydides' account and explanation of the course of the Peloponnesian War compare with those offered or accepted by his contemporaries, and by later ancient writers who knew of the earlier opinions and also those of Thucydides. The results seem to me to shed revealing light on some of the aims of the historian and also on the purposes and character of his great work. One scholar has made the shrewd observation that Thucydides' *History* "is sometimes a revisionist, often a polemical work."[15] Independently, I called him "the first revisionist historian."[16]

In this book I examine some of the most important interpretations Thucydides offers for events in the war and compare them with the evidence that he and other ancient sources provide. In each case I arrive at different conclusions from those of the great Athenian historian. In undertaking this bold and dangerous course I follow the suggestion of a brilliant modern historian of the ancient world whose advice influenced me at the very beginning of my studies. In writing of the alleged unpopularity of the Athenian empire he challenged the picture painted by Thucydides: "This," he said,

is what Thucydides wanted his readers to believe. It is undoubtedly the conception he himself honestly held. Nevertheless, his own detailed narrative proves that it is certainly false. Thucydides was such a remarkably objective historian that he himself has provided sufficient material for his own refutation. The news columns in Thucydides, so to speak, contradict the editorial Thucydides, and the editor himself does not always speak with the same voice.[17]

These observation are acute and helpful. They remind us that Thucydides is not infallible and that we must test his conclusions as we would those of any writer. Only when we do that and compare the results with the historian's interpretations can we have fuller access to the mind of Thucydides. The differences and contradictions provide us with some of the most creative contributions he makes. They are his explanations and arguments that mean to correct the understandings of events that were common in his time which he believed erroneous.

Only when we take note of these divergences can we ask why Thucydides differed so markedly and frequently from opinions held by his contemporaries and so obtain a deeper understanding of his methods and purposes.

CHAPTER ONE

Thucydides the Revisionist

W HAT IS A REVISIONIST? How can Thucydides be considered a
revisionist, when he seems to have been the first man to write
a history of the Peloponnesian War? What received opinions existed for
him to revise? In a sense all historians are revisionists, for each tries to
make some contribution that changes our understanding of the past.
When we use the term *revisionist*, however, we generally mean something more fundamental: a writer who tries to change the reader's mind
in a major way by providing a new general interpretation, one that sharply
and thoroughly reexamines the established way of looking at a matter.

Given that Thucydides believed in the practical importance of history, we should expect him to be eager to set straight any errors of fact or
interpretation that he found. But his critical spirit was brought to bear on
a larger scale than merely factual detail. He uses the evidence of Homer,
for instance, to show that it was the poverty of the Greeks, not the bravery of the Trojans, that was responsible for the length of the siege of
Troy. He seems to have been the first to present the view that the Peloponnesian War was a single conflict, not a series of separate wars. Many
other and greater and more controversial revisions will be discussed in
this and later chapters.

If we grant that Thucydides had the instincts of a revisionist, what
was there to revise? The answer is: the not yet fully formed or written
opinions of contemporaries. In our own day these are easy to identify.
Some of us still remember them from direct experience, and, in any case,
modern revisionists usually confront and argue against their opponents. Thucydides' method is different. He argues with no one by name

and presents no labeled alternative views, even to refute them, but gives the reader only the facts and the conclusions distilled from them that he deems necessary after careful investigation and thought. He has been so successful with this approach that for more than twenty-four hundred years few readers have been aware that any other point of view existed. But a careful reading of Thucydides himself and other ancient sources shows that there were different opinions in Thucydides' time and that his *History* is a powerful and effective polemic against them. Recovering these forgotten and obscured contemporary opinions and comparing them with Thucydides' own interpretations casts an interesting light on his mind and the significance of his work.

The Greatness of the War

The *History* begins as follows: "Thucydides, an Athenian, wrote an account of the war between the Peloponnesians and the Athenians, having begun it immediately when it started and expecting that the war would be more worthy of the telling than those that came before" (1.1.1). This last assertion would have elicited at least a modicum of surprise in his contemporaries. They would have countered immediately with the Trojan War, celebrated in Homer's epics, which the Greeks—and Thucydides himself—treated as fundamentally historical, and would have questioned whether any other war could compare with that titanic struggle of gods and heroes. Then they would have thought of the Persian Wars, during which the vast army and navy of the great Persian Empire attacked the Greek states; occupied much of Greece, including Attica; and threatened to conquer it all, enslaving its population and smothering its brilliant culture in its cradle.

To meet such anticipated objections Thucydides defended and extended his bold assertion, arguing that in the Peloponnesian War "both sides were at the height of their power in every respect, and seeing that the rest of the Greeks were taking sides with one or the other, either immediately or after thinking about it. For this was the greatest distur-

bance to have stirred the Greeks, involving even some part of the barbarian world, one might even say the greater part of mankind" (1.1.1). This
characterization of the relative impotence of the competitors in earlier
wars requires demonstration. Thucydides concedes that the passage of
time has made it impossible for him to discover with certainty the nature
of those conflicts, but his most careful investigation has allowed him to
be confident that those earlier events "were not great either as regards
war or anything else" (1.1.2).

Sections 2–21 of the first book of the *History* tell the story of the development of Greek society from earliest times until the rise to comparable
power of the two great antagonists in the Peloponnesian War, Sparta
and Athens. The purpose of the entire section is to support Thucydides'
novel assertion that the war was the greatest conflict ever known. His approach is remarkably sophisticated, employing reasoned inferences from
material remains and a critical analysis of information provided by the
poets, chiefly Homer's epics. He uses the resulting evidence to advance
a new, thoroughly rational, theory of the economic and social development of the Greek world.

In earliest times people were migratory, without settled homes. There
was no agricultural surplus and no trade. No one planted orchards because
their settlements were unwalled, and they were too poor and weak to resist
raiders who would seize their products. Since they needed to be ready to
move to a new location when attacked, their towns were neither very large
nor wealthy. The most fertile and desirable lands were also most subject to
invasion, and they were also troubled most by internal strife. As support
for his argument, Thucydides uses the example of Athens—a land of relatively poor soil that avoided civil war and foreign invasion, "and the same
people dwelt in it always." That factor made it possible for its population to
grow, while the migrations of other peoples prevented their number from
increasing. From early times it became a solidly established community,
attracting the most notable refugees from other areas of Greece. After a
time Athens could not hold its burgeoning population and began to establish colonies as far away as Ionia across the Aegean Sea (1.2).

Further evidence for the relative weakness of early times is that, in
Homer's time, a general name for Greece—*Hellas*—and the Greeks—
Hellenes—did not even exist yet, so his poems do not use the term *barbarian* to distinguish other peoples from the Greeks. No significant common
undertaking was possible until the Greeks had acquired the ability to
navigate the seas, and it was only after they were able to do so that they
could launch the Trojan War (1.3). That day had been long delayed because no one state had the wealth and power to suppress rampant piracy
at sea or plunder and insecurity on land. In fact, the absence of walled
settlements and the general insecurity made it necessary for the Greeks
to carry weapons wherever they went, and they lived just like barbarians. Because of these dangers, Thucydides observes, the earliest Greek
settlements were built at some distance from the sea to escape piratical
raids, while those established later, "after it was safer to sail the seas and
they accumulated a surplus of wealth, built walled towns right at the seashore and on the isthmuses for the purposes of trade and defense against
their neighbors" (1.7). Already Thucydides indicates some key elements
needed for civilization, greatness and military might: wealth, walled cities,
and navies.

Assuming Greek tradition to be based fundamentally on fact, he
cites King Minos of Crete as the first to acquire a navy, which he used to
suppress piracy as best he could, "so as to collect his revenues with less
trouble" (1.4). While Minos thereby helped create more secure conditions that permitted the Greeks to take common military action in the
form of the Trojan War, even that famous conflict did not amount to
much. Its leader was Agamemnon, king of the fortress city of Mycenae,
capital of the Argolid. Tradition attributed his assumption of leadership
of the campaign to his position as brother of Menelaus, the husband of
the beautiful Helen who ran off to Troy with the seductive Paris. Hel-
en's father, Tyndareus, the story went, had made all her suitors swear
an oath to protect the marriage rights of the man of her choice. Without
denying the historicity of the events described, Thucydides rejects the
oath as the true source of Agamemnon's leadership. Revising the tale in

characteristic fashion, he concludes that the Greek chieftains accepted Agamemnon's command because he "was preeminent in power among the princes of that time" (1.9.1). That superior position he had inherited along with a great fortune from his ancestor Pelops, who brought it from Asia and became the ruler of all the Peloponnesus, to which he gave its name. His wealth and power increased under his son Atreus, who passed it on to his own son, Agamemnon. With that legacy Agamemnon was able to acquire a navy greater than all the others, which enabled him to bring the other princes under his command against Troy, "not so much because of loyalty [to the oath] as to fear" (1.9.3).

By careful calculation from the *Iliad*'s catalogue of ships and other details in Homer's epic Thucydides defends the poet's description of the size of the Greek expedition, asserting that it was "greater than any that came before it" (1.10.3). At the same time he makes the argument that, even if one does accept Homer's (probably exaggerated) numbers, the force was small compared with those of Thucydides' time. If we estimate the number of men on the Greek ships at Troy by taking the average of the crews mentioned in Homer's catalogue, "they appear to have been not many, since they came from all Greece in common" (1.10.5).

The weakness of the expedition did not lie chiefly in the shortage of men, however, but rather in the lack of funds. Thucydides concludes that there were plenty of men available for a larger invading force but not enough supplies available to maintain them, which forced the Greeks to take only as many as could live off the land around Troy. These forces had to scatter and turn to farming and pillaging in the neighborhood, making it easier for the Trojans to hold out for ten years. "The facts show that because of the lack of wealth earlier undertakings were feeble, and the Trojan War itself, although more famous than those that came before, was inferior to what was said about it and as it is still believed to be, thanks to the influence of the poets" (1.11.2). The elements that Thucydides would come to see as decisive in the great war of his own day—wealth and naval power—he asserted to be crucial, too, in the great war far back in the Bronze Age.

The period after the Trojan War, Thucydides tells us, produced no action of great size. Quarrels in the cities drove the losing factions into exile, where some of them founded new cities, and new migrations caused further disruption. Only after the passage of many years did Greece become pacified and secure enough to support the growth of a surplus population to found colonies as far off as Asia Minor in the east and Italy and Sicily, and even France and Spain, in the west. The ensuing growth of wealth and power enabled the emergence of tyrannies in many cities, which appeared in association with the first important navies since those of Minos of Crete. The Corinthians held a strategic position on their isthmus, which allowed them to profit from commerce by both land and sea, and they used the income to build a fleet, drive out piracy, and thus make themselves still more rich and powerful. Without naming Cypselus, the founder of Corinth's dynasty of tyrants, or any of his successors, Thucydides asserts that the Corinthians appear to have been "the first to manage naval matters in something like the modern manner, and Corinth was where the first triremes were built" (1.13.2). Triremes came to be the characteristic Greek warships, for centuries invincible against any other naval force and the vessel of choice for both sides in the Peloponnesian War.

Other Greek states also developed significant naval forces. Polycrates, the tyrant of the important island of Samos, became strong enough at sea to conquer other Aegean islands to create what the Greeks called a *thalassocracy*, a naval empire. Thucydides also mentions Phocaea, an Ionian city that established a colony as far away as Massalia (modern Marseilles) and defeated the mighty Carthaginians in a naval battle when challenged.

All these cases support Thucydides' theme that the measures of greatness in wars are to be found in wealth and navies, and while he describes the growth of both during the centuries after the Trojan War, he makes it clear that none of these new powers of the Archaic period of Greek history really amounted to much. He speaks of "the most powerful of the navies" (1.14.1) of the period, but these employed only a few triremes. These fleets primarily consisted of pentecontors, fifty-oared ships, and

"long boats," meaning warships, not merchantmen; both types soon became obsolete and were woefully inferior to the triremes that succeeded
them. Only several Sicilian tyrants and the Corcyraeans in the Ionian
Sea acquired a notable number of triremes before the Persian invasion
of Greece. The famous and extended naval war between Athens and
Aegina was no exception: the fleets involved in the conflict were small
and consisted chiefly of pentceonters. The Athenians built the fleet of
triremes with which they won the battle of Salamis only a few years prior
to the great Persian conflict, and even these ships were without full decks
(1.14.3).

On land the situation was much the same as at sea. Wars were small
affairs between two neighbors arising from border disputes. There were
no expeditions for conquest far from the homeland. No single power
emerged either as the ruler of a land empire or even as the leader of a coalition of states. The first example of a conflict involving multiple states
was the Lelantine War, named for the plain that lay between the chief
combatants, the cities of Chalcis and Eretria on the island of Euboea.
Although its date is uncertain, it seems to have come to an end in about
700,[1] after a number of important states came to the aid of each side, but
it certainly did not rank as a great war.

Given their resources and power, the tyrants might have been expected to undertake major military actions, but none did. They were on
the whole conservative rulers, concerned chiefly with their own safety
and prosperity and that of their families. When they did undertake any
noteworthy action, it was always a single ruler challenging one of his
neighbors. "So for a long time, in every direction, Greece was in such
a condition that no impressive achievement could be attained either in
common or by individual states" (1.17).

Then, says Thucydides, came the Spartans. Overcoming a long early
period of internal conflict, they adopted a good constitution and were
always free of tyrants. This excellent and uniquely stable form of life and
government had lasted for more than four hundred years, dating back
from the end of the Peloponnesian War (404). "Because of this the Spar-

tans became powerful and established control of other states, too" (1.18.1).
Finally, they succeeded in putting down tyranny throughout Greece.
Thucydides' thumbnail sketch of the rise of Sparta is overly simple and
exaggerates its role in ending Greek tyranny. Tyrannies rose and fell at
Argos, within the Peloponnesus, and at Corinth and Megara, just outside
it, without any record of Spartan intervention. No doubt the antityran-
nical reputation Sparta enjoyed in his day and its crucial role in bringing
down the Peisistratid dynasty in Athens in 510 influenced Thucydides
in his assessment, but this passage also provides a starting point for the
rise of the Spartans to the hegemony of the Peloponnesus and to Sparta's
place as one of the principal powers in the great war to come.

Sparta was already in that position when the Persian invasion came
in 480. Thucydides acknowledges that the Persians "sent a great fleet
against Greece to enslave it," that the Greek defense was a common
effort, that the Spartans took the leadership of those states that chose
to resist, and that the Athenians were compelled to flee their country,
"board their ships and become sailors" (1.18.2). The Persian War, he says,
"was the greatest action" before the Peloponnesian War; nonetheless it
was quickly decided by two battles at sea and two on land" (1.23.1). The
Peloponnesian War, by contrast, stretched out for a long time, and never
before had so many disasters occurred in an equivalent span of time.

> Never had so many cities been captured and devastated, some by the
> barbarians and some by the Greeks themselves as they fought one an-
> other (some of the cities, after they were taken experienced a change
> of their inhabitants); never had there been so many exiles and so much
> slaughter, whether in the war itself or in civil strife. Stories about ter-
> rible events in the past that had rarely been confirmed by fact now no
> longer seemed unbelievable; for example about earthquakes, which
> were very violent and occurred in many places, and eclipses of the sun,
> which happened more frequently than at any time previously remem-
> bered and great drought that caused famines and, what caused the most
> harm and destroyed a considerable part of the population, the pestilen-

tial plague. For all of these fell upon them at the same time during this war. (1.23.1–3)

With these dramatic words Thucydides concludes the long, argumentative narrative he presents to refute common opinion and to justify his bold claim that the Peloponnesian War was "the greatest disturbance to have stirred the Greeks" and "more worthy of the telling than those that came before." But to convince his listeners or readers requires something more: Thucydides needs to demonstrate that common opinion is often wrong, and that his own account deserves greater credence.

After a brief description of the development of Sparta and Athens since the Persian War he observes, "Such was the way I found that things were in early days, although it is hard to believe every bit of evidence we find in turn. For men accept what they hear from one another about past events without putting them to the test, even if it is about their own country" (1.20.1). As an example he offers the majority of Athenians, who continue to believe that Hipparchus was tyrant when he was assassinated by the tyrannicides Harmodius and Aristogeiton. They are not aware that it was in fact his older brother, Hippias, who was on the throne after the death of their father, Peisistratus, nor do they have their facts straight about other details of the murder. But it is not only ordinary people who are misinformed. "The rest of the Greeks are mistaken about many other things that have not been forgotten because of the lapse of time but exist in the world today" (1.20.3). They believe, for example, that the Spartan kings have two votes, not one, and that there is something called a Pitana company in the Spartan army, when there never has been any such thing. To be sure, these are small details, but Thucydides' target here is not actually the common man, but Herodotus himself, the father of history.[2] "So careless are most people in the search for truth; they are more inclined to accept the first story that comes to hand" (1.20.3).

But not Thucydides. His reader will not go wrong in accepting his interpretations, for his account is superior to that of the poets, who exaggerate and embellish their subject, or the storytellers in prose, who design their tales to please the ear in public recitations rather than to report the truth. "Their stories cannot be tested and, for the most part, because of the passage of time, have won their way into the realm of mythology and cannot be trusted" (1.21.1). He knows that it is human nature, while a war is in progress, to regard it as the greatest in history, but when it is over to marvel more at older ones. Repeating his claim, however, he assures his reader that by judging the facts themselves they will see "that this war was greater than any that came before it" (1.21.2).

To support this claim Thucydides now sets out to describe the methods he has employed in composing his *History*. He divides his explanation into two parts: his reports of speeches (*logoi*) and his accounts of the "facts [*erga*] of the events of the war" (1.22.1–2). These passages make it clear that Thucydides claims the diligent and demanding effort of accuracy in his search for the truth of the events he describes, and hardly any careful student of the *History* has doubted him.

But why does he take the trouble to elucidate his method so clearly and so powerfully, when no other ancient historian has done the same? His explanation comes in the greater claim that he presents next: that he intends his work to be "a possession forever" meant to be useful to "such men as might wish to see clearly what has happened and what will happen again, in all human probability, in the same or a similar way." For that to be possible his account must be scrupulously correct, for any error of fact could result in an error of understanding that would mislead the extraordinary reader using his work to make important decisions. Given its position, moreover, this unique description of Thucydides' methods is a final support for his argument about the historical predominance of the Peloponnesian War.

But what, precisely, constituted the Peloponnesian War? While it is possible that Thucydides was the first to define the events that took place from the spring of 431 to the spring of 404 as constituting a single war— *the* war between the Spartans and the Athenians—this was by no means the only way of interpreting them. The two sides had earlier fought what modern scholars call the First Peloponnesian War between about 460 and 445, and some consider that to be the actual first act in the long war that occupied most of the rest of the century. On the other hand, writers contemporary with Thucydides and in the years afterward treated the several episodes of fighting between 431 and 404 as independent wars.[3] In what has been called a second introduction, after he reports the treaty that ended the first phase of the war in 421, Thucydides makes an argument in favor of the unity of the war and his own view of its extent that is so pointed and emphatic as to remove any doubt that it serves as a revision of what was a common opinion at the time.

> The same Thucydides, an Athenian, wrote the history of this period in the order in which the events happened, by summers and winters, to the time when the Spartans and their allies put an end to the Athenian empire and took the Long Walls and Piraeus. The whole war had then lasted for twenty-seven years. And if anyone should think that the period in which there was a treaty was not part of the war he would be wrong. (5.26.1–2)

As he did earlier in making the case for his view of the stature of the war, Thucydides argues for this interpretation based on what he deems to be the relevant facts. How can anyone consider peace to be genuine when neither party to the truce carried out its territorial provisions, not to mention that during the putative Peace of Nicias both sides fought against each other at Mantinea and Epidaurus? Or when the Peloponnesians' allies in Thrace remained openly hostile to Athens, and the Boeotians refused to join in the peace but made only consecutive ten-days truces? Thucydides concludes that "counting the first war of ten years, the suspect truce that followed it and the war that came after it, one will find that, calculating by seasons, the war lasted just as many years as I have said plus a few days over" (5.26.3).

Here, too, having put forward a new and challenging interpretation, he feels the need to defend its reliability:

I lived through the whole war, being of an age to understand the events, and giving my attention to them in order to know the precise truth about them. It also happened that I was sent into exile for twenty years after I was general at Amphipolis; and being in touch with both sides, especially the Peloponnesians because of my exile, I had leisure to learn rather more about the events. (5.25.5)

These revisions were important to Thucydides, and he argued for them in a vigorous manner. Neither, however, was as controversial as others to come; they would require no less vigor but much more ingenuity.

CHAPTER TWO

Causes of the War—Corcyra

ONE OF THE KEENEST controversies surrounding the Peloponnesian War is the question of its causes. The Peloponnesians, of
course, blamed the Athenians for provoking it, based on alleged violations of the peace in the form of actions taken against Sparta's allies. Even
before its outbreak, however, Athens itself was sharply divided about the
war's necessity (1.44).[1] At least two actions proposed and defended by
Pericles, were met with severe criticism. The first, the decision in 433
to send aid to Corcyra, threatened by Corinth, in the form of only ten
ships, when hundreds were available, was superseded at a later assembly
and resulted in the dispatch of twenty more. (1.50.5). Critics complained
that the original force was "too small to help but big enough to serve as
a pretext for war."[2]

The second was a decree barring the city of Megara, a member of
the Peloponnesian League, from the use of the Athenian Agora and the
harbors of the Athenian Empire. This proved to be the most significant
grievance of the Peloponnesians, who, in the end, pronounced themselves willing to preserve the peace on the condition that the Athenians withdraw the bar. The Athenians took this offer seriously, and
their final debate on peace or war focused chiefly on the Megarian Decree, since the Spartans had indeed dropped all their other demands.
"Many others came forward to express their opinions on each side of
the question, either to go to war or that the decree should not be a
barrier to peace but should be withdrawn. At last Pericles, the leading man among the Athenians at that time and the most formidable in
speech and action, came forward and advised them" (1.139.4). He urged

the Athenians not to give way, advice they accepted, and the war commenced the following spring.

In 430 the Peloponnesians invaded and devastated Attica a second time without serious hindrance, and a great plague broke out, killing tens of thousands of Athenians locked up inside their city. The people "changed their minds and laid the blame on Pericles for persuading them to go to war and for the disasters that had befallen them" (1.59.2). Although Pericles would recover his influence and be reelected to office after being dismissed, the charge that he was the cause of the war continued to flourish.

In the winter of 425, the sixth year of the war, the comic poet Aristophanes produced *Acharnians*, which won first prize at the Lenaean Festival, which only citizens attended. Thousands of Athenians gathered to see a humorous performance that satirized real Athenian citizens, especially politicians, and joked, sometimes with serious intent, about the events of the day. Dicaeopolis, the comic hero of the play, is tired of the war and insists on peace negotiations at once, enraging the warlike citizens of the township of Acharnae. To make his case he argues against what must have been a common opinion that the Spartans were the aggressors. He tries to justify the Spartan action in going to war against Athens. Like the angry Acharnians, he, too, hates the Spartans. His vines, too, they have cut down: "But come," he says, "for only friends are here, why do we blame the Laconians? Some of our men (I do not say the state, mind you, I do not say the state), some vice-ridden wretches, men of no honor, false men, not even real citizens, kept denouncing Megara's little coats; and if anyone ever saw a cucumber, a hare, a suckling pig, a clove of garlic, or a lump of salt, all were denounced as Megarian and confiscated."[3]

Next he tells of the theft by some drunken Athenians of a Megarian woman and the countertheft by the Megarians of three prostitutes from the house of Pericles' beloved Aspasia. Pericles, in his fury, "enacted laws that sounded like drinking songs, 'That the Megarians must leave our land, our market, our sea and our continent.' Then, when the Megarians were slowly starving, they begged the Spartans to get the law of the three harlots withdrawn. We refused, though they asked us often. And from that came the clash of shields."[4]

None of this should be taken literally, for the main aim of the poet is a good laugh. The story is in fact a parody of the rape of Helen, which was the cause of the Trojan War, and possibly also of the reciprocal rapes reported by Herodotus as the ultimate cause of the Persian Wars. The terms of the decree and the severity of its results are comically exaggerated, and the portrayal of Aspasia as the madam of a brothel and the instigator of Pericles' support of the decree are malign jokes, but at the core of the scene is the malicious charge that Pericles was responsible for the war because of his insistence on the Megarian Decree. That certainly reflected a significant segment of public opinion both during the crisis preceding the outbreak of the war and after it was underway.

In the spring of 421, in the tenth year of the war, the idea that Pericles bore culpability for the war still had a strong hold on the minds of Athenians, a notion that Aristophanes exploited in his *Peace*. There he presented a comic explanation for the onset of the war, which was remembered and taken seriously even in later centuries. His chorus asks: "But where has Peace been all this long time, tell us, Hermes, most benevolent of the gods." Hermes replies: "O, you very wise farmer, listen to my words if you want to hear why she was lost. The beginning of our trouble was the disgrace of Phidias; then Pericles, fearing he might share in the misfortune, dreading your ill nature and stubborn ways, before he could suffer harm, set the city aflame by throwing out that little spark, the Megarian Decree."[5]

Such conceptions of the Megarian Decree were no novelty by 421, but Aristophanes probably invented the connection between the trial of the sculptor Phidias, a charge against Pericles, and his deliberate use of the Megarian Decree to bring on war as a distraction to prevent his embarrassment. Certainly, the simple farmers to whom Hermes explains the link seem never to have heard this rationale before. The comic hero Trygaeus says: "By Apollo, no one ever told me that! Nor did I think there was any connection between Phidias and Peace." The chorus is equally surprised: "Nor did I, until just now. That is why she is so beautiful, since she is related to him. My, how many things escape our notice."[6]

The absurdity and humor of Aristophanes' comic invention are made all the clearer by what follows, for it turns out that the Spartans entered the war for money, bribed by Athenian allies who were anxious to cease paying the tribute.[7]

The reference to Phidias concerns a series of legal attacks that had been launched against Pericles, probably around 438. Plutarch had Thucydides and many other sources before him when he wrote of the affair in second century of our era. He, too, mentions Pericles' political troubles as the bases of the allegation that he brought on the Peloponnesian War to escape these attacks. Plutarch says that the worst charge of all, but the one with the most support, was that Phidias, a close friend of Pericles and the sculptor and contractor of the great gold and ivory statue of Athena on the Acropolis, was charged with embezzlement. Behind the accusation, explains Plutarch, were men jealous of Phidias' influence, but also those who wanted to use the prosecution as a test case to see how juries would act in a trial involving Pericles. Although Phidias was able to prove his innocence, he was later condemned for including his own and Pericles' portraits in the sculptures on the Parthenon. The assembly passed a decree giving the informer, Menon, who had worked with Phideas, immunity from taxation and personal protection.[8]

At the same time, Aspasia was tried for impiety, and a certain Diopeithes introduced a bill that would have made atheism and "teaching about the heavens" public crimes. This proposal, says Plutarch, was aimed at "directing suspicion against Pericles through Anaxagoras."[9] The people were pleased by these measures, and while they were still receptive, a hostile politician, Dracontides, moved that Pericles be required to deposit his accounts with the council and that his case should be decided by jurors voting with specially sanctified ballots. Hagnon, a friend and ally of Pericles, amended the bill so that any suits arising from the investigation should be tried in the ordinary way before a jury of fifteen hundred Athenians. Plutarch tells us that Pericles was able to save Aspasia by weeping at her trial, but he was forced to send Anaxagoras away out of fear for his safety. Finally, fearing for his own safety in the trial to come, Pericles passed the Megarian Decree and launched the war to save himself. All this Plutarch reports as one explanation for the coming of the war; he himself acknowledges that the truth is not clear.[10]

Diodorus of Sicily, writing in the first century B.C.E., specifically cites Ephorus, a fourth-century historian, as a source for much the same story, adding one fine tale to it. In his version Pericles was guilty of misusing the imperial funds for his own purposes. When called upon to account for them, he worried about how to respond. His nephew Alcibiades advised him not to seek a way to render his accounts but rather a way not to render them. There soon followed the prosecutions of Phidias, Aspasia, and Anaxagoras, and to save himself Pericles proposed the Megarian Decree and brought on the war.[11] From Plutarch's remark that this version had the most support, and from its persistence through the centuries, it is clear that this interpretation of the cause of the war had become the prevalent one.

No serious person, much less so careful a historian as Thucydides, could accept such tales. But Thucydides was convinced that even the historical kernel giving rise to them—namely, the widespread contemporary belief that blamed the war on the policies of Pericles or, for that matter, on the specific actions taken by Athens or Sparta in the years leading up to the war—was wrong. After concluding his argument for the supreme greatness of the Peloponnesian War he sets down his belief about its causes:

> The war began when they violated the Thirty Years' Peace that they had made after the capture of Euboea [445]. First I have set forth why they broke it and the reasons for their disputes so that no one may ever have to ask what was the cause of so great a war among the Greeks. I think that the truest explanation, although it has been the least noticed, was the growth of Athens to a great power, which brought fear to the Spartans and compelled war. But the complaints publicly stated on either side that led them to break the truce and to choose war were these. (1.23.5–6)[12]

In this critical passage Thucydides clearly distinguishes the "truest explanation" from the events of the period after 435 that gave rise to the specific complaints he dismisses as merely for public consumption.

These conclusions are a far cry from those of his contemporaries, yet he has persuaded almost all readers in the succeeding millennia in the validity of his interpretation and all but obliterated any other opinion. How did he accomplish this most significant revision? After stating his bold new conclusion he launches on an analytic narrative of the events of the final crisis, from the start of the involvement of Corcyra in the civil war at Epidamnus in 435 to the Spartan decision that Athens had broken the Thirty Years' Peace in the summer of 432 (1.24–87).

He then concludes his account of these quarrels and complaints, by dismissing their relevance and asserting that the Spartans voted to go to war, "not so much because they had been persuaded by the arguments of their allies as because they were afraid that the Athenians might become more powerful, seeing that the greater part of Greece was already in their hands" (1.88). This in effect attributes to the Spartans the same appraisal of the situation as his own. His assertion is then supported by a long excursus whose purpose is to show the degree to which Athenian power had grown and alarmed the Spartans (1.89–118). It has the effect of demonstrating that the origins of the Peloponnesian War must be sought long before the trouble at Epidamnus. Finally, at the end of that excursus he makes it clear that the decision for war was merely the last step in a continuous process that began immediately after the Persian War.

> All these actions that the Greeks performed against each other and against the barbarian took place in the period of about fifty years between the retreat of Xerxes and the beginning of this war. In this time the Athenians established and reinforced their empire, and themselves attained great power. Although the Spartans perceived this, they made only a small attempt to prevent it and remained quiet for the greater part of the time. For even before this they had never been quick to go to war unless they were compelled, and in this period they were hindered,

to a degree, by wars at home. This quiet lasted until the power of the Athenians began to manifest itself and to lay hold on their allies. Then the situation became unendurable and the Spartans decided they must try with all their resolution to destroy that power if they could and to launch this war. (1.118.2)

The last two sentences reaffirm Thucydides' revision, stated twice before and fortified by the detailed account of the more recent events and by the briefer narrative of the *pentekontaetia,* the half-century between the Persian and Peloponnesian Wars.

Since the immediate causes are dismissed as incidental; since the growth of Athenian power from the time of the Persian War is offered as the "truest cause," and since Thucydides presents no way of preventing the growth of that power or the fear it engendered, we can only conclude that he meant us to think that the war was inevitable once the Athenian Empire was permitted to come into existence.

These statements of Thucydides' own opinion, confidently asserted and bolstered by well-placed historical narratives, are not, however, the only techniques by which he conveys his challenge to received opinion. Close examination of the First Peloponnesian War strongly suggests that Thucydides' verdict on the causes of the great war of 431 applies equally well to the earlier one. The rivalry between Sparta and Athens initially developed in the decades after the Persian War as the Delian League grew in success, wealth, and power and was gradually transformed into the Athenian Empire.

From the first, there was a faction in Sparta that, suspicious and resentful of the growth in Athenian strength, opposed the Athenians' desire to rebuild their walls after the Persians had fled. When the Athenians rejected such views in no uncertain terms, the Spartans made no formal complaint, "but they were secretly embittered" (1.92.1). By 475 resentment had grown to the point that a proposal emerged in the Spartan senate (*gerousia*) to go to war against the Athenians in order to destroy their new alliance and gain control of the sea.[13] After some debate the

Spartans rejected the plan, but the event reveals that an anti-Athenian faction continued to exist. In the early years of Athenian power, however, the memory of their recent collaboration in the great war of Greek independence against Persia argued against a conflict. The Athenians, meanwhile, appeared to be continuing the good fight against the Persians and for the liberty of the Greeks. The Spartans, moreover, would soon be distracted by troubles closer to home in the form of wars within the Peloponnesus. By the time the danger from Athens could no longer be ignored its might was daunting, and the Spartans' capacity to overcome it was open to question.

There was no trouble for some time, but in 465 the Athenians besieged the island of Thasos, where they met fierce resistance. The Thasians sent to the Spartans, urging them to come to their aid by invading Attica. In a secret decision, unknown to the Athenians, they made a promise to do so and, Thucydides tells us, the Spartans "meant to keep it" (1.101.1–2). They were prevented from doing so, however, by a terrible earthquake in the Peloponnesus that led to a major revolution of the helots, conquered people who worked the Spartans' land. Unable to drive the rebels from their mountain stronghold, the Spartans called on their allies for help. Among those who came were the Athenians, still formally tied to the Spartans under the terms of the Greek alliance against Persia sworn in 481, and famous for their skill at siege warfare.

Before long the Spartans asked the Athenians to leave, alone among their allies, on the specious grounds that they were no longer needed. Thucydides reports the true motive: "The Spartans were afraid of the boldness and the revolutionary spirit of the Athenians, thinking that . . . if they remained they might be persuaded . . . to change sides. . . . It was because of this expedition that the Spartans and Athenians first came to an open quarrel" (1.102.1–3).

The incident, clear evidence of the suspicion and hostility felt by many Spartans, brought about a political revolution in Athens and then a diplomatic one in Greece. The Spartans' insulting dismissal of the Athenian army brought down Cimon's pro-Spartan regime, which had maintained friendly relations between the two powers since the Persian Wars. The anti-Spartan group, which had opposed sending help to the Peloponnesus, drove Cimon from Athens, withdrew from the old alliance with Sparta, and made a new one with Sparta's old and bitter enemy, Argos (1.102.4).[14]

Relations between Sparta and Athens soon deteriorated further. When the besieged helots could hold out no longer, the Spartans allowed them to leave the Peloponnesus under a truce, provided they never return. The Spartans must have thought they would scatter harmlessly, but the Athenians settled them as a group in the city of Naupactus, which Athens had recently acquired, at a strategic site on the north shore of the Corinthian Gulf, "because of the hatred they already felt toward the Spartans" (1.103.3).

Next, the Athenians took an action that annoyed the Spartans even more. Two allies of Sparta, Corinth and Megara, were at war over the boundary between them. Megara was losing, and the Spartans did not choose to become involved, so the Megarians proposed to secede from the Spartan Alliance and join with Athens in exchange for help against Corinth. This incident starkly reveals how the breach between Athens and Sparta created a new instability in the Greek world. So long as the two hegemonal states were on good terms, each was free to deal with its allies as it chose; dissatisfied members of either alliance had nowhere to go. Now, however, dissident states could seek support from their leader's rival. In fact, the very existence of the rivalry encouraged dissent.

Megara, on Athens' western border, had great strategic importance. Its western port, Pegae, gave access to the Corinthian Gulf, which the Athenians could normally only reach by a long and dangerous route around the entire Peloponnesus. Nisaea, its eastern port, lay on the Saronic Gulf, from which an enemy could launch an attack on the port of Athens. Even more important, Athenian control of the mountain passes of the Megarid—a situation possible only with a friendly Megara—would make it difficult if not impossible for a Peloponnesian army to invade Attica. An alliance with Megara would, therefore, bring Athens enormous advantages, but it would also involve it in a war against Corinth and probably with Sparta and the Peloponnesian League. The Athenians accepted Megara, nevertheless, "and it was chiefly because of this action that Corinth's powerful hatred of the Athenians first arose" (1.103.4).

Although the Spartans did not become directly involved in the conflict for several years, this incident marked the beginning of the First Peloponnesian War. After the Spartan rejection of Cimon's troops, it could scarcely have been avoided. It is interesting to apply Thucydides' judgment of the "truest cause" of the later war to the outbreak of this one. "I think that the truest cause but the one least spoken of was that the Athenians had grown powerful, which presented an object of fear to the Spartans and forced them to go to war." In this case his assessmet appears to be right in every particular. The power of Athens had grown enormously since 479, the point at which Thucydides begins his analysis. Fear of Athens was manifest in the debate in the Spartan senate (*gerousia*) of 475, in the promise to help Thasos in 465/4, and finally in the expulsion of the Athenian hoplites in 462/1. The expression of that fear, moreover, was internal and did not need outside goading. When the Spartans made the fateful decision to expel the Athenians, they needed and received no urging from Corinthians, Aeginetans, or Megarians.

The Spartan attitude reflected an important fact about the condition of the Greek world from 479 to 461: its stability was only apparent. The alliance that did exist between Sparta and Athens was not one of states but of factions. The faction of Cimon in Athens and the faction that would be headed by King Archidamus in Sparta were prepared to accept limits to the hegemonal claims of their respective states, but in each case there were significant elements of the population who were not. The political positions of Cimon and the Spartan peace party were not strong enough to resist their opponents indefinitely. The Spartans were simply not yet prepared to share hegemony with Athens, nor were the Athenians prepared to accept Spartan checks on their ambitions. It is easy to believe that if the dismissal of the Athenians troops had not occurred, another casus belli might soon have been found.

The war lasted for more than fifteen years, including periods of truce and lapses of action, and, at one time or another, involved the Athenians fighting from Egypt to Sicily. It ended when the Megarians defected from the Athenian alliance and returned to the Peloponnesian League, opening the way for the Spartans to lead a Peloponnesian army into Attica. The Athenian army marched out to defend their land, and a decisive battle seemed certain but, at the last moment, the Spartans returned home without a fight. A short while later the Spartans and Athenians concluded a peace treaty.

Since the Thirty Years' Peace ended the war in 445 and lasted until 431 any argument that the war could not be avoided after the emergence of the Athenian Empire must demonstrate that the peace of 445 was doomed from the start. The treaty was ratified in the winter of 446/5, and although we do not have its text or a single full account of all its provisions, its essential elements are clear. In the only territorial clause, the Athenians agreed to give up the Peloponnesian lands they had acquired during the war. In return, the Spartans granted what amounted to official recognition of the Athenian Empire, for Sparta and Athens each swore the ratifying oaths on behalf of their allies. The Greek world was now formally divided in two by a provision forbidding the members of each alliance to change sides, an obvious attempt to prevent a recurrence of another war, as the last one had begun when Megara did precisely that. A clause that looked to the future did permit neutrals to join either side, an apparently straightforward and sensible item that would in fact cause a surprising amount of trouble. The most novel and interesting provision required both sides to submit future grievances to binding arbitration, a plan that seems to be the first attempt in history to maintain perpetual peace through such a device.

Some peace treaties end a conflict in which one side is destroyed or thoroughly defeated, such as the last war between Rome and Carthage (149–146 B.C.E.). Others, like the peace that Prussia imposed on France in 1871, impose harsh terms on an enemy who has been defeated but not destroyed. This kind of treaty often plants the seeds of another war because

it humiliates and angers the loser without destroying the capacity for revenge. A third sort of treaty ends a conflict, usually a long one, in which
each side has become aware of both the costs and dangers of continuing
the war and the virtues of suing for peace, whether or not there has been
a clear winner on the battlefield. The Peace of Westphalia in 1648 ending
the Thirty Years' War and the settlement with which the Congress of
Vienna concluded the Napoleonic Wars in 1815 are good examples of this
type. Such a treaty does not aim at destruction or punishment but seeks
instead a guarantee of stability against the renewal of war. The success
of this kind of peace requires that it accurately reflect the reality of the
military and political situation and that it rest on a sincere desire of both
parties to make it work.

The Thirty Years' Peace of 446/5 belongs in this last category. In the
course of a long war both sides had suffered losses and experienced dangers. Neither could win a decisive victory; the sea power had been unable
to sustain its victories on land, and the land power had been unable to
win at sea. The peace, therefore, was a compromise that contained the
essential elements required for success. It accurately reflected the balance
of power between the two rivals and their alliances. It committed both
sides to maintain the status quo in regard to each other and their allies.
By recognizing Sparta's hegemony on the mainland and Athens' in the
Aegean it accepted the dualism of the Greek world and so provided hope
for a lasting peace.

Like any peace treaty, this one also contained elements of possible
instability. In each state a minority faction remained dissatisfied: Some
Athenians favored expansion of the empire, while some Spartans resented sharing hegemony with Athens. Others, including a number of
Sparta's allies, feared Athenian ambition, believing that the very existence of a powerful Athenian naval empire threatened the independence
of the other Greeks. Athenians were well aware of these suspicions,
which led them to suspect that the Spartans and their allies were not
truly committed to peace but were only waiting for a favorable opportunity to renew the war. Some Spartans were frustrated with the way the

war had ended, confident that total victory had been at hand when King Pleistoanax withdrew their army from Attica without engaging in battle. The Corinthians were still angry at Athens for its interference against the Megarians; Megara, itself, was now ruled by oligarchs who had massacred an Athenian garrison in gaining control of their city, and they were as bitterly hostile to Athens as the Athenians were to them. Boeotia, and especially its chief city, Thebes, were also under the control of oligarchs who resented the Athenians' imposition of democratic regimes in their land during the late war.

Any or all of these factors might one day threaten the peace, but the men who agreed to it, made weary and cautious by the war, intended to preserve it. The arbitration clause was not conventional boilerplate, but a fresh new idea. Its acceptance suggests that both the Spartans and Athenians were ready to seek unusual means to avoid wars in the future. To do so each side needed to allay suspicion and build confidence; in each state the friends of peace had to remain in power; each state needed to control any tendency its allies might have to create instability. When the peace was ratified there was reason to believe that all this was possible.

The next five years tested the peace twice, the second time more severely. In 444/3 Sparta and Athens received a request from citizens— some of them Athenians who had joined as individuals—of the recently reestablished colony of Sybaris in southern Italy. Decimated by quarrels and civil wars, the Sybarites had sent to mainland Greece for help in founding a new colony at nearby Thurii. Sparta had no spare population to provide colonists and in any case had earlier indicated a lack of interest in the project.[15] The Athenians agreed to help, but in an unusual manner: they sent messengers throughout Greece to advertise for settlers for a new colony, that was not, however, to be an Athenian but rather a Panhellenic colony. This was a thoroughly new idea, without precedent. Why did Pericles and the Athenians conceive it?

It might be suspected that the Athenians were expansionists without limit and that the foundation of Thurii was merely part of a plan for uninterrupted Athenian imperial growth, in the west as well as the east. But,

apart from Thurii, the Athenians actually sought neither territory nor allies in the west in the years between the Thirty Years' Peace and the crisis
that brought on the Peloponnesian War, so the test of the theory must
be Thurii itself. In that colony Athenians made up only one of the ten
tribes in the city, the largest single group of which were Peloponnesians,
so Athens could not have reasonably hoped to control the place and use it
for its own purposes. The city's early history, moreover, reveals that Athens had never intended to control it. No sooner was Thurii founded than
it fought a war against one of Sparta's few colonies, Taras. Thurii lost, and
the winners set up a trophy of victory and an inscription at Olympia for
all the assembled Greeks to see: "The Tarantines offered a tenth of the
spoils they took from the Thurians to Olympian Zeus."[16] If the Athenians
had seriously intended Thurii to be the center of an Athenian Empire in
the west they should have taken some action in the matter, but they did
nothing, allowing the Spartan colony to flaunt its victory in the most
public gathering place in Greece.

A decade latter, in the midst of the crisis that led to war, a dispute
arose in Thurii as to the ownership of the colony. The priests at Delphi
declared that Apollo was the founder of the colony, which settled the
matter. That decision effectively reaffirmed the Panhellenic character of
Thurii and denied its connection with Athens, yet again Athens did nothing, even though Delphic Apollo was friendly to Sparta, and the colony
could be useful to the Spartans in case of war. The Athenians clearly continued to regard Thurii as a Panhellenic colony and consistently treated
it as such.

How can we explain the Athenians' actions? If they had no designs
on the west and wished to avoid provoking such Peloponnesian states
as Corinth, which did have colonies and interests in that direction, they
could simply have refused to take part in the establishment of Thurii.
Such inaction would have attracted little notice, but by inventing the
idea of a Panhellenic colony and planting it in an area outside Athens'
sphere of influence, Pericles and the Athenians may have been sending a
diplomatic signal. Thurii would stand as tangible evidence that Athens,

rejecting the opportunity to establish its own colony, had no imperial ambitions in the west and would instead pursue a policy of peaceful Panhellenism. The reception and persuasiveness of that message would soon be tested.

In the summer of 440 a war broke out between Samos and Miletus over control of Priene, a town lying betwen them. The island of Samos was autonomous, a charter member of the Delian League, and the most powerful of the only three allies that paid no tribute and possessed their own navies. Miletus had also been a member of the league from the first, but it had twice revolted and been punished accordingly, as the Athenians subjugated it, deprived it of its fleet, and forced it to pay tribute and to accept a democratic constitution. The Athenians now asked the Samians to submit the quarrel to arbitration, but they refused. Athens could not ignore this defiance of its leadership and authority, so Pericles himself led a fleet against Samos, replacing the ruling oligarchy with a democratic government, imposing a large indemnity, taking hostages as a guarantee of good behavior, and leaving an Athenian garrison to guard the island.

The Samian leaders responded by turning to outright revolution. Some of them persuaded Pissuthnes, the Persian satrap in Asia Minor, to help them against Athens. He allowed them to hire a mercenary army in his territory and stole the hostages from the island where the Athenians were holding them, thereby freeing the rebels to go forward with their plan. Joined by their mercenary army, the rebels surprised and defeated the democratic government and the Athenian garrison on Samos. As a supreme act of defiance they sent the captured garrison and other Athenian officials to the Persian satrap.

News of these events sparked further trouble in the empire. Byzantium, an important city located at a choke point on the Athenian grain route to the Black Sea, also revolted. Mytilene, the chief city of the island of Lesbos and another autonomous ally possessing a navy, awaited only Spartan support before joining the rebellion. The danger to Athens was acute, and two elements of the coalition that would later cause the defeat of Athens in the great Peloponnesian War were now in place: revolt in the empire and support from Persia. For now, everything depended on Sparta, for without its commitment the rebellions would be defeated and the Persians would draw back. Sparta's decision, in turn, was sure to be influenced by Corinth for, in case of a war against Athens, the Corinthians would be the most important ally expected to produce a fleet.

The test of the peace, and of Athenian policy since its conclusion, was at hand. If that policy, especially in the west, seemed to Sparta and Corinth to be aggressive and ambitious, this was the time to seize the incomparable opportunity to make a sudden attack on Athens while her sea power was seriously engaged. The Spartans called a meeting of the Peloponnesian League, proving that they took the matter seriously. The Corinthians later claimed it was they who decided the question, saying: "We did not vote against you when the other Peloponnesians were divided in their voting as to whether they should aid the Samians" (1.40.5). The decision went against attacking Athens, which was then free to crush the Samian rebellion and thus to avoid a general uprising aided by Persia, and a war that might have destroyed the Athenian Empire.

Why did the Corinthians, whose hatred of Athens dated back for two decades and who would be the major agitator for war in the final crisis, intervene to save the peace? The most plausible explanation is that they had understood the signal sent by the Athenian action at Thurii, for they would have certainly been inflamed had they believed the colony was meant to be part of a new Athenian expansion in the western regions so important to Corinth.

If the Samian crisis produced a dangerous threat of war, its outcome strengthened the possibility of peace. Since the agreement of 446/5 both sides had shown restraint and a refusal to seek advantages that might endanger the status quo. Prospects for the future were hopeful when a quarrel in a remote city created new and unexpected problems.

Epidamnus, where the trouble began, was governed by an aristocracy, but internal struggles against the democratic faction and a war against neighboring non-Hellenic Illyrian tribes had weakened the city and the aristocrats' hold on it. When the democrats gained the upper hand and drove their enemies from the city, the defeated aristocrats joined forces with the Illyrians and attacked their homeland. Since Epidamnus had been founded by Corcyra about two centuries earlier, the democrats within the city sent to the mother country, asking for help in ending the fighting. The Corcyraeans, who had done well by their policy of isolation from the brotherhood of Corinthian colonists as well as from any other alliance, refused. The desperate and beleaguered Epidamnians then turned to Corinth, offering to become a Corinthian colony in return for assistance. Corinth had founded Corcyra and, as was customary, had provided the founder for the city established by its own daughter city. The Corinthian proposal was a dangerous action, for unlike Corinth's warm ties with her other foundations, relations between Corinth and Corcyra were bad. For centuries the two cities had quarreled, warring often over control of some colony that both claimed as their own.

The Corinthians therefore joined in the conflict with enthusiasm, knowing full well that they would thus annoy the Corcyraeans, probably to the point of war. No tangible benefits compelled the Corinthians to intervene; since the Corcyraeans had remained aloof, no interest of the Corinthians was threatened, nor any diminution of their power or prestige. They seized the opportunity primarily to humiliate their insolent colony, sending a considerable garrison to reinforce the faction in Epidamnus and bringing along many whom they invited to be permanent settlers of the reestablished colony.

The Corcyraeans in turn sent a fleet to Epidamnus and presented their demands: the faction holding Epidamnus must send away the garrison and colonists sent by Corinth and take back the exiled aristocrats. These terms were rejected, as Corinth could not agree to them without disgrace, and the faction holding Epidamnus could not accept them in safety.

The Corcyraeans' confident arrogance rested on their naval superiority. They had dispatched forty ships to besiege the city, while the Epidamnian exiles and their Illyrian allies besieged it by land. But in relying on the correlation of forces at the beginning of the quarrel the Corcyraeans made a great mistake. Corinth was rich, adaptable, angry, and determined. It was allied to Sparta and a member of the Peloponnesian League. In the past the Corinthians had more than once been able to use those alliances to their own advantage, and they expected to do so again against Corcyra. The Corcyraeans should have been able to foresee the danger, but they were blinded by their own anger.

Corinth responded with vigor, announcing the foundation of a completely new colony at Epidamnus and inviting settlers from all over Greece to join it. Many responded and were sent to Epidamnus, accompanied by thirty Corinthian ships and three thousand soldiers. Additional help came from several cities asked by Corinth to supply ships and money. Several of them, including the major states of Megara and Thebes, were members of the Spartan Alliance, but the Spartans themselves gave no help. Even a token force from the Spartans might have intimidated the Corcyraeans, but we have no evidence that the Spartans were asked for support. Perhaps the Spartans had already expressed disapproval of the Corinthian expedition.

Shaken by these developments, the Corcyraeans sent negotiators to Corinth "with Spartan and Sicyonian ambassadors, whom they had invited along" (1.28.1). They repeated their demands that the Corinthians withdraw from Epidamnus. Failing that, Corcyra was willing to submit the dispute to arbitration. If the Corinthians refused and insisted on war, Corcyra would be forced to seek friends elsewhere—the unnamed "friends" obviously being the Athenians.

A minor incident in a remote corner of the Greek world had produced a crisis that now began to threaten a serious and widespread war. The Spartans, foreseeing the danger, agreed to lend their presence to the diplomatic effort for peace, but still the Corinthians would not yield, and after some maneuvering the negotiations failed. The Corinthians declared war and sent a fleet of seventy-five ships and two thousand infantrymen to Epidamnus. On the way they met a Corcyraean force of eighty ships and were thoroughly defeated at the battle of Leucimne. On the same day Epidamnus surrendered to the Corcyraean besiegers. To add to the Corinthians' humiliation, they could not prevent the Corcyraean fleet from ravaging and burning the territory of their allies in the west (1.29–30).

The Corinthians' answer to defeat was to spend the next two years preparing for revenge. They built their largest fleet ever and hired experienced rowers from throughout Greece, including cities in the Athenian Empire. The Athenians did not object, which may have strengthened the Corinthians' opinion that Corcyraean threats to seek help from Athens were unrealistic. Corcyra, frightened by Corinth's preparations, therefore sent an embassy to Athens to seek an alliance and assistance against Corinth. When the Corinthians heard about the mission they, too, sent ambassadors to Athens, "to prevent the addition of the Athenian fleet to the Corcyraeans' since that would impede their victory" (1.31). The crisis was about to reach a higher and more dangerous level, involving at least one of the great powers and alliances of the Greek world.

The Corcyraeans argued for the moral justice of their cause and for the legality of the alliance they proposed, since the Thirty Years' Peace expressly permitted alliance with a neutral. The Athenians, however, were more concerned with questions of security and their own interest, and the Corcyraeans were prepared to satisfy them: "We have a navy that is the greatest except for your own"—in other words, a force that could be added to strengthen Athenian power.

The most powerful appeal, however, was to fear. The Athenians needed the alliance as much as those proposing it, and they needed it at once, for a war between Athens and the Spartan Alliance was now inevitable. "If any of you thinks it will not happen his judgment is in error, and he does not see that the Spartans are eager for war out of fear of you, and that the Corinthians have great influence with them and are your enemies" (1.33.3). Since war could not be avoided, Athens must accept the Corcyraean alliance. "There are three fleets worthy of mention in Greece, yours, ours, and the Corinthians'; if the Corinthians get control of us first, you will see two of them become one, and you will have to fight against the Corcyraean and Peloponnesian fleets at once; if you accept us you will fight against them with our ships in addition to your own" (1.36.3).

For their part the Corinthians made a not very persuasive case on moral and legalistic grounds. They reminded the Athenians of past favors they had received from Corinth, especially during the Samian uprising when they helped to dissuade Sparta and the Peloponnesian League from attacking Athens at a moment of great danger. In response to the most telling argument of the Corcyreans—that war was inevitable, and in that war the Athenians must be sure to have the Corcyrean fleet on their side—the Corinthian answer was very simple: They merely denied that the war *was* unavoidable, arguing that it was precisely the Athenian decision about the alliance that would determine whether or not war would come. "The imminence of war, with which the Corcyreans frighten you and bid you do wrong is still uncertain" (1.42.2), they insisted, urging the Athenians not to turn the hostility of Corinth from a possibility into a certainty.

Thucydides' account of the debate indicates that the inevitability of the war was indeed a central issue. As the historian was certainly present on this crucial occasion, we should not doubt his accuracy in reporting it. Moreover, because thousands of Athenians were also present, if Thucydides reported the debate falsely, presenting an argument as being central when it was in fact only peripheral, many of his readers would know it at once, and his credibility would be destroyed. Like all the speeches at Athens that Thucydides reports took place before his exile, those of the Corcyraeans and Corinthians in September 433 must be authentic. It is worth considering that Thucydides' own conviction of the war's inevitability might well have been influenced by hearing these debates.

The Athenians now faced the most difficult of choices. If they accepted the Corcyraean alliance, it would surely draw them into war against Corinth and, sooner or later, probably against the Spartans and their allies. If they refused, they ran the risk of a Corinthian victory, Corinth's possible capture of the Corcyraean fleet, and the resulting major change in the balance of forces at sea. In case of a future war against the Peloponnesians, that change would put Athenian security at a fearful risk. As Thucydides describes the scene:

> Having heard both sides, the Athenians met in two successive assemblies. In the first they inclined toward the Corinthians, but in the second they changed their minds and decided to make an alliance with the Corcyraeans. But they did not agree to have the same friends and enemies [a *symmachia*, or offensive and defensive alliance] for then, if the Corcyraeans asked them to sail against Corinth, they would be breaking the treaty with the Peloponnesians. Instead they made a defensive alliance [*epimachia*] in which each side would assist the other if anyone should attack Athens or Corcyra or the allies of either. For they believed a war against the Peloponnesians was bound to come. Athens did not want so great a fleet as the Corcyraeans' to fall under Corinthian control. They also hoped that the two sides would wear each other down as much as possible in fighting each other so that, if war did come, the Corinthians and other naval powers would be weaker. (1.44)

Although almost all debates in the Athenian assembly typically ended in a single day, the argument over the Corcyraean alliance required a second meeting—one that produced a policy that ultimately led to the great war. The Athenians voted for an alliance that was defensive only, the first instance we hear of such a treaty in Greek history. At this point Thucydides, who has just reported speeches by the two foreign ambassadors, letting their words reveal their arguments, does not report any of the Athenian speeches but confines himself to the briefest summary of *what he believes* were the reasons for the action they took. He does not even tell us who proposed or argued for the new motion that gave rise to the final decision. For that we must rely on Plutarch, who reveals that it was Pericles who "persuaded the people to send help to the Corcyraeans

who were fighting the Corinthians and to attach themselves to a vigorous island with naval power."[17]

Even from this brief account it is obvious that there must have been a
long, contentious debate that involved a significant difference of opinion
within the assembly. At least two sharply opposed viewpoints must have
been presented—a situation that is ideal for a typically Thucydidean device: a pair of speeches, an antilogy, used to illustrate a situation most
graphically. This is precisely the method he will choose when he later
takes us into the Spartan assembly to hear the debate between Archidamus
and Sthenelaidas on its decision for war. Surely, on the Athenian side,
Cleon, the great war hawk, took part in the debate, probably in favor of
the offensive alliance, and it is possible that Thucydides son of Melesias,
the leader of the conservative, aristocratic Athenians, having returned
from his ostracism, spoke against it. At the second meeting, if Plutarch is
correct, Pericles himself spoke in favor of the defensive alliance, an idea
that was newly introduced. That suggestion might have drawn opposition from either of the two factions just mentioned. Whatever the case,
each assembly offered a golden opportunity for a dramatic presentation
of the issues at stake based not on the interpretation of the historian but
on the very words of the speakers and their reactions to one another.

Why, then, did Thucydides reject this opportunity? One inevitable
consequence of reporting the speeches directly would have been to emphasize in a striking way that at the start of the debate, at least, most
Athenians did *not* believe that war was inevitable. In fact at the end of
the first day they inclined against the policy of an offensive alliance after
hearing the Corcyraeans' claim that war was unavoidable and the Corinthians in turn deny it. At the second meeting they could be brought
round only by softening the policy to a defensive alliance, which might
allow them to take no action at all, and which was likely to encounter
challenges from both those who still thought the new proposal too dangerously strong and those who thought it inadequate and weak. A report
of the several speeches at both assemblies must have included arguments

against inevitability, further emphasizing the contemporary differences of opinion on that point.

Convincing a majority to support the defensive alliance at the second meeting surely demanded a speech by Pericles, and therein lay another problem for Thucydides. It is likely that Pericles' speech was characteristically impressive and that he carried the day, as he usually did. The result would have been to confirm the impression that it was Pericles who "persuaded the people to send help to the Corcyraeans," a policy that gave rise to the war that caused such suffering and ended so badly.

The common view, as we have seen, held Pericles responsible for bringing on the war. This was precisely the opinion Thucydides wanted to refute, and the technique he chose to do so was to treat the Athenian decision impersonally, as a consequence of all the Athenians' deliberations and as an inevitable response to the situation.

CHAPTER THREE

Causes of the War—From Corcyra to the Megarian Decree

WHY, many must have asked, should the Athenians risk war on behalf of Corcyra when any danger Athens faced was remote and uncertain? The choice of a defensive alliance in place of an offensive one, is certainly, consistent with a policy aimed not at preparing for war but at deterring it. In this case it represented a middle way between the unpleasant choices of refusing the Corcyraeans, thereby risking the loss of their fleet to the Peloponnesians, and accepting an offensive alliance likely to bring on an unwelcome war. At the time Pericles continued to shape Athenian policy, and the Athenians' subsequent behavior in the crisis indicates that he, and they, chose this policy of moderation and deterrence and held to it as long as possible.

As tangible and visible evidence of their commitment the Athenians sent a fleet to Corcyra, and its numbers, leadership, and instructions neatly illustrated the principles of the Periclean policy. Only ten ships were dispatched, of the hundreds that might have been sent, a force that was obviously meant to be more symbolic than militarily significant. Had Pericles seriously intended to fight the Corinthians, in preparation for a war against the Peloponnesians or otherwise, he should have sent at least two hundred warships. If a battle ensued, such a force, combined with the Corcyrean fleet, would have guaranteed a smashing victory and possibly the obliteration of the enemy's navy. The small force of ten ships, however, would make little difference in a battle if their presence alone failed to deter the Corinthians. Among the three commanders sent to Corcyra was Lacedaemonius son of Cimon. Although he was a seasoned soldier we know nothing of his actual naval experience. His choice as a general of this expedition cannot have been a coincidence. His paternity, and his own name, made plain his family's close friendship with the Spartans, and his selection for this assignment was clearly a gesture meant to disarm Spartan suspicion.

The generals were ordered not to enter into battle against the Corinthians unless they attacked Corcyra itself and were about to land on its territory; only then should the Athenians engage, to prevent a landing. "These orders were given in order not to break the treaty" (1.45.3), but proved to be a nightmare for the commanders who had to interpret them on the scene. How, in the midst of a naval battle, could a man be certain of the intentions of the participants? The Corinthians might approach Corcyra as part of a tactical maneuver, with no plans of landing, but this might not be clear until the last moment—by which point it might be too late to prevent a landing if that was what the Corinthians had really intended. In the event of an unnecessarily aggressive action that brought on a war it would be especially helpful if the crucial decision were made by Lacedaemonius, a well-known friend of the Spartans.

The arrival of the small Athenian squadron at Corcyra, however, did not deter the Corinthians, who sailed toward their hated colony with the largest fleet they had yet amassed: ninety ships of their own and sixty from their colonies and allies. Only two allied cities, Elis and Megara, took part in this campaign, near the island of Sybota, compared with the eight who had contributed to the battle of Leucimne. While the remaining six may have been dissuaded by the involvement of Athens, it also seems likely that the Spartans had applied some pressure on their allies to stay out of the conflict. Against this powerful armada the Corcyreans put to sea with one hundred and ten ships, accompanied by the ten from Athens. After a while the Corinthians gained the upper hand, and the Athenians were gradually forced to take part in the battle.

As the Corinthians drove their opponents back towards their island, the Corcyreans, reinforced by an Athenian contingent ready to fight, reorganized their forces and prepared to defend their land from invasion. But having sounded the signal to attack, the Corinthians suddenly began to back water. Why had they pulled back from delivering the coup de grâce? The answer came when twenty Athenian warships appeared on the horizon. They had been sent twenty-three days after the first group, when the Athenians decided that a larger force would be needed. Pericles had been compelled to yield to the more hawkish element in the city, who had no faith in the delicacy of his policy. At home as well as on the seas it was becoming increasingly difficult to hold to a thoroughly reasoned and carefully measured course of action once a commitment had been made and passions began to rise.

The Corinthians could not have known the size of the Athenian reinforcement, and given that the twenty ships they had spotted might be only the first squadron to arrive of many, they withdrew to avoid being caught between the two fleets. Night fell without further fighting, and when the following day the Corcyreans, strengthened by thirty undamaged Athenian ships, came out to fight, the Corinthians would have none of it. Not only had the balance of forces changed to their disadvantage, but they could still not be sure that further reinforcements were not on the way. They were also afraid that the Athenians might regard the previous day's skirmish as the beginning of a war against Corinth, giving them an excuse to destroy the Corinthian fleet on the spot.

In fact, both sides moved cautiously to avoid an irrevocable conflict and the blame for a formal breach of the peace. The Corinthians sent some men to talk to the Athenians, but without the herald's wand that was the equivalent to a flag of truce, for carrying that stick would be a formal admission that a state of war existed. The messengers accused the Athenians of breaking the treaty by preventing the Corinthians from punishing their enemies. "If you intend to prevent us from sailing to Corcyra or anywhere else we like," they said, "and in this way to break the treaty, first seize us and treat us as enemies" (1.43.2). The Corcyreans were most enthusiastic about this suggestion and urged the Athenians to kill the envoys. Instead, the Athenians returned a very careful answer in perfect accord with their strict orders and limited objectives:

We are not beginning a war, O Peloponnesians, nor are we breaking the treaty, but we have come to bring help to our Corcyrean allies. If you want to sail anywhere else we will not hinder you, but if you mean to sail against Corcyra or some part of her territory, we will not permit it, insofar as it is in our power. (1.53.4)

Each side, for its own reasons, was scrupulous in trying to avoid responsibility for breaking the treaty. The Corinthians knew that any chance they might have of winning a war against Athens depended on embroiling the Spartans and the Peloponnesian League. But because the Spartans had already indicated their disapproval of Corinthian policy, if the Corinthians could be shown to have been the first to break their oaths the chance of involving them in the Corinthian cause would be even slimmer. The Athenians were obviously concerned not to give the Spartans reason to take part in the quarrel by violating the treaty, but beyond that, their policy was to try to avoid war altogether, and they could hope that the hard evidence of their commitment and seriousness to that goal as demonstrated at Sybota might still deter Corinth from carrying the contest farther.

The most clear-cut instance of the Athenians' preparation for war against Corinth came in the winter following Sybota, in the form of an ultimatum they delivered to Potidaea, a city in the northern Aegean. The Potidaeans were members of the Athenian alliance and at the same time colonists of Corinth, unusually close to the mother city. Knowing that the Corinthians were planning revenge, the Athenians feared they might join with the hostile king of neighboring Macedon to spark a rebellion in Potidaea. From there it might spread to other states and cause serious problems in the empire.

Without any specific provocation, the Athenians ordered the Potidaeans to pull down the walls that protected them on the seaward side, to send away the magistrates they annually received from Corinth, and to give hostages. These actions would remove the city from Corinthian influence and place it at the mercy of Athens. Once again, the Athenian action should be understood as a diplomatic response to a looming problem, a moderate choice between unwelcome extremes. Taking no action might invite rebellion; sending a military force to gain physical control of Potidaea would make the city safe for Athens, but it could be provocative. Issuing the ultimatum was a matter of imperial regulation, clearly permitted by the Thirty Years' Peace.

The Potidaeans sent an embassy to Athens to object to the ultimatum, and discussions went on all winter, until the Athenians finally became suspicious and ordered the commander of an expedition they had previously sent to Macedonia "to take hostages from the Potidaeans, pull down their walls, and keep watch on the cities near by so that they would not rebel" (1.57.6). The Athenian suspicions were justified; at the same time the Potidaean sent envoys to Athens they had secretly dispatched another embassy to Sparta, where, supported by the Corinthians, they asked for help in their rebellion. In a remarkable reversal of policy, Spartan magistrates, no doubt the ephors, promised to invade Attica if Potidaea launched a rebellion. It remained to be seen if the assembly would endorse this agreement.

During the same winter (in close proximity to the Potidaean ultimatum, but whether before or after it is unclear) the Athenians took still another provocative action when they passed the decree barring the Megarians from the harbors of the Athenian Empire and from the Athenian Agora, its marketplace and civic center. While economic embargoes are sometimes used in the modern world as diplomatic weapons, as means of coercion short of war, in the ancient world we know of no previous embargo employed in peacetime.

This was certainly another of Pericles' innovations, for contemporaries blamed the subsequent war on the decree and on him for using the decree, although he defended it stubbornly to the end, even when it appeared to become the sole issue on which war or peace depended. Why did the Athenian leader introduce the decree, and why did he and the majority of Athens' citizens approve and hold fast to it? Modern commentators have seen it variously as an act of economic imperialism, a device intended deliberately to bring on the war, an act of defiance to the Peloponnesian League, an attempt to enrage the Spartans into violating the treaty, and even the first act of war itself. The official version was that the decree was provoked by the Megarians' cultivation of sacred land claimed by the Athenians, by their illegal encroachment upon borderlands, and by their harboring of fugitive slaves (1.139.2). The modern theories do not bear close scrutiny, and the ancient complaints are a mere pretext. The purpose of the Megarian Decree should be understood to have been a moderate intensification of diplomatic pressure to help prevent the spread of the war to Corinth's allies. The Corinthians could succeed only if the other Peloponnesians, especially Sparta, could be induced to join the fight. Corinth had defied Spartan wishes by rejecting a negotiated peace. Megara had done the same by sending help to Corinth at Leucimne and also at Sybota, even when most of the other Peloponnesian states had refrained from doing so. In time, other states might join the Corinthians in some future encounter with Athens; if enough of their allies took that step, the Spartans could stay aloof only at the risk of their leadership of the alliance and their own security. Pericles and the Athenians accordingly decided to punish the Megarians in order to deter further help to Corinth.

Once again, the Athenian action should be seen as a middle path. To do nothing might encourage further assistance to Corinth by Megara itself and might make it easier for other states to join them. To attack the city by any military means would be a breach of the treaty and would draw Sparta into the war against Athens. The embargo was not designed to bring Megara to its knees or do irreparable damage, but rather to cause general discomfort to most Megarians and do significant harm to the men who prospered from trade with Athens and her empire—some of whom, no doubt, were members of the oligarchic council that governed the city. The punishment might also persuade Megara to stay out of future trouble and serve as a warning to other trading states that they were not immune from Athenian retaliation, even in a period of formal peace.

For all its intended moderation, the Megarian Decree was not without risks. The Megarians were sure to complain to the Spartans, who might feel compelled to come to their aid, although there was reason to doubt that they would respond. But once again, the measure had been carefully crafted not to violate the terms of the treaty, which said nothing about trade or economic relations. In any case, Pericles was a personal friend of Archidamus (2.12.4), the only king in Sparta (Pleistoanax had been sent into exile in 445). He knew that Archidamus favored peace and could expect that his royal friend would understand his own peaceful intentions and the limited purposes of the decree and would help the other Spartans to understand, as well. Pericles was right about Archidamus, but he underestimated the passions aroused in some Spartans by the combination of events that had taken place since the alliance with Corcyra.

Although the Spartan magistrates had secretly promised the Potidaeans to invade Attica, that agreement was not endorsed by the Spartan assembly and therefore not executed in the spring of 432. Neither their king nor a majority of the Spartans was yet prepared to go to war, but an influential faction was eager to change their minds.

The Potidaeans, unaware of Spartan hesitation, launched their rebellion nonetheless, and the Athenian force dispatched to prevent an uprising was too little and arrived too late. Potidaea had organized a corps of "volunteers" commanded by a Corinthian general who led a force of Corinthians and Peloponnesian mercenaries, which forced the Athenians to send for reinforcements from Athens. By the summer of 432 a large force of men and ships surrounded the city, beginning a siege that lasted more than two years and cost a vast sum of money.

The Athenians were besieging a city defended by Corinthians and other Peloponnesians, whatever their informal status, and since the Megarians were injured and insulted by the Athenian embargo, the Corinthians now had grievances other than their own with which to inflame the Spartans against Athens. They in turn encouraged all the states that had complaints about Athens to put pressure on the Spartans as well. At last, in July 432, the ephors called a meeting of the Spartan assembly, inviting any allied state with a case against Athens to come to Sparta. This was the only known occasion when allies were invited to speak, not at a meeting of the Spartan alliance, but in the Spartan assembly. In spite of their promise, the ephors had not been able to get a vote for war against Athens in the assembly on their own. The most plausible explanation for this unique invitation is that the bellicose ephors did not believe they could bring the majority of the Spartans around to their view unaided, so they summoned the angry allies to help make the case.

Several spokesmen addressed the assembly, the most vehement being the Megarians, but the Corinthians were the most effective. Their strategy was to persuade Sparta that its traditional policy of caution and reluctance to fight was disastrous in the face of the dynamic power of Athens.

> They wear out their entire lives with danger, and they enjoy what they have the least of all men because they are always engaged in acquisition and because they think their only holiday is to do what is their duty and also because they consider tranquil peace a greater disaster than painful activity. As a result one would be correct in saying that it is their nature neither to enjoy peace themselves nor to allow it to other men. (1.70)

The Corinthians concluded with a threat: the Spartans must come to the aid of Potidaea and their other allies and invade Attica, "lest you betray your friends and kinsmen to their worst enemies and turn the rest of us to some other alliance" (1.71.4). The ultimatum was empty; there was no other alliance to which they could turn, but it had an effect nonetheless. Sparta's security and its way of life rested, to some considerable degree, on the integrity of its alliances, so even the suggestion of defections that might lead to dissolution was alarming.

The next speaker was a member of an Athenian embassy who, Thucydides says, "happened to be present beforehand on other business" (1.72.1). We are not told what that "business" might be, and it seems clear that it was merely a pretext to allow the Athenians to present their views.

For Pericles and the Athenians it was important not to send an official spokesman to a Spartan assembly to answer complaints, for that would concede Sparta's right to judge Athenian behavior rather than to submit disagreements to arbitration, as the treaty required. At the same time, they wanted to affect the debate. The Athenian representative intervened to prevent Sparta from making a serious mistake by yielding to the arguments of its allies, and to argue that Athens had gained her power justly, while stressing that Athenian power was formidable. He ascribed the growth of Athens' empire not to ambition but as a response to a series of necessities imposed by the demands of fear, honor, and a reasonable self-interest—principles that the Spartans, who exercised a similar power, should understand. His tone was not conciliatory, but businesslike, and his conclusion insisted on the precise letter of the treaty: the submission of all disputes to arbitration. Should the Spartans refuse, however, "we shall try to take vengeance on those who have started the war when you have led the way" (1.78.5).

Thucydides plainly states his opinion that the Athenian embassy had been sent not to bring on the war but to try to preserve peace: "They wanted to make clear the power of their city, to offer a reminder to the older men of what they already knew and to the younger men the things of which they were ignorant, thinking that because of their arguments the Spartans would incline to peace instead of war" (1.72.1). The Athenians placed their hopes for peace in a combination of deterrence and the honorable alternative to war of arbitration.

As Thucydides wrote this passage he knew that the effort had failed and that war would come. Subsequently, as we have seen, many Athenians blamed the coming of the war on Pericles, a charge that Thucydides believed was woefully mistaken. Yet Pericles was the chief shaper of Athenian policy throughout this period. To send a delegation to Sparta with instructions to intervene in the debate if the opportunity seemed appropriate required a vote of the Athenian assembly. On most occasions such envoys were instructed very carefully about the nature of their mission and even how to carry it out. It is inconceivable, therefore, that the

Athenian spokesman in Sparta did not follow the spirit of his instructions. It is likewise inconceivable that those instructions were contrary to the wishes of Pericles, for if they were, Thucydides would surely have said so. When the effort failed, and the debate in Sparta resulted in a resolution that Athens had broken the peace, critics of the Periclean policy would surely have made this incident part of their complaint against him.

Like them, some modern writers have understood the Athenian ambassador's speech as deliberately provocative, intended to incite the Spartans to violate their oaths and start the war. Thucydides, however, was convinced that such a judgement was wrong, and that the speech's consequences were unwanted by Athens, but merely demonstrated the truth of the historian's interpretation that war was now inevitable. The Spartans could have avoided war simply by keeping their oaths and abiding by the arbitration clause in the treaty. That they did not demonstrates that the growth of Athenian power and the danger it presented—a peril powerfully argued by the Corinthians—had so frightened the Spartans that war could not be avoided.

Thucydides helps his reader to reach such a conclusion by delicate means, as well as a more obvious one. He was surely present at the assembly that voted to send a mission to Sparta, selected its members, and gave them their instructions, yet he fails to report any of the relevant speeches or even to mention the assembly at all. He does not say who introduced the motion or who argued for and against it or the nature of the debate. He says the envoys "happened to have been present [in Sparta] beforehand on other business" (1.72.1), but it is hard to imagine what that "other business" might be, if it was not to assess the situation among the Spartans, to report that back home, and, if the situation called for it, to deliver a prepared message to the assembly in Sparta. There were no commercial treaties to negotiate, no cultural exchanges or any more plausible matters to attend to, nor were ambassadors in Sparta in pursuit of their own affairs. The Athenian spokesman himself makes it clear that he and his colleagues came to deal with "those things for which the city sent us" (1.73.1).

There is every likelihood that Pericles or one of his supporters made the proposal for the mission in the Athenian assembly, and that it contained both the names of the ambassadors (also likely to be his supporters) and, in a general way, the character of the message they should deliver to the Spartan assembly if they found it expedient to speak there. But focusing attention on the freely chosen decision that was part of a failed policy—a policy that would rightly be attributed to Pericles—would have had exactly the wrong effect, from the historian's point of view.

Thucydides was convinced that these negotiations were not crucial and were doomed from the start, because greater issues and events, dating back decades, had made the war inescapable. He therefore omits to reveal the originator of the plan, the true purpose of the mission, the members of the embassy, and the instructions they received. He does, however, report speeches by King Archidamus, who was opposed to war at that time, and the presiding ephor, Sthenelaidas who, insisting that Athens had broken the treaty, favored war at once. The vote was for war. Then, to be sure that his readers derived the correct understanding from his description of the assembly in Sparta, Thucydides adds, as we have seen: "The Spartans voted to go to war, not so much because they had been persuaded by the arguments of their allies as because they were afraid that the Athenians might become more powerful, seeing that the greater part of Greece was already in their hands" (1.88), a variation on his statement of the "truest explanation" of the coming of the war. How he knew with certainty what was in the hearts and minds of the Spartans is not clear.

The vote for war opened the way for an invasion of Attica, an action that would have redeemed the Spartan's promise to the Potidaeans, only carried out months late. The simple preparations for the invasion needed no more than a few weeks, and September and October would provide good weather either for a battle or for doing harm to property if the Athenians should refuse to fight. Although the Athenian grain crop had long since been harvested, there was still time to do significant damage to grapevines and olive trees and to the farmhouses outside the walls. If the Athenians were going to come out and fight, as the Spartans expected, a September invasion would give them plenty of incentive to do so.

All this argued for an immediate advance into Attica, but the Spartans and their allies took no military action for some nine months. Even then, it was the Thebans, attacking Athens' allies the Plataeans without consulting Sparta, who began hostilities in March 431. In the interim, moreover, the Spartans sent no fewer than three peace missions to Athens, of which at least one seems to have been sincere (1.126–139). The long delay of the onset of the war and the attempt at negotiation suggest that after the emotion of the debate had passed the cautious and sober arguments of Archidamus asserted themselves and restored the mood in Sparta to its usual conservatism. Perhaps war might yet be averted.

The first Spartan mission demanded that the Athenians "drive out the curse of the goddess" (1.126.2–3), a reference to an act of sacrilege committed two centuries earlier by a member of Pericles' mother's family, with which Pericles was widely associated. The demand was not intended seriously but meant only to embarrass Pericles. The Spartans thought it would be easier to win concessions from the Athenians if Pericles were banished, but they had no real hope of bringing about his exile. They hoped, instead, that he would be blamed for Athens' troubles and discredited, because, "as the most powerful man of his time and the leader of his state, he opposed the Spartans in everything and did not allow the Athenians to yield but kept driving them toward war" (1.126.3). The Spartans' effort at such psychological and political warfare, however, suggests that they did believe there was enough opposition in Athens to both Pericles and his policy to make it worthwhile. Pericles, however, was himself experienced and skilled in the art of political propaganda, and the Athenians rejected the proposal.

Undaunted by this rebuff, the Spartans sent envoys making various demands, but finally settling on one: "They proclaimed publicly and in the clearest language that there would be no war if the Athenians withdrew the Megarian Decree" (1.139.1). This demand reflected a compromise and indicated a change in Sparta's political climate since the vote for war. Plutarch says that Archidamus "tried to settle the complaints of the allies peacefully to soften their anger,"[1] but neither he nor his opponents were firmly in command. If Archidamus were in control he could have submitted the complaints to arbitration; if the advocates of war had the upper hand they could have ended negotiations after the failure of the first embassy. Archidamus, apparently, was strong enough to force a continuation of negotiations, but his opponents could demand concessions without arbitration. The compromise still rejected arbitration but reduced the demands to one.

The Megarian offer was no light concession by the Spartans, for it amounted to a betrayal of Corinthian interests. On the other hand, by supporting and protecting the Megarians without submitting to arbitration, the Spartans demonstrated their power and reliability as leaders of the alliance, thereby isolating Corinth. If the Corinthians threatened to secede in those circumstances, Archidamus and the majority of Spartans were ready to let them try to do so. Perhaps the time had come to show Corinth who was leader of the alliance.

In spite of the softened Spartan position Pericles remained obdurate, insisting on nothing less than arbitration, as required by the treaty. The Spartans' offer of compromise did, however, persuade many Athenians. By dropping all their other demands the Spartans made it seem that Athens was willing to go to war simply over the Megarian Decree, which, after all, had originally been intended as a mere tactical maneuver and in itself was certainly not worth fighting over. Pericles could not, therefore, ignore the pressure for a response. The official charges that had ostensibly provoked the embargo were now embodied in a formal decree and sent to Megara and Sparta as a defense of the Athenian action. "This decree was proposed by Pericles and contained a reasonable and humane justification of this policy," says Plutarch.[2] In answer to repeated Spartan requests, Pericles explained his refusal to rescind the embargo by pointing to some obscure Athenian law that forbade him from taking down the tablet on which the decree was inscribed. The Spartans replied,

"Then don't take it down, turn the tablet around, for there is no law against that."[3] True or not, the story reflects what must have been great pressure to yield, rescind the decree, and avoid war, but Pericles held fast and kept the majority with him.

The Spartans now sent a final embassy with an ultimatum: "The Spartans want peace, and there will be peace if you give the Greeks their autonomy" (1.139.3). This amounted to a demand for the dissolution of the Athenian Empire, and Pericles would have liked the argument in the Athenian assembly to focus on that obviously unacceptable requirement, but his opponents were able to set the terms of the debate. The Athenians "resolved to give an answer after having considered everything once and for all" (1.139.3). Here again, as in the debate on the Corcyraean alliance, was a classic opportunity to present a pair of competing speeches, each making the case for one of the different policies. Once again, Thucydides was surely in attendance and heard all that was said at the assembly.

Although the historian tells us that "many others spoke, some arguing that the war was necessary, others that the decree should not be a hindrance to peace but should be withdrawn," he reports only one speech, the one made by Pericles. On this occasion he introduces him as "Pericles the son of Xanthippus, the foremost man at that time among the Athenians and the most powerful in speech and in action" (1.139.4).

In the first part of his speech Pericles defends his policy, pointing out that the Spartans had consistently refused to submit to arbitration, as the treaty required, but instead sought to win their point by threats or force. "They want to resolve their complaints by war instead of discussion, and now they are here, no longer requesting but already demanding. . . . Only a flat and clear refusal of these demands will make it plain to them that they must treat you as equals" (1.140.2, 5). Pericles was willing to yield on any specific point. If the Spartans had submitted to arbitration, he would have been compelled to accept the decision and was ready to do so. What he could not accept, however, was direct Spartan interference in the Athenian Empire at Potidaea and Aegina, whose representatives at the Spartan assembly in 432 had also made a complaint, or with Athenian commercial and imperial policy as represented by the Megarian Decree. That would in effect be a concession that Athenian hegemony in the Aegean and control of her own empire depended on the sufferance of the Spartans. If the Athenians gave way when threatened now, they would abandon their claim to equality and open themselves to future blackmail. Pericles carefully spelled this out in his speech to the assembly:

> Let none of you think that you are going to war over a trifle if we do not rescind the Megarian Decree, whose withdrawal they hold out especially as a way of avoiding war, and do not reproach yourselves with second thoughts that you have gone to war for a small thing. For this "trifle" contains the affirmation and the test of your resolution. If you yield to them you will immediately be required to make another concession which will be greater, since you will have made the first concession out of fear. (1.140.5)

Pericles' statement is a classic rejection of appeasement under pressure, but was it justified? For many Athenians it must have been difficult to understand why they should be willing to fight for this seeming trifle of a decree. But the apparently trivial source of contention masked significant political and strategic considerations.

The grievances at hand were not important in themselves. Sparta's single nonnegotiable demand contained nothing of material or strategic importance to the Athenians. If the Athenians had withdrawn the Megarian Decree, the crisis would probably have blown over. That danger averted, several circumstances might have encouraged a continuation of the peace. Sparta's betrayal of Corinth would surely have led to a coolness between the two states, a rift that might have distracted the Spartans from conflict with Athens. Other distractions might arise in the Peloponnesus, as they had in the past. The longer the peace, the greater the chance that all would be reconciled to the status quo. These and other arguments were available to the opponents of Pericles, and many of them would likely have been used in their speeches, but Thucydides chose not to report them. Individually and collectively they would have powerfully suggested a war between Athens and Sparta was not inevitable if the current crisis could be overcome. All the Athenians need do was withdraw the Megarian Decree and peace would be preserved.

Once again, as in the debate over Corcyra, that conclusion was precisely what Pericles and Thucydides believed was mistaken. In his speech Pericles tried to turn his audience's attention to a broader view of their situation than the immediate Spartan proposals and demands: "It was already clear in the past that they were plotting against us and now it is even clearer" (1.140.2). This assertion was meant to remind the Athenians of the long history of Spartan hostility dating back to the Persian War, of their opposition to the Athenians' rebuilding their walls just after the Persian War, to the Spartans' serious consideration of challenging Athenian leadership of the Delian League soon after its foundation, to their promise to the rebellious Thasians to invade Attica in 465, to their insulting dismissal from the Peloponnesus of the Athenian army in the next year, to the decade and a half of the First Peloponnesian War, and to Sparta's openness to launching another war against Athens during the Samian rebellion of 440.

If any were so credulous as to believe that the Spartans were now ready faithfully to observe the Thirty Years' Peace, they needed to take note that, "although the treaty stipulated that each side should submit complaints to arbitration while each kept what it had, they have never yet asked for arbitration themselves nor do they accept it now that we offer it. They want to resolve complaints not by words but by war, and now they are here, not arguing their case but already giving orders" (1.140.2).

The Athenians, Pericles insisted, should send an embassy to Sparta to say that Athens would allow free access to the Megarians "when the Spartans exempt us and our allies from their laws expelling aliens from their territory (for the treaty contains nothing that forbids either action)." We should also say that we are willing to submit to arbitration according to the treaty, that "we will not start a war but will defend ourselves against those who do begin it. That is an answer that is both just and

that suits the dignity of this city. *But we must know that war is inevitable"*
(1.144.2–3).

Thucydides concludes his account of this fateful debate in the assembly by telling us: "So spoke Pericles. The Athenians, believing that he had
given the best advice, voted as he directed and answered the Spartans
accordingly. . . . And the Spartans went home and sent no more embassies" (1.145). Since the reader has been told none of the opposition's arguments he is ill equipped to question the eloquent and powerful ones made
by Pericles and the skillful frame for them constructed by the historian.
The widespread contemporary opinion that blamed Pericles and his policies for the outbreak of the war is buried in silence and the overwhelming
sense of its inevitability.

CHAPTER FOUR

The Strategy of Pericles

W E HAVE SEEN that Thucydides gives a full and unequivocal endorsement to Pericles' strategy for victory in the great war that
began in 431:

> As long as he led the state in peacetime he kept to a moderate policy
> and kept it safe, and it was under his leadership that Athens reached her
> greatest heights; and when the war came it appears that he also judged
> its power correctly.
>
> Pericles lived for two years and six months after the war began, and
> after his death his foresight about the war was acknowledged still more.
> (2.65.5–7)

The strategy Pericles had proposed was this: "if the Athenians stayed
on the defensive, maintained their navy and did not try to expand their
empire in wartime, thereby endangering the state, they would win out"
(2.65.7). But after his death they abandoned his program and pursued
others, and when their efforts failed they undermined the state's conduct
of the war.

> And yet, after losing most of their fleet and all their other forces in Sic-
> ily, with revolution already breaking out in Athens, they still held out
> for ten years against their original enemies, with the Sicilians now by
> their side and against their own allies, most of whom had revolted, and
> against Cyrus, son of the King of Persia, who later joined the other side
> and provided the Peloponnesians with money for their fleet. And they

did not give in until they had destroyed themselves by their own internal conflicts. So immensely great were the resources that Pericles counted on at the time through which he foresaw an easy victory for Athens over the Peloponnesians alone. (2.65.12–13)

Such was Thucydides' interpretation of events, but it was not in fact the way his contemporary Athenians viewed them. In the first year of the war the Spartans invaded Attica. So long as they confined their devastation to the northwestern corner of Athenian territory the people were willing to follow Pericles' orders without complaint and stay behind their walls, avoiding battle:

But when they saw the army in the neighborhood of Acharnae, only sixty stadia from the city, they thought the situation no longer tolerable; on the contrary, it naturally appeared to them a terrible thing when their land was being ravaged before their eyes, a sight that the younger men had never seen, or even the older men except in the Persian War; and the general opinion, especially on the part of the younger men, was that they ought to go out and put a stop to it. They gathered in knots and engaged in hot disputes, some urging that they should go out, others opposing this course. Oracle-mongers were chanting oracles of every kind, as each man was inclined to hear them. And the Acharnians, thinking that no insignificant portion of the Athenian people lived at Acharnae, insisted most of all upon going out, as it was their land that was being devastated. Thus in every way the city was in a state of irritation; and they were indignant against Pericles, and remembering none of his earlier warnings they abused him because, though their general, he would not lead them out, and considered him responsible for all their sufferings. (2.21.2–3)

In the spring of 430 the poet Hermippus presented a comedy that gives us an idea of what must have been a common charge leveled against the reluctant general: cowardice. He addresses Pericles as follows: "King of the Satyrs, why won't you ever lift a spear but instead only use dreadful words to wage the war, assuming the character of the cowardly Teles. But if a little knife is sharpened on a whetstone you roar as though bitten by the fierce Cleon."[1]

Anger toward and criticism of his policies became so fierce that Pericles feared that the Athenian assembly might reject his strategy and force a battle on land.

> Pericles, however, seeing that they were angry at the current situation and that they were not thinking at their best, and convinced that his judgment was right about refusing to go out, would not call a meeting of the assembly or any gathering whatever, for fear that if they got together there would be an outbreak of passion without judgment that would end in some serious error. (2.22.1)

Here is Plutarch's account of the situation:

> And he would not call the people to assembly, afraid that he would be compelled against his own judgment . . . but he used his own calculations, paying little attention to the complainers and those who could not bear the suffering. Still, many of his friends pressed appeals on him and many of his enemies threatened him and made accusations against him. Choruses sang mocking songs of ridicule, insulting his generalship for its cowardice, and its abandonment of everything to the enemy. Cleon, too, was already harassing him, making use of the anger of the citizens against him to gain ground toward his own leadership of the people.[2]

Pericles was able to hold his critics at bay, but his military plan did not work. The aim of his strategy was not to defeat the Spartans in battle but to convince them that war against Athens was futile. His goals, therefore, were entirely defensive, and his tactics, almost completely so. The Athenians were to reject battle on land, abandon their fields and homes in the country to Spartan devastation, and retreat behind their walls. Meanwhile, their navy would launch a series of commando raids on the coast of the Peloponnesus. The naval raids and landings were not meant to do serious harm but merely to annoy the enemy and to suggest how much damage the Athenians could do if they chose. The intent was not to exhaust the Peloponnesians physically or materially but psychologically. This program would continue until the frustrated enemy was prepared to make peace.[3]

No such strategy had ever been attempted in Greek history, for no state before the coming of the Athenian imperial democracy had ever had the means to try it. Even then, this unprecedented plan ran directly against the grain of Greek tradition, in which willingness to fight, bravery, and steadfastness in battle were the essential characteristics of the free man and the citizen. Most Athenians, moreover, were farmers whose lands and homes were outside the city walls, and they were required to look on idly while their houses, crops, vines, and olive trees were damaged or destroyed. It is hard to understand, even in retrospect, how Pericles could convince the Athenians to accept such conditions.

When Pericles died the Athenian treasury was running dry, his plan lay in ruins, and there was no prospect for victory. Only when his successors turned to a more aggressive strategy did the Athenians level the playing field and achieve a position that allowed them to hold out for twenty-seven years and almost achieve victory.

Why did Pericles' strategy fail?

To evaluate his plan objectively we need to determine how long Pericles expected the Spartans to hold out before they saw reason. That question is not generally asked by those who regard the outcome of the Archidamian War (431–421) as justification for his strategy, but implicit in their reasoning is the fact that a war of ten years duration did not lie outside his calculations. Pericles rightly argued that, while the Peloponnesians lacked the resources to launch the kind of campaign that would have seriously endangered the Athenian Empire, nothing prevented them from continuing to invade and devastate Attica annually. These invasions lasted no longer than a month, and the only cost to the invaders was the soldiers' food. The important question is, how long could the

Athenian treasury hold out at the annual rate of expenditure required to sustain the Periclean strategy?

We can get some idea of its average yearly expense by examining the first year of the war, when Pericles was firmly in control and his strategy applied to the letter. It was as unadventurous a year as any could be while Athens was still in good fighting condition. By three different calculations it becomes clear that Pericles must have expected to spend at least 2000 talents a year to carry on the war;[4] three years of such a war would cost 6000 talents. In the second year of the war the Athenians voted to set aside 1000 talents from this fund to be used only "if the enemy should make a naval attack against the city and they should have to defend it" (2.24.1). This left a usable reserve fund of 5000 talents; if we add three years of imperial revenue or 1800 talents, we get a total of 6800 talents. Pericles, therefore, could maintain his strategy for three years but not for a fourth.

He could calculate these sums as well as we can, so we must not imagine that he actually expected a war of ten years, much less the twenty-seven it ultimately lasted. His goal—to bring about a change of opinion in Sparta—was not unreasonable when we remember how unwilling the Spartans were to go to war in the first place, given the long interval between their vote for war and their first action, their attempt to negotiate a peace in the interim, and the great and continuing reluctance of Sparta's king to begin hostilities. For Pericles' scheme to succeed the Athenians needed merely to help restore the natural majority that kept Sparta conservatively and pacifically inside the Peloponnesus, as it typically was.

In light of these facts Pericles' decision seemed to make excellent sense. His main tactical problem was the defensive one of restraining the Athenians from offering battle in Attica. The offensive naval actions were deliberately unimpressive, for they were intended only as evidence that an extended war would be damaging to the Peloponnesians. The overall policy of restraint at home and abroad could reasonably be expected to bring the friends of peace to power in Sparta eventually. Pericles might well have anticipated such a change in Spartan opinion to come quickly—as early as after only one campaigning season. Perhaps it would take two years, but surely not more than three, for it would be wildly unreasonable for Sparta to continue to beat its fist without effect against the stone wall of the Athenian defensive strategy.

The plan, however, did not work, and signs of trouble appeared in the very first year. The Athenians stayed behind their walls and refused to fight a land battle; their ships sailed around the Peloponnesus devastating coastal regions of several enemy states, defeating small armies that came against them, and capturing several strategic ports. After the Spartans withdrew from Attica, Pericles himself led a large Athenian army against Megara and thoroughly ravaged its land. Yet in spite of this careful adherence to his plan, the end of the war was nowhere in sight.

In a war of attrition the side that does the greater damage will win in the end, and the Spartans had so far done most of the damage. In addition to paying the psychological price of watching their crops cut down, their vines and olive trees destroyed or damaged, their houses demolished or burned, the Athenians had lost the grain they needed for food. This could be replaced by imported supplies, but at a cost. The exports typically used to maintain a balance of trade were olive oil and wine, but their sources were no longer available. Payment for the imported foodstuffs, whether privately or publicly funded, reduced the financial resources of the Athenians and, in turn, the amount of time they could hold out. By comparison, the attacks on the Peloponnesus, apart from extra-Peloponnesian Megara, were mere pinpricks, irritating but with little long-term strategic significance, for they did not weaken the enemy's capacity or will to fight. The Athenians were also disappointed when the resistance of the Potidaeans continued.

The Athenians had spent considerable time and money with little to show for their expenditure. They had already been compelled to borrow from the reserve fund in the sacred treasuries some 1300 to 1400 talents, more than a fourth of their disposable war chest. The Peloponnesians showed no sign of discouragement, but would return the following spring with the spirit to destroy the large portion of Attica they had left untouched. There is no evidence of dissension within the Peloponnesian League during this period, or of a growing influence of the friends of peace in Sparta. As the first year of the war came to an end the pressure on Pericles and his strategy only increased.

Even Pericles could not ignore the discontent, so, "because he wanted to cure these ills and also because he wanted to do some harm to the enemy,"[5] he himself led an expedition against the Peloponnesus in May of 430 with a very large force, with the mission of doing more damage than had been inflicted the previous year. "When they arrived at Epidaurus in the Peloponnesus they ravaged most of the land. And when they made an attack on the city they arrived at the hope of taking it, but they were not successful. Leaving Epidaurus, they ravaged most of the land of Troezen, Halieis, and Hermione, which are all on the coast of the Peloponnesus. From there they sailed to Prasiae, a coastal town of Laconia; they ravaged its land, took the town, and sacked it. When they had done this they returned home" (2.56.4–6). This campaign did not represent an actual change in strategy but merely an intensification of it to speed up the education of the Peloponnesians.

The Peloponnesians' second invasion was merciless, sparing no part of Attica. The army remained for forty days, their longest stay of the war, wreaking havoc across the entire country and leaving only when its supplies ran out. Instead of becoming more inclined toward peace as their strategic expectations were refuted, both sides became more bitter and determined, and increased their efforts accordingly.

Then disaster struck the Athenians. During the years 430 and 429 a plague broke out and raged with unprecedented ferocity; after a hiatus, it reappeared in 427 and before running its course it killed as many as one third of the city's inhabitants. Because the entire population of Attica had been crowded into the walled area, it was especially virulent. The plague had a crushing effect on Athenian morale, and it severely undermined Pericles' position, popular confidence in his strategy, and the continuation of a war that was increasingly blamed on his policy.

At least part of this disapproval was the result of a religious reaction among the people. The Greeks had always thought of plagues as divine punishments for human actions that angered the gods. Such was the plague at the beginning of Homer's *Iliad*, sent by Apollo to avenge Agamemnon's insult to his priest. But pestilences were also often connected with the failure to heed divine oracles and with acts of religious pollution. At the onset of the plague at Athens the older men recalled an oracle from the past that said "A Dorian war will come and a plague with it" (2.54.2). That implicitly cast blame on Pericles, the firmest advocate of war against the Dorian Peloponnesians and a man known for his rationalism and for associating with religious skeptics. The pious linked his impiety to Athenian suffering, pointing out that the plague that had ravaged Athens had not entered the Peloponnesus.

Some had more plausible complaints, accusing Pericles of imposing a strategy that made the effects of the plague far more terrible than if the Athenians had been scattered around Attica, as they usually were. The people were persuaded by his enemies that the plague had been caused by the crowding of the masses from the countryside into the city, where, during the summer, many were jammed together in small huts and stifling tents; they were forced to spend their time inactive at home instead of in the pure open air as before. Pericles had allowed them to be penned up like cattle to fill one another up with corruption, providing no change or rest.[6]

As a result of all these factors, the Athenians finally turned sharply against him and his policies. Pericles could no longer prevent a meeting of the people, and contrary to his wishes the Athenian assembly sent ambassadors to Sparta to ask for peace. We are not told what terms were discussed, but evidently even the Athenians who wanted peace thought them too harsh, for they rejected them and continued the war. The Spartans probably insisted on the conditions of the ultimatum they had issued before the war: that Athens should free the Greeks—that is, abandon its empire. The failure of this mission struck a blow from which the peace faction at Athens did not recover for almost a decade. Their attempt to negotiate an acceptable agreement at a time of weakness proved that

Pericles had been correct in his main contention: the Athenians could achieve no satisfactory peace until they had convinced the Spartans that Athens would not yield and could not be defeated. Some within the peace faction, however, appear not to have given up hope of renewing negotiations, but they were thwarted by the influence and eloquence of Pericles. Frustrated, they launched a personal attack on Pericles, and he rose to defend himself in his last reported speech.

Never since his rise to leadership had his popularity and influence been at a lower ebb, but his standing was mitigated by the character of his leadership. He was that rare political leader who had always told the people the truth, even while pursuing disputed and unpopular policies. No one could claim that he had not presented the issues clearly and honestly, or that they had not been fully and freely debated by the public. If he had underestimated the fierceness of Sparta's anger and determination, the people had been permitted to dispute his assessment when they voted on his policies. The Athenians, like most groups suffering misfortune, forgot their own responsibility and miscalculation and sought a scapegoat, but Pericles' record of forthrightness gave his angry listeners no opportunity. "If," he said to them, "you were persuaded by me to go to war because you thought I had the qualities necessary for leadership at least moderately more than other men, it is not right that I should now be blamed for doing wrong" (2.60.7).

The Athenians sent no more embassies to Sparta and took up the war with renewed vigor, but the advocates of peace persisted in their campaign. In September of 430, the Athenians deposed Pericles from his office as general to stand trial on a charge of embezzlement. It seems likely that the city's two extreme factions—the supporters of peace at almost any price, and their opposite numbers, the faction favoring a more aggressive war, led by men like Cleon—joined forces to remove the moderate leader who stood in the way of both.

In light of the misery caused by the plague, and the evident inadequacy of his strategy, with no immediate prospect of either victory or an acceptable peace, it is not surprising that Pericles was convicted and punished with a heavy fine. That sentence appears to have carried with it disenfranchisement, which means that the verdict removed Pericles from public life. No doubt Pericles, perhaps helped by his friends, soon paid the fine, but beginning in September 430 he was out of office and away from the conduct of government affairs.

The following spring, however, the Athenians elected him general once again. Thucydides offers an explanation for this reversal of opinion: "Not much later, as the mob loves to do, they elected him general again and turned everything over to him, for their individual feelings were less keen over their private misfortunes whereas for the needs of the state as a whole they judged him to be the ablest" (2.65.4). This account says more about Thucydides' view of Athenian democracy than about the cause of the shift in public sentiment. The passage of time had accustomed the Athenians to their sufferings and had revealed that the removal of Pericles had had no useful consequences. They must also have missed his outstanding talents, his experience and confidence, and the sense of security he fostered. It is also true, however, that the unnatural coalition that had brought about his downfall could not last, and the great moderate bloc that Pericles himself had formed and consolidated over the years gradually reasserted itself.

By midsummer 429, when he resumed office, Pericles was mortally ill and had only a few months to live. The disease that killed him did not attack him suddenly but lingered, "using up his body slowly and undermining the loftiness of his spirit."[7] Near the end of his biography of Pericles Plutarch describes the great Athenian leader on his deathbed. The best men of Athens and his personal friends gathered in his room were discussing his virtues and the power he held. Thinking he was asleep, "they added up his achievements and the number of his trophies, for as general he had set up nine commemorating a victory on behalf of the city."[8]

But Pericles was awake and responded to the encomiums of his military prowess. He expressed astonishment that they should be praising what was actually as much the result of good fortune as of his own talents and what many others had accomplished. Instead, he said, they should be celebrating the finest and most important of his claims to greatness: "that no Athenian now alive has put on mourning clothes because of me."[9] That assertion, the last words of Pericles reported to us, must have astounded his audience, as they would have surprised any other Athenian. Even his friends would have had to admit that his policy had contributed at least something to the coming of the war, and that his strategy had been in part culpable for the intensity of the destruction caused by the plague. Nevertheless, his final words reveal how deeply he felt the wounds caused by the widespread accusations hurled against him, as well as his stubborn refusal to admit he had been wrong. He had applied his great intelligence to his city's needs, and reason told him that he was not responsible for the results, which he must have believed to be temporary. If his fellow citizens would have the wisdom and courage to hold to his strategy they would win out. So he believed, and so did his great contemporary Thucydides.

But, as we have seen, at the time of his death Pericles' strategy was unequivocally a failure. His expectations about the Spartan reaction had proven to be overly optimistic, which in turn left his estimate of the adequacy of Athenian resources incorrect. By 428 the reserve fund was all but exhausted, and his successors were compelled to resort to a direct tax to carry on the war, perhaps the first in Athenian history, and to an increase in the tribute—neither measure having been planned for by Pericles or even mentioned by him at the beginning of the war. The direct tax was always unpopular with the propertied classes and might have undermined Pericles' control of Athens had he tried to institute it. Nor could he have counted on the great increase of the tribute, for in normal times it would have provoked rebellion. In 425, however, Cleon and Demosthenes, departing sharply from Pericles' policy, won a great victory that struck a blow to Sparta's prestige and raised that of Athens. No ally dared rebel at that moment, which made it possible for the tribute to be raised to generate the revenue needed to continue the war. This was the result of a strategy employed by Pericles' more aggressive successors, without which Athens could not have continued the war and achieved the peace that concluded the Ten Years' War and left it with its walls, fleet, empire, independence, and power intact. Whatever security Athens gained by the Peace of Nicias in 421 was attributable to the new strategy and was "owed above all to the abandonment of the plan of war that Pericles had advised."[10]

Thucydides, in contrast, insists that the failure of Pericles' strategy was due to its abandonment by his successors, who "did everything contrary to his plan in every way" (2.65.7). But Pericles' plan remained intact for two years after his death without showing any promise of success, and its flaws had already been demonstrated while he was still alive. The chief proof is the decision by the Athenians in the second year of the war, despite Pericles' opposition, to send an embassy to Sparta to ask for peace. Although they chose not to, the Spartans could at that point have offered terms favorable enough for the Athenians to accept while still falling far short of what Pericles sought. Had such terms been accepted, the war would have effectively been lost, at least in Pericles' definition.

The Athenians who blamed Pericles for launching the war and imposing a cowardly and ineffective strategy, who rejected his guidance and sought peace may, of course, have been wrong, but the analysis offered here suggests otherwise. Once again, however, most readers, including many fine scholars, have agreed with the interpretation offered by Thucydides. The great modern historian of the Peloponnesian War, Georg Busolt, for instance, concedes that Pericles' strategy "was somewhat one-sided and doctrinaire, and in its execution it was lacking in energetic procedure and the spirit of enterprise." But he has no doubt that, in general, the plan "was fundamentally right."[11] How has Thucydides managed to persuade so many of the soundness of the Periclean strategy?

The most important device is his powerful, unequivocal statement elaborated in section 2.65. But that assertion would have been seriously weakened had Thucydides included various pieces of evidence he possessed that would tend in a different direction. The first of these has to do with the financial implications of the Periclean program. In many passages of his work Thucydides demonstrates the clearest understanding of the importance of money in war. One of the most critical differences between previous wars and the great modern war of his day was the availability of vast accumulations of money, first by Athens and then, after the Persians joined them, by the Peloponnesians. As we have seen, Thucydides connects the rise of civilization itself with the amassing of money: "After it was safer to sail the seas *and they accumulated a surplus of wealth*, they built walled towns right at the seashore and on the isthmuses for the purposes of trade and defense against their neighbors" (1.7). A further critical development was the suppression of piracy by King Minos of Crete, which he did "so as to collect his revenues with less trouble" (1.4). Similarly, it was not some sacred oath but inherited wealth that made Agamemnon the generalissimo of the Trojan expedition (1.9.1). The Trojan War itself was petty compared to the Peloponnesian War, and it took so long for the Greeks to seize the city because they lacked funds (1.11.2). The accumulation of wealth made it possible for tyrants to gain power and hold it (1.13.1).

Thucydides is careful to tell us the precise amount that the members of the Delian League were assessed and that the Athenians held the office of Treasurer of the Greeks (*Hellenotamias*), who collected the money (1.86.2). He reports a Corinthian speech to the Peloponnesians on the eve of the war which tries to allay fears about Athenian financial, and therefore naval, superiority: "As for the navy, in which they are stronger, we shall be able to outfit a fleet from the funds that each of us has on hand, and also by borrowing money from the treasuries at Delphi and Olympia" (1.21.3).

Pericles himself was likewise keenly aware of the central role of money, and the fleet it would finance, in the strategy with which he proposed to win the war, and Thucydides reports his thinking on the matter:

> The Peloponnesians farm their lands themselves; they have no money, either private or public. Then, too, they have had no experience in lengthy wars or those fought across the sea since, because of their poverty, they

only wage short campaigns against one another. Now people so poor cannot be manning ships or frequently sending out expeditions by land, since they would thus have to be away from their lands and at the same time would be spending their own money, and also are barred from the sea. Accumulated wealth, and not taxes imposed under compulsion, supports wars. . . . The greatest thing is that they will be hindered by lack of money and delayed by their difficulty in procuring it; but the opportunities of war do not wait." (1.141.3–5; 1.142.1)

When the Peloponnesians were on the point of invading Attica, Pericles once again spoke to the Athenians, urging them to keep a firm rein on their allies, "for their strength derived from the money they received from them as, for the most part, wars were won by superiority in money and wise policy" (2.13.2–3). This was followed by a thorough and remarkably detailed account of Athens' annual income, its reserve fund, and even what sources of wealth were available in case of emergency (2.13.3–6). These and other facts and arguments he presented to them, "as he usually did, to show that they would win the war" (2.13.9).

Given Thucydides' keen awareness of the centrality of money in Pericles' calculations in adopting his strategy for victory in the war, it is surprising that he does not make the types of calculations we have made. He could have easily done so, discussing Pericles' expectations for the cost of conducting such a plan and the time limitations they might impose on it.

In the fourth year of the war—in the year after Pericles' death—the Athenians found themselves in a critical situation. Led by the important city of Mytilene, one of only two remaining autonomous allies of Athens, all but one of the cities of the great island of Lesbos rebelled. When the Athenians were informed of the uprising they thought it "a big event" (*mega ergon*), so serious that at first they refused to believe it. When the truth became inescapable the Athenians sent a fleet to the rebellious island and were soon engaged in a difficult and expensive siege. In the spring of 428 the Mytileneans sent ambassadors for help to the Spartans, and met them at Olympia, where the sacred games were in progress. There they made a long speech in the course of which they pointed out that this was an "opportunity like none before" for a decisive action. The Spartans and their allies the Boeotians had helped plan the rebellion (3.2.3), and the time was ripe to bring over the entire island of Lesbos to the Peloponnesian side. Besides, they argued, "the Athenians have been ruined by the plague and the expenditure of money" (3.13.3). They further emphasized the crucial role of money:

> This war will not be decided in Attica, as some people think, but in those places from which Athens gets its support. For her revenues come from her allies, and they will be still greater if we are conquered. No one else will rebel and our wealth will be added to hers, for we will be treated worse than those who were enslaved earlier. But if you come to our aid with vigor, you will enroll among your allies a state that has a great navy, which you need most of all, you will defeat the Athenians more easily by drawing their allies away from them (for every one will proceed more boldly after you have assisted us), and you will escape the charge which you now have of not helping those who rebel from Athens. If, however, you show yourselves openly to be liberators you will more surely have victory. (3.1.5–7)

Although the Spartans accepted the alliance on the spot, the other Peloponnesians were less enthusiastic. "They collected slowly because they were in the midst of harvesting the grain and reluctant to serve" (3.1.5.2) and so delayed any meaningful action.

The Athenians were well aware that the actions of Mytilene and the willingness of the Spartans to support them were at least in part motivated by the belief that Athens was too weak and exhausted to face this new challenge. They decided, therefore, to put to sea a fleet of one hundred triremes to circle the Peloponnesus, making raids as in the past and demonstrating their confidence in their ability to ward off any contemplated Spartan attack.

This show of strength placed a fearful strain on the Athenians' already stretched resources, and they were forced to adopt measures never contemplated in Pericles' plans. The siege of Mytilene, which became effective at the very onset of winter, called for such extraordinary steps as having the hoplites who were needed for the operation serve as rowers as well. There can be no doubt that the attempt to save money was the incentive for their double duty.[12] By the winter of 428/7 the available reserve fund seems to have been dipped to below one thousand talents.[13] Busolt noted that if the Athenians did not open a new source of income, if they renewed their naval operation in only a moderate way, and even if there were no new emergencies, "the exhaustion of the treasury could be expected within three or four years" of the start of the war.[14] The Lesbian rebellion and the Spartan response proved, however, that the Athenians would need to use their navy frequently and heavily and also that emergencies should be expected. The financial crisis was not a few years off; it was immediate.

The Athenians, therefore, undertook two emergency measures. First, they announced a reassessment of the tribute from the allies, aimed at raising revenue.[15] Normally the deadline for collecting the tribute was the Dionysiac festival in the spring, but in the winter of 428/7 the Athenians needed money quickly, so they sent out a fleet to collect the newly assessed taxes, with ultimately little profit.

This small increment of money from the empire would not, in any case, have solved their financial problems, so the Athenians decided on an even more desperate step: "Being in need" of money for the siege, they themselves introduced for the time a direct tax (*eisphora*) in the amount of two hundred talents" (3.19.1). No one doubts that such a tax had not actually been imposed in a very long time or that it was regarded as extraordinary and painful, especially by the propertied classes, on whom the *eisphora* fell exclusively. The danger of imposing this direct tax was that it could sap enthusiasm for the war by the propertied classes, who formed the bulk of support for the moderate faction. The amount collected in 428, moreover, although presumably as much as the traffic could bear, likewise did not significantly alter Athens' financial problem. We need not wonder that Pericles himself never suggested such expedients in his public discussion of Athenian resources.

It is inconceivable that Pericles did not know how long Athens' finances would permit the pursuit of his original strategy, given that other Greeks had made reasonable calculations. Thucydides states that, at the beginning of the war, "some thought that Athens could hold out for a year, some for two, but no one for more than three years" (7.28.3). He reports this fact, however, not in the context of Pericles' war plans, where it would have made plain the strategic miscalculation and the failure of Pericles' program, but much later in his work. In fact, at the moment when the abandonment of that plan is at hand, Thucydides makes no mention whatsoever of the financial crisis that loomed before the Athenians, for had he done so he would only have drawn attention to the failure of the Periclean strategy. By not discussing these financial issues Thucydides makes it easier to focus on his own interpretation, in support of that strategy.

The historian uses another powerful technique to achieve the same result. While the plague was raging in the summer of 430 popular opinion turned sharply against Pericles and his policies. The withdrawal of the Spartan army had ended the immediate military emergency, and, with his popularity eroded, Pericles could no longer prevent the meeting of an assembly. He rose to defend himself in his last reported speech.

In the course of this turbulent time many public speeches were delivered while Thucydides was in Athens and could hear them. The man who introduced the motion to discuss peace with Sparta must have made a speech in its favor, and it is inconceivable that no one spoke in opposition. Even after the discussions came to nothing and the Athenians abandoned hope of a negotiated peace, "they were vexed by their sufferings; the ordinary people, having less to begin with, were deprived even of that, while the powerful had lost their beautiful estates in the country, buildings and expensive furnishings, and the greatest thing was that they had war instead of peace" (2.65.2). Still blaming Pericles for their miseries, some Athenians brought charges against him. The formal complaint was embezzlement.[16]

The process for such an action was an indictment (*eisangelia*) taken to the assembly by a private citizen acting as prosecutor. If the assembly accepts such a case it orders the council to draw up a motion (*probouleuma*) stating the charge, regulating the procedure, and fixing the sentence. The assembly discusses, possibly modifies, and votes on this *probouleuma* at its next meeting. If the assembly passes the motion, it either tries the case at a third meeting or refers it to the law courts. In the trial of Pericles, the first assembly's vote, which initiated the *eisangelia*, must have been the occasion of at least two speeches, one by the prosecutor and another against the proposal. In the second assembly, during which the *probouleuma* was passed to the law court, at least two additional speeches would have been presented—by the prosecutor, and by Pericles or someone representing him. Thucydides, Diodorus, and Plutarch all agree that the case went to trial; therefore, two further speeches must have been delivered in the popular court that tried the case.[17]

Thus the process of removing Pericles from office, bringing him to trial, and convicting him could not have involved fewer that six public speeches—at least four in the assembly and at least two in the law court. All were heard by hundreds or thousands of Athenians, yet Thucydides does not record a single one. Instead he reports at considerable length one speech by Pericles, presented after the peace mission to Sparta had failed, introducing it as follows:

> After the second invasion of the Peloponnesians the Athenians, now that their land had been devastated a second time while the plague and the war together weighed heavily upon them, changed their minds. They blamed Pericles for having persuaded them to go to war and held him responsible for the misfortunes which had befallen them, and were eager to come to an agreement with the Lacedaemonians. They even sent envoys to them, but accomplished nothing. And now, being altogether at a loss, they attacked Pericles. And when he saw that they were angered

by the present situation and were acting exactly as he had expected, he called a meeting of the assembly—for he was still general—wanting to calm them, and by cooling their anger, to bring them to a milder and less fearful frame of mind. (2.59)

Pericles' speech is most importantly an argument against those Athenians who had sought to negotiate with Sparta to end the war and were still working for immediate peace in spite of Sparta's recalcitrance. The sufferings of the Athenians and the failure of their recent military attempts had given the peace advocates a large and receptive audience, and it was to them that Pericles directed his oration. He reaffirmed the necessity of war, for the choice was either to accept orders from the Spartans and their allies or to endure an unwelcome conflict in order to maintain independence and freedom of action. In such circumstances the man who resists is less culpable than the man who yields. Pericles reminds his audience that he is the man to whom the people gave their trust and whose policy they supported; it is only the sudden and unforeseeable misfortune of the plague that has made them repent of their previous decisions. That is understandable, but not becoming to citizens of a city whose greatness and character Pericles has described in the Funeral Oration. Private misfortunes must be set aside for the more pressing concern of the safety of the city (2.61).

Even at this difficult moment, however, there is reason for confidence: the greatness and power of the Athenian Empire. That empire, and especially the naval force on which it rests and to which it contributes, enables Athens to master not only its allies but the entire realm of the sea. No one, not even the Great King, can limit Athenian movement on the sea, its only restriction being the desire of the Athenians. Compared to this the loss of land and houses is nothing, "a mere garden or other adornment to a great fortune. Such things can easily be regained if Athens retains her freedom, but should she lose her freedom all else will be lost as well" (2.62).

This is a striking departure from the previous position taken by Pericles. Since the Thirty Years' Peace of 445 he had always counseled the Athenians to be satisfied with what they had and not to try to extend their empire. He especially emphasized this theme during the early stages of the war, and we have no reason to think he ever changed his opinion that the Athenian Empire was large enough, that to try to expand it was madness. Nevertheless his words in this speech seem to encourage expansionism. Pericles himself explains his change in attitude: "I did not speak of this in my previous speeches, nor would I use such language now—for it seems rather boastful—if I did not see you depressed beyond reason" (2.62.1). He is willing to risk rousing such feelings since the menace, for the moment, is from a direction opposite to what he expected. The earlier attacks on him came from those forces who wanted to fight more aggressively. In the present calamity their voices were stilled.

Pericles was not content merely to remind the Athenians of their present benefits and future hopes. They should also fear a policy of making peace and withdrawing from empire, for not only would Athens then become subordinate to the greater power of Sparta and her allies, but, by now abandoning the source of their power was too dangerous. Plainly, the advocates of peace were critical of the empire and talked of giving it up, for the Spartans had made it a barrier in the way of peace, if we have approximated the Spartan peace terms correctly. It is such Athenians Pericles addresses when he says, "It is not possible for you to withdraw from this empire, if any in the present situation out of fear or from love of tranquility [apragmosyne] has decided to become honest. . . . Such men would quickly destroy a state if they persuaded others even if they had an independent state for themselves. For the lover of tranquility [apragmon] cannot be preserved except in alliance with the active man, and it is of no use for the citizen of an imperial city to seek safety in slavery; that is expedient only in a subject state" (2.63.2–3).

Pericles' remarks indicate that the opposition had revived the moral argument as a weapon against the imperial policy and the war. The supporters of Thucydides son of Melesias had complained more than a decade earlier that the empire was tyrannical and therefore immoral because it used funds from the league for the benefit of Athens alone. On that occasion Pericles had rejected the charge of tyranny, but had been glad to emphasize the rewards of empire received by the Athenian people.[18] For this speech, however, he does not reject the charge of tyranny against the empire but instead uses it as a weapon with which to defend his policy. The time for morality is past; it is now a matter of survival. He therefore urges the Athenians to reject the advice of the *apragmones*, and not to turn against Pericles and his policy either because the enemy did what was expected or because the plague brought suffering that could not be expected. They must act in a manner worthy of their city and bear their misfortunes with courage, for it is a city that has "the greatest name among all men because it has not yielded to misfortunes but has given life and labor in war and possesses the greatest power up to this time" (2.64.3).

There follows a section which seems fully in order for Pericles in 430:[19]

Even if we should now be compelled to give way to some degree, for all things which have grown also decline, the memory will remain that no Greeks ever ruled over so many Greeks, that we opposed in the greatest wars alliances and individual enemies, and that we have inhabited a city which was both the richest and the greatest. No doubt the *apragmon* would complain of these things, but the man who wishes to accomplish something will strive after them and whoever does not possess them will be jealous. To be hated and odious for the moment is the fate of all who have tried to rule others, but whoever accepts this jealousy with a view towards the greatest things judges well. For hatred does not last long, but the splendor of the present and the glory of the future remain in memory forever. And with the foreknowledge that you will have a noble future as well as a present free of shame, and that you will obtain both by your zeal at this time, do not send heralds to the Spartans and do not let them know that you are tormented by your present sufferings. For those whose spirits are least troubled in the face of misfortunes and

who resist them most in their actions, they are the strongest, whether
they be states or individuals. (2.64.3–6)

The speech is a most powerful presentation of Pericles' views, which
Thucydides himself endorses. We are reminded that the war was not op-
tional but was forced on Athens by necessity, a version of the argument
from inevitability. And it is necessity, too, that makes the arguments of
the *apragmones* wrong and irresponsible, for the abandonment of the empire would bring vengeance and disaster upon Athens.

Earlier in the speech Pericles, far from seeking sympathy or forgive-
ness for the current terrible consequences of his policies, boldly insists
on his superiority in the qualities that make for effective leadership of
a state. The case for persevering in the war and against the *apragmones*,
who have become foolish, cowardly, and selfish through their misfortune and fear, is made by a brave, old, and wise man with the outstanding qualities of a true leader.

That, at least, is how Pericles presents himself in his potent speech,
and that is how the historian portrays him. In his long period as leader
Pericles kept the city safe and prosperous, and Athens "reached the height
of her greatness." Pericles was correct in his conduct of the war and, unlike his successors, always pursued the city's interest and not his own.

Pericles, who owed his power to his excellent reputation and quality of
judgment, and had shown himself obviously incorruptible, restrained
the many in a liberal manner, and was their leader rather than being
led by them, because he did not speak to please them, seeking power
improperly, but was able because of his high reputation to speak against
their desires, even to the point of angering them. Whenever, in fact,
he saw them unreasonably bold and arrogant, his words would reduce
them into fear; and, on the other hand, when he saw them unreasonably afraid, he would restore them to confidence again. And so Athens,
though in name a democracy, gradually became in fact a government
ruled by its foremost citizen. (2.65.8–10)

Thucydides' view of the true character of Athenian government is open to challenge (and will be discussed in chapter 5), but the historian's description of the wisdom and character of Pericles and the unique admiration and power he enjoyed as the gift of the citizens of Athens is the most powerful and convincing endorsement of his policies that one can imagine.

But, as we have noted, there were speeches given in this period that might have shed a different light on events had Thucydides chosen to report them. Here was an occasion of the type that the historian uses so dramatically and effectively at a number of places throughout his history to set out conflicting political opinions. In this case, however, the reader is invited simply to accept the policy of Pericles as both correct and inevitable, and to see its opponents as merely short-sighted, self-centered, and lacking in courage, determination, and wisdom. Pericles alone is permitted to speak, and the force of his words is magnified by the thorough endorsement of the historian, who speaks in thunder, like a deus ex machina.

CHAPTER FIVE

Was Periclean Athens a Democracy?

A s controversial as any statement made by Thucydides is his claim that, under the leadership of Pericles, Athens, "though in name a democracy, gradually became in fact a government ruled by its foremost citizen" (2.65.10). Scarcely any modern scholar would accept that assertion. While recent scholarship has offered numerous challenges to the claim that classical Athens was a democracy, they come from a thoroughly different perspective. Many critics insist that, to qualify as a democracy, a state must offer full constitutional and political protections and opportunities to all who have legal permanent residence within its borders and desire citizenship.

But the Athenians limited the right to vote, hold office, and serve on juries to adult males who were citizens; slaves, resident aliens, women, and male citizens under the age of twenty were denied these privileges. In excluding such groups the Athenians were like every other society from the invention of civilization (about 3000 b.c.e.) until only recently. What sets them apart are not their exclusions but the unusually large degree of *inclusion*, as well as the extraordinarily significant and rewarding participation of those included. It is useful to remember that what has been called the Jacksonian democracy coexisted with slavery, that women were everywhere denied the right to vote until the twentieth century, and that we continue to limit political participation to those of a specified age. None of these restrictions has prevented Europeans and Americans from regarding the people of the United States, for instance, as living under a democratic government. The fundamental understanding of the meaning of the term *democracy* through the ages has been a significant participation in self-government by those designated as citizens, if that status is not limited to a small number of people. To deny that Periclean Athens was a democracy because of its exclusions is to employ a parochial and anachronistic set of criteria that produces paradoxical results.

It was on just such a broad understanding of democracy that Thucydides based his claim that, under Pericles, Athens was ceasing to be a democracy. His point was that there was less democracy in Periclean Athens than met the eye; that the power of even the freeborn adult native Athenian male was more apparent than real; and that Pericles, because of his extraordinary talents, personal and political abilities, and unrivaled stature, was the true ruler of Athens, not its assemblies and law courts. So fine a historian as Georg Busolt agreed with that assessment, arguing that aspects of Pericles' leadership (such as his great building program) resembled those of the sixth-century tyrant Peisistratus, who led, in effect, a democratic monarchy. Both regimes were concerned with the relief of the lower classes, the attempt to provide a livelihood, and also with the acquisition of overseas possessions and the provision of landed property for many citizens. Pericles' colonization of the Chersonnese and his restoration of circuit judges join directly with the tradition of the time of the Peisistratids.[1]

Busolt regarded Pericles' defeat in 443 of his chief political opponent, Thucydides son of Melesias, as a turning point in Athenian political and constitutional history.

> The oligarchic party lost, with its organizer, its firm coherence and its capacity for robust opposition. Pericles was thus without a rival, and therefore, in the eyes of the people, attained a new stature. If he had earlier felt himself compelled to be at the people's disposal and to yield to the wishes of the masses, he now began to behave independently and to take command. By using the force of his personality he ruled the state—on the one hand by means of the official authority given to him, on the other hand by means of his decisive influence on the decisions of the popular assembly. For a fifteen-year period he was elected to the general-

ship annually. In difficult times of war he was granted the supreme command, and at the beginning of the Peloponnesian War he was also given extraordinarily full powers. Although he did not usually have greater official power than the other generals, he nevertheless held the authoritative position in the college of the generals and thereby effectively led its conduct of the military, maritime, financial, and administrative affairs that were in its competence. The unbroken continuity of office, in fact, released him still further from the principle of accountability and gave him an exceptional position.

Pericles succeeded by dint of his firmly based authority, his proven political insight, the integrity of his character, the dignity of his bearing, and the power of his speech. As he did not first need to acquire influence by improper means and was not accustomed to speak in order to please but, on the contrary, by virtue of the esteem in which he was already held, he could, under certain circumstances, even sharply oppose the people. He thus would not be led by the people, but instead he led them. As a result there developed a regime that was a popular government in name but one ruled by the first citizen—in fact, a monarchical leadership on a democratic base.[2]

Few scholars have accepted these views, and even Busolt was compelled to temper them somewhat.[3] Still, ancient writers do make the case that Pericles' leadership of Athens had an authoritarian element. By birth he was an aristocrat of the bluest blood: "He was of the first families and households on both sides, Xanthippus, who conquered the generals of the King at Mycale, married Agariste, granddaughter [niece, in fact] of that Cleisthenes who nobly drove out the Peisistratids and put down their tyranny and established a constitution with laws best fitted to harmony and safety."[4] No modern parallel exists for the extraordinary advantages that the sons of Xanthippus and Agariste inherited. If an Adams of Massachusetts had married a near descendant of George Washington, and if the Adamses had been rich and famous aristocrats of long standing, their son's political prospects might almost be comparable to those accorded the young Athenian.

The Chian poet Ion described Pericles' speaking style as "presumptuous and arrogant," suggesting a haughtiness in which there was contempt and disdain for others.[5] Even friendlier accounts portray an impressive but somewhat remote and forbidding individual. These qualities likewise raised questions as to whether the young aristocrat could truly be considered a democrat.

If noble birth and distant manner were not enough ammunition against any claim to populism Pericles' physiognomy gave further support to critics. Plutarch tells us that as a young man he was very careful not to appear in the public arena too often because he was thought to look like the tyrant Peisistratus. Old men who had lived under the tyranny were said to marvel at the resemblance when they heard the young nobleman's sweet voice and swift and artful rhetoric.

Plutarch, Pericles' ancient biographer, suggests that the Athenian statesman used a democratic platform as a means to achieve power, but subsequently ruled the people, benevolently but firmly. In 443 he defeated and expelled his chief political opponent and achieved a secure political position. Thereafter, Pericles

was not the same man, submissive to the people and ready to obey and give in to the desires of the masses as a steersman yields to the winds. Instead he gave up this lax and effeminate demagogy . . . and tightened up the management of the state in an aristocratic and royal way. He used his leadership for the best interests of all in a straight and upright manner. In most things he led a willing people, persuading and teaching the masses, but sometimes, when they were very angry with him, he tightened the reins and compelled them to do what was good for them, very much like a physician who treats a complicated and chronic illness, sometimes with harmless goodies that please his patient, but sometimes with bitter medicine that brings them salvation.[6]

Plutarch's account squares with the interpretation of Thucydides, but its shortcomings are quickly apparent. In the years immediately following the ostracism of Pericles' formidable opponent, Thucydides son of Melesias, Athens' comic poets launched a campaign of attack and ridicule against Pericles that lasted until the end of his life. Some years before, he had divorced his Athenian wife and brought into his house a Milesian woman, Aspasia. She was a *hetaira*, a kind of high-class courtesan who provided men with erotic and other kinds of entertainment. She clearly had a keen and lively intellect, and Socrates himself thought it worth his time to talk with her in the company of his followers and friends. In the dialogue *Menexenus*, Plato jokingly gives her credit for writing Pericles' speeches, including the Funeral Oration.

The scandal surrounding Pericles' liaison with Aspasia was immense, and the comic poets made the most of it. They called her a whore and her son a bastard; they called her Omphale, after the legendary Lydian queen for whom the hero Heracles had worked as a slave; and Pericles' enemies carried this image even further by comparing her with Thargelia, a beautiful and clever Ionian courtesan who had consorted with many important Greek men and used her influence to bring them over to the Persian cause. The implication was clear: Pericles was enslaved by the charms of this foreign woman, and she was using her hold over him for her own political purposes.

The Samian War, which arose in 440 over a quarrel between Aspasia's native Miletus and Samos, intensified these allegations, for the story spread that Pericles had launched the war at her bidding. After Pericles' death, Aristophanes revived these old charges and comically worked them around to blame Aspasia for the Peloponnesian War, as well.

The slanders swirling about Aspasia touched Pericles, too, and not merely because of his association with her. In the comedy *Cheirones*, performed in 440, Cratinus satirized them together: "In olden days Faction and Cronus married and she bore him the greatest tyrant of all, whom the gods call Head-collector. And on Lewdness he begot Aspasia as his Hera, a dog-eyed whore."[7] In this passage the jokes are thickly packed. The Titan Cronus, instead of being married to Rhea, as in the myths, is married to Faction (*Stasis*), a reference to Pericles' rise to power out of party conflict. Cronus' son was Zeus, whom Homer calls "Cloud-gatherer"; Cratinus' Zeus is Pericles, whom he calls "Head-gatherer," making fun of both the odd shape of his head and of his position of leadership. Homer admiringly called Zeus' wife Hera "the Ox-eyed lady," but Cratinus calls Pericles' consort "the dog-eyed whore."

Crantinus' reference to tyranny had particular political significance. The pattern of a popular leader's rising out of factional strife and making himself tyrant was common in Greek history and had special meaning for the Athenians. The tyrant Peisistratus had come to power in just that fashion, and the behavior of his tyrant-sons, including their treasonous dealings with the Persians, left a bitter memory for all Athenians. Any association with that memory was bound to be damaging to an Athenian politician, a problem that was compounded by the fact that Peisistratus, like Pericles, had been a great builder. When Cratinus joked about Pericles and his most recent construction project in the comedy *Thracian Women*, performed not long after the ostracism of Thucydides, he may have intended a subtle reminder of that fact: "Here comes squill-headed Zeus with the Odeum on his cranium, now that the ostracism is over."[8] And when people pointed out that the roof of the Odeum was just like the one on the pavilion of the Great King of Persia, they may have been inferring monarchical pretensions.

These representations appeared in comedies performed before the entire Athenian population. Their personal ridicule of Pericles and his common-law wife and their political innuendo are simply inconceivable in a state that was a de facto monarchy or dictatorship. Some have tried to compare the leadership of Pericles with the Principate of Augustus in Rome, but the analogy is entirely inappropriate, if revealing. No one could imagine the first Roman emperor, however he sought to conceal the authoritarian nature of his monarchy behind the title of Princeps, submitting to such public verbal assaults launched with complete impunity. These are the products of a remarkably free democracy, and possible nowhere else.

In 438, Pericles' new political opponents found another way to undermine him, launching a series of attacks against his friends using the pretext of irreligion. The rebellions at Samos and Byzantium that had threatened Athens' safety were less than two years in the past. The siege of Samos had been long and costly, in both casualties and money, and his enemies now claimed that Pericles had been led into the venture not by necessity but on behalf of Aspasia. The time was ripe for attack, and the unveiling of Phidias' statue in the Parthenon provided the occasion. Phidias, the great sculptor who was Pericles' friend and the supervisor of his building program on the Acropolis, had been working on the enormous and expensive gold and ivory statue of Athena to be placed in the cella of the Parthenon when he was charged with stealing some of the gold consigned to him for the statue. The target was especially attractive, not only because Phidias was so close to Pericles but also because Pericles, as a member of the board of supervisors of the project, would share responsibility. According to Plutarch, some of the accusers were personal enemies of Phidias, but others, as we have seen, "were testing out what sort of a judge the people would be in a case involving Pericles."[9] Pericles, however, had ordered Phidias to put the gold on the statue in such a way that it could easily be removed in an emergency, such as a protracted war in which the Athenians might run short of money; the gold could then be taken down, melted, and used for public purposes. On this occasion, Pericles asked Phidias to take down the gold plates and have them weighed; the results showed that no gold was missing.

That was not the end of Phidias' troubles, however. He was next charged with impiety because, in the scene of the battle with the Amazons he had carved on Athena's shield, one of the figures "suggested himself as a bald old man lifting on high a stone with both hands," while another was an excellent likeness of Pericles fighting an Amazon. Plutarch, who had seen the sculptures himself, remarks: "The arrangement of the hand, holding out a spear in front of Pericles' face, is cleverly worked to hide the resemblance, but it is perfectly obvious when seen from either side."[10] This was a daring and dangerous joke to play in the fifth century. No living human being had ever been shown on a Greek temple before Phidias put a great number of anonymous Athenians on the frieze of the Parthenon. To carve recognizable people on the statue of the goddess, however, was far too bold a gesture for the ordinary citizen, who was likely to consider it an act of hubris that could endanger the entire city.

Because most Athenians remained pious in the traditional way, religious fears and superstitions always lay close to the surface, and an attack such as the one conducted against Phidias brought them into the open. The sculptor was convicted and went off into exile. That success encouraged the attackers to bring a charge of impiety against Aspasia. Plutarch says that in addition to this charge she was alleged to have procured free women for Pericles' enjoyment. No doubt the plaintiffs hoped that the general prejudice against Aspasia, amplified by the resentments against her festered by the Samian War, would weigh more heavily than any specific details of her alleged crimes. Pericles, in any case, took the threat very seriously, for the proud, reserved "Olympian" came into court and broke down in tears as he successfully begged the jurors to acquit her.[11]

In the same year a bill providing that "those who do not believe in the gods or who teach doctrines about the heavens should be impeached"[12] was introduced by the oracle-monger Diopeithes. Pericles' teacher and friend Anaxagoras was the obvious target. This was one challenge that Pericles did not dare meet head-on, and no trial appears to have taken place. As one scholar has remarked, "In this crisis, the spirit of Galileo rather than that of Socrates prevailed, and the scientist was sent out of town."[13]

Pericles' position had been weakened by these attacks, and his enemies now took aim at their real quarry. A certain Dracontides proposed a bill that required Pericles to place his public financial accounts in the hands of the Prytanies, the presidents of the council, and to answer a charge of stealing sacred property. Pericles' enemies meant to use the prejudices of religious orthodoxy aroused by the other trials and legislation to embarrass and, perhaps, convict him. An unusual, perhaps unique, proviso required the jurors to use "ballots that had lain at the altar of the goddess on the Acropolis."[14] The sacred character of this procedure "would make superstitious jurymen almost duty-bound to find Pericles guilty."[15] At this point, his friend, the prestigious general Hagnon, came to the rescue. He amended the bill, requiring that the case be tried by a jury of fifteen hundred using ordinary procedures. That put an end to the entire plan, for nowhere in Athens could a jury of fifteen hundred men be found to convict Pericles of anything, much less a charge of stealing public property. There is no reason to believe that the case ever came to trial.

Such assaults in the courts against a political leader are rare enough even in democratic states and are inconceivable under any authoritarian regime. Much like Augustus in Rome and the Medici in Florence, Peisistratus, the sixth-century tyrant of Athens, shrewdly tried to govern under the apparent rule of law as much as possible, even appearing in court to answer a charge of homicide, "but the frightened accuser did not appear."[16] That is not how the system worked, however, in Periclean Athens. His enemies not only appeared to make their charges against Pericles in Athenian courts, but succeeded in driving his friends from the city, in humiliating Pericles by bringing him to tears in defense of his beloved consort, and by bringing charges against Pericles himself. This, however, required that they remove the case from the popular courts to a venue likely to be hostile to him. When the case was remanded to a court of ordinary Athenians the accusers abandoned their efforts. There is not a hint that any action was taken against them; they could continue to operate with impunity.

The most serious and effective case, of course, is the one brought against Pericles in 430. Its details are significant. The first step required that he be formally removed from his position as general by vote of the popular assembly. After that the case came before a popular court, where he was tried for embezzlement of public funds, convicted by a large jury of Athenian citizens, and fined an uncertain but extraordinarily large amount.[17]

A period of weeks, perhaps months, passed between his indictment and his trial, which offered sufficient time for an autocrat, however disguised his power might be, to intimidate or eliminate his accusers or to seize power in a more public way, but that was beyond the capacity of Pericles or any other individual in Athens from the time that Cleisthenes established the democracy in 508/7 until late in the Peloponnesian War in 411. On that latter occasion, moreover, it was not an individual autocrat but an oligarchical conspiracy that seized power in a coup d'état.

Here again a comparison with Augustan Rome is instructive, for to suggest any similarity between it and Periclean Athens is at once to underscore the differences. The rule of Augustus rested on his absolute control of an enormously powerful military, the only one left in the Mediterranean world. Pericles controlled no army, not even a police force, but depended entirely on the continued and freely expressed support of the Athenian people. All decisions of the state were decided by a majority in the assembly, where all elections were also held without coercion. Pericles' only office was that of general, a position that was subject to yearly elections and public inspection of his accounts, and was constantly open to recall and public trial. There can be no doubt that such a regime was a true democracy.

A brief description of the workings of the Athenian constitution only makes that argument clearer. The center of political power and action was the assembly (*ekklesia*), which was open to all adult male citizens of Athens—during Pericles' lifetime, perhaps forty to fifty thousand men. Most Athenians lived many miles from the city and few owned horses, so attendance required a long walk to town. As a result, the number actually taking part on any given occasion was probably from five to six thousand, although some actions did require a quorum of six thousand. The meetings took place on a hill called the Pnyx, not far from the Acropolis and overlooking the Agora, where the citizens sat on the earth of the sharply sloping hill, and the speakers stood on a low platform.

The assembly had four fixed meetings in each of the ten periods into which the official year was divided, and special meetings were called when needed. Topics included approval or disapproval of treaties and issuing declarations of war, assigning generals to campaigns and deciding what forces and resources they should command, confirmation of officials or their removal from office, whether or not to hold an ostracism, questions concerning religion, questions of inheritance, and, in fact, nearly every other issue of civic concern. In the second meeting of each period "anyone who wishes can address the people on whatever subject he likes, whether private or public," and the third and fourth meetings discussed "all other kinds of business," whatever they might be.

The gravest questions of international relations, of matters of war and peace, arose frequently in Periclean Athens. Each time, the popular assembly held a full debate and made the decision by raising their hands in a vote determined by a simple majority—strong evidence for the full and final sovereignty of the Athenian people.

An assembly of thousands, of course, could not conduct its business without help. For that it relied on the Council of Five Hundred, chosen by lot from among all the Athenian citizens. Although it performed many public functions that the larger body could not handle efficiently, its main responsibility was to prepare legislation for consideration by the people. In this respect, as in all others, the council was the servant of the assembly. The assembly could vote down a bill drafted by the council, change it on the floor, send it back with instructions for redrafting, or replace it with an entirely different bill. Full sovereignty and the real exercise of public authority rested directly with these great mass meetings. Almost no constitutional barrier prevented a majority of the citizens assembled on the Pnyx on a particular day from taking any action it chose.

In Athens, what we would call the executive was severely limited in extent, discretion, and power, and the distinction between legislative and judicial authority was far less clear than in our own society. To begin with, there was no president, prime minister, cabinet, or any elected official responsible for the management of the state in general, for formulating or proposing general policy. There was no body that Americans would call an "administration" or that the British would call a "government." The chief elected officials were the ten generals, all serving one-year terms. As their title indicates, they were basically military officials who commanded the army and navy, and could be reelected without limit. Although extraordinary men like Cimon and Pericles were elected almost every year, their cases were most exceptional. The political power such men were able to exercise was limited by their personal ability to persuade their fellow citizens in the assembly to follow their advice. They had no special political or civil authority, and, except on military and naval campaigns, they could give no orders.

Even in military matters, the powers of the generals were severely restricted. Leaders of expeditions were selected by vote of the full Athenian assembly, which also determined the size of the force and its goals. Before the generals took office they were subjected to a scrutiny of their qualifications by the Council of Five Hundred. After completing their year of service, their performance on the job, and especially their financial accounts, were subject to audit in a process called *euthyna*. Aristotle describes how the process could continue, even after that hearing:

> Officials called Examiners sit during the regular market hours at the statue of the eponymous hero of each tribe. If any citizen wishes to prefer a charge, either of a private or public nature, against any of the officials who have rendered their accounts at an euthyna, within three days he must write on a whitened board his own name, and the name of the man he accuses, the offense with which he charges him, and the fine he considers appropriate.[18]

If the examiner decided that the charge had any merit, he passed it on to the appropriate popular law court for final judgment.

This was not the only control the people had over the few officials chosen by election. Ten times a year the popular assembly voted "to determine whether [the generals'] conduct of military affairs appears satisfactory; and if the people vote against someone's confirmation in office

he is tried in a law court. If he is found guilty they assess his punishment or fine; if he is acquitted he resumes office."[19] Since elected office
conferred prestige, elected officials were carefully monitored lest they
undermine the rule of the people.

Even with these severe controls, the Athenians filled only a few other
public offices by election, including generals, naval architects, some of
their treasurers, and the superintendents of the water supply. All other
officials were chosen by lot, in accordance with the democratic principle that any citizen was capable of performing civic responsibilities well
enough, and its corollary that the concentration of executive or administrative power in the hands of a few men, even those with experience or
special abilities, was unacceptable.

A partial list of the allotted offices in Athens indicates the breadth of
public-service positions that were entrusted to the average citizen chosen at random. First came the Council of Five Hundred, whose members could not serve more than two terms and whose duties included
preparing legislation for the assembly and receiving foreign heralds and
ambassadors. From this group came a board of presidents of the council,
a foreman of that board, the officials who presided over meetings of the
assembly, and the chairman of each day's meeting. The vendors, who
farmed out public contracts to work the publicly owned mines and to collect the state's taxes, were also chosen by lot. So, too, were the receivers,
who collected public revenues and distributed them to the appropriate
officials; the accountants, who checked the accounts of those officials;
the examiners, already mentioned, who sat in the Agora to receive public complaints against public officials; and commissioners, who were responsible for maintaining public sanctuaries.

It is worth quoting Aristotle's description of the duties of another
board of allotted officials, the city commissioners, for it provides a picture of Athenian life not often discussed:

> They see to it that the flute-girls, harp-girls, and lyre-girls are not hired
> for more than two drachmas, and if several men are eager to hire the

same girl they cast lots between them and assign her to the winner. They also take care that none of the dung-collectors deposits the dung within ten stadia of the city walls. They don't allow people to let their buildings encroach on the street, to build balconies that extend out over the street, to make drainpipes that discharge into the street from above, or to have windows that open onto the street. They also remove the bodies of people who die in the streets, using public slaves [owned by the Athenian state] for the purpose.[20]

The Athenians also chose their market inspectors by lot; their duties included inspecting the purity of articles for sale. Commissioners of weights and measures supervised the honesty of purveyors, while grain commissioners saw to it that there was no price gouging for grain and bread and that the loaves were of full weight. There were many other such positions, and to a degree that is amazing to the modern mind the Athenians kept the management of their public life in the hands of the ordinary citizen, away from professionals, experts, bureaucrats, and politicians.

The Athenian judicial system may appear even more striking to our contemporary sensibilities than the rest of the constitution. The distinction between assembly and law courts, for example, was almost a technicality. The underlying principle behind both institutions was the same: full, direct, popular sovereignty. The panel of six thousand jurors who enlisted to serve in the courts each year, in fact, was called the Heliaea, a name given in other states to the assembly. From this panel on any given day jurors were assigned to specific courts and specific cases. The usual size of a jury was 501, although there were juries composed of from 51 to as many as 1501 jurors, depending on whether the case was public or private and how important it was. To avoid any possibility of bribery or partiality, the Athenians evolved an astonishingly complicated system of assignments that effectively prevented tampering.

Legal procedure was remarkably different from what takes place in a modern American court. There were no public prosecutor or defense attorneys. Complaints were registered and argued by private citizens. Anyone was free to hire a speechwriter help him prepare his case. There was no judge; the jury was the sole arbiter. No self-respecting Athenian democrat would allow an individual, whatever his qualifications, to decide what constituted relevant evidence, or which laws and precedents applied in a given case. That would give too much weight to learning and expertise; it would also increase the danger of corruption and of undemocratic prejudice. It was, therefore, up to the contestants in the case to cite the relevant laws and precedents and up to the jurors to decide between the respective merits of their arguments.

In the courtroom, the plaintiff and defendant each had an opportunity to present his case, rebut his opponent, cite the law, produce witnesses, and offer a concluding summary. Each phase was limited to a specific amount of time, which was marked by an official using a water clock, and no trial lasted more than a single day. Finally, the case went to the jury, which received no charge or instruction. It did not deliberate but merely voted by secret ballot. A simple majority decided the issue. If a penalty was called for and not prescribed by law (as few were) the following procedure applied: the plaintiff proposed one penalty, the defendant another; the jury voted to choose one of these but could not propose any other. Normally, this process led both sides to suggest only moderate penalties, for the jury could be displeased by an unreasonable suggestion. Although critics complained that democracy made the Athenians litigious, the system contained a device intended to promote restraint: if the plaintiff did not win a stated percentage of the jurors' votes he was required to pay a considerable fine, a measure that must have served as significant deterrent to frivolous, malevolent, and merely adventurous suits.

For all its flaws, the Athenian system was simple, speedy, open, and easily understood by its citizens. It contained provisions aimed at producing moderate penalties and at deterring unreasonable lawsuits. It placed no barriers of legal technicalities or expertise between the citizens and their laws, counting as always on the common sense of the ordinary Athenian. If such a regime as has been described here is a concealed autocracy, it is like no other ever seen in this world.

Ancient critics of Periclean Athens, unlike their recent counterparts, were confident that it *was* a democracy and, therefore, by its very nature, bad. The "Old Oligarch," the name often given to the unknown author of an antidemocratic pamphlet written a few years after the death of Pericles, simply assumes that democracy promotes the interests of the poor at the expense of the rich. According to this writer, the Athenians chose democracy because "they preferred that the masses should do better than the regular citizens."[21]

Plato cited Pericles as an especially heinous demagogue, the first who "gave the people pay and made them idle and cowardly and encouraged them in the love of talk and money."[22] Aristotle links Pericles with the radical democrat Ephialtes as one of those who "sought favor with the people as with a tyrant and brought the constitution to the current democracy."[23] So far as we know, Thucydides was the only ancient writer to suggest that Periclean Athens was anything but a thoroughgoing democracy.

Pericles himself experienced the reality and power of the Athenian democracy when he was deposed, tried, convicted, and fined. A modern scholar has drawn the obvious conclusions:

> Now if democracy means and is government by the citizens, if the *ekklesia* [assembly] decided policy by vote, if free elections persisted at their constitutional intervals, if Pericles was at all times responsible to the sovereign demos, and if an unoppressed political opposition survived, as it surely did—if all this is so, then Athens was as democratic, not only in theory but in day-to-day practice, as government can conceivably be.[24]

All this is to say that Thucydides' judgment on the nature of the government of Periclean Athens is altogether incorrect, as demonstrated by the evidence of his own history. Unable to credit the debased democracy

of the last days of the fifth century with the ability to achieve the greatness that was midcentury Athens, he was led to deny that the two political systems were fundamentally indentical. The historian was convinced
that success in the political realm required a rare kind of wisdom, one
possessed by only a few. A democracy that placed the common opinion
of all, who did not possess such political gifts, above that of that rare
individual who did, could not be successful. Only when the untalented
citizenry submitted to the leadership of the man of political genius could
the state hope to achieve success. Thucydides' denial that Periclean Athens was a democracy was an especially bold attempt at revising a very
widespread contemporary opinion.

CHAPTER SIX

Cleon's Lucky Victory at Pylos

C LEON SON OF CLEAENETUS, as we have seen, was a leading critic of Pericles and of his strategy for the war from its very beginning.[1] After Pericles' death in the autumn of 429 he became a chief competitor against Nicias son of Niceratus for the leading position in Athenian politics. Thucydides introduces Cleon into his history for the first time in 427, although he had been prominent in Athenian politics for some years, and calls him "the most violent of the citizens and at that time by far the most influential with the people" (3.36.6).

This is a rare instance of direct characterization of an individual by Thucydides, and its harshness is uniquely applied to Cleon. His introduction stands in direct contrast to Thucydides' first description of Pericles as "the foremost man in Athens at that time and the most powerful in speech and action" (1.139.4). Cleon surely loomed large in Thucydides' mind when he drew the contrast between the wise and austere Pericles who stood above all other politicians, who restrained and cowed the masses, who was not led by them but led them, while "those who came later who were more on a par with each other, each seeking to be first and sought to please the people, even turning the management of public affairs over to them" (2.65.10).

Thucydides was hardly alone in depicting Cleon in a hostile manner. Aristophanes mocked him as a tanner and a leather merchant,[2] a "coward and a pervert,"[3] "a criminal and a slanderer,"[4] and called him a thief and brawler whose voice "roared like a torrent" and "sounded like a scalded pig's." The comic poet depicts him as always angry, a lover of war who constantly stirs up hatred. These may be considered the exaggerated epithets of Athenian comedy, but Aristotle presents the same negative characterization: Cleon "seems to have corrupted the people more than anyone by his attacks; he was the first to shout while speaking in the assembly, first to use abusive language there, first to hitch up his skirts [and move about] while addressing the people, although the other speakers behaved properly."[5] Plutarch gives an even harsher account: Cleon came to have "so much reputation and power that he launched out into oppressive arrogance uncontrolled rashness and inflicted many disasters which worked especially to his own advantage. Worst of all, Cleon stripped the bema of its dignity, and he was the first of the demagogues to shout when he addressed the people, throwing back his robe, slapping his thigh, and running about while speaking. In this way he infused those who managed the city's policies with recklessness and contempt for propriety."[6] The contrast with "Olympian" Pericles could not have been greater.

Most scholars have judged Nicias and Cleon to be very different from one another: Nicias a follower of the policy of Pericles, an advocate of peace, a man of probity and reserve, a gentleman; Cleon an opponent of Pericles, an advocate of war, a demagogue, a vulgarian. But it is arguable whether the two men were as different as they are usually depicted. Both came from the same class of "new men" without noble lineage. Nicias made his money from the rental of slaves to work in the silver mines of Attica. Cleon's father owned a tannery that made hides into leather and did well enough at it to become quite rich, for only a rich man could afford to be a *choregos* at the dramatic festivals, as Cleaenetus was in 460/59. Not only was neither source of wealth aristocratic, but each could be considered vulgar, and even embarrassing. In both cases the father is the first member of the family known to us. One scholar has traced each man's descent and concludes: "The two genealogies show a similar pattern. Nicias and Cleon are the first members of their families known to have won any great distinction; their fathers were probably both wealthy but not especially prominent in the city."[7]

Likewise, Nicias and Cleon were not as opposed in their attitudes toward the war as is usually thought. Neither favored the peace negotiations with Sparta that Pericles also opposed. There is no clear record of any disagreement between the two until the Pylos affair in 425, but the usual assumption that Nicias must have opposed the harsh measure proposed by Cleon in 427, which would have put the Mytilenean rebels to death, is probably correct. Nicias, nevertheless, seems to have been the most active general in the Archidamian War.

Still, while few men could have been more different in personality, character, and style, in 428 the two men found their interests to be identical, since a negotiated peace was impossible. The empire had to be kept safe for Athens, the Athenians had to be imbued with the spirit to carry on the war, resources had to be husbanded and new ones identified, and some way had to be found to resume offensive operations if the war was ever to be brought to a successful conclusion. The two men therefore had a motive to cooperate, and there is no reason to think that they did not.

In that year, as we have seen, Mytilene rebelled and brought about a severe crisis. The Peloponnesians were slow to come to their aid, and the Athenians were able to encircle the city and lay siege to it, until the following year Mytilene was compelled to surrender. In the debate over what to do with the captive Mytilenaeans Cleon proposed that all the men be killed and the women and children sold as slaves. The frightened and angry Athenians approved his proposal and sent a ship to Lesbos to carry out the sentence, but overnight they had second thoughts. At a second assembly the next day Thucydides reports a debate in which Cleon defended the original sentence and a man called Diodotus, otherwise unknown, argued for greater clemency.

Just as Thucydides' report of Pericles' speech in 430 supports his analysis of Pericles' unique position in Athens so, too, does his account of Cleon's speech about Mytilene fortify the impression created by his introduction of this "new politician."[8] Cleon argued that the rebellion was unjustified; justice, therefore, required swift and severe punishment. No distinction, he insisted, should be made between common people and oligarchs, for both took part in the action. Cleon, moreover, believed that leniency would only encourage further rebellion, while a uniformly harsh punishment would deter it: "We should never have treated the Mytileneans differently from the others and then they would not have reached this point of insolence. In general, it is the nature of man to despise flattery and admire firmness" (3.39.5). His implication was that the Athenians ought to have deprived Mytilene of its autonomy long since, and the failure to have done so was only one of many past errors. "Consider your allies: if you impose the same penalties upon those who rebel under constraint by the enemy and on those who rebel of their own free will, tell me who will not rebel on the smallest pretext when the reward for success is freedom and the price of failure is nothing irreparable?" (3.39.7).

If the Athenians continued their policy of softness, misplaced pity, and clemency, "we shall risk our lives and money against each rebellious state. If we succeed we will recover a state that has been destroyed, only then to be deprived for the future of its revenue, which is the source of our strength. If we fail we will add new enemies to those we have already, and the time we should devote to fighting our present enemies we will spend combating our own allies" (3.39.8). Cleon's address amounted to nothing less than a full-scale attack on the imperial policy of Pericles and the moderates. He recommended instead a calculated policy of terror to deter rebellions, at least in wartime.

Cleon's speech also gave Thucydides an opportunity to contrast powerfully the great leader he admired with his unworthy successor. The very words that begin Cleon's speech remind us unmistakably of Pericles: "I am the same and do not change. [*Ego men oun ho autos eimi têi gnômêi*]" (3.38.1). On the eve of the war Pericles says: "Men of Athens, I hold to the same opinion as always. [*Tes men gnômês O Athenaioi aiei tês autês echomai*]" (1.140.1). In 430 he firmly declares: "I am the same and do not retreat [*Kai ego men ho autos eimi kai ouk existamai*]" (2.61.2) while Cleon says: "I am the same in my opinion [*Ego men oun ho autos têi gnômei*]" (3.38.1). As a keen scholar has observed, "In the order in which we read the speeches, Kleon is the imitator, taking up for violent and (in comparison) trivial purposes the phrases in which Perikles had displayed his steady insight into the largest issues."[9] Even more striking is Cleon's statement that "you [Athenians] hold the empire as a tyranny [*tyrannida echete tên archên*]" (3.37.2), echoing Pericles' statement in 430 that "Already you hold the empire as a tyranny [*Hos tyrannida gar êdê echete autên*]" (2.63.2). Again, the contrast between the two political leaders and how they use the same phrase is inescapable. Pericles was pointing out a hard truth for his audience's safety, to remind the people that any thought of abandoning the empire to gain peace was suicidal. Cleon makes the point to convince the Athenians that the road to safety requires the use of unprecedented terror.

We have seen that Thucydides was eager to show that, while Pericles had been entirely correct in his views of the conduct of the war, his successors took a different and disastrous path. The same shrewd scholar has neatly described the connection between that purpose and the speeches about Mytilene:

> Thucydides' own analysis, in terms of the less secure influence of Perikles' successors, their struggles for the people's favour, their quarrels and irresponsibility, has been given directly in 2.65; here we have an indirect counterpart, one of the disruptive elements, the portrait of the demagogue in action. . . . Kleon exhibits the qualities credited to him in 3.36.6, violence and the ability to sway the people. His energy stands out all through; he violently discredits his opponent in advance, working on the plain man's distrust of the clever and his readiness to suspect bribery; he appeals to unregulated emotion to carry his violent proposal.[10]

Cleon and Diodotus, who represented the extreme positions in 427, were only two among several speakers on the Mytilene situation. Others who "expressed various opinions" (3.36.6) surely spoke of justice and humanity, since Cleon's reported speech rebuts those considerations, and Thucydides tells us that the second assembly had been specifically convened to address the Athenians' concern that the penalty chosen was "cruel and excessive" (3.36.4).

For Diodotus Mytilene represented an isolated case, which made the policy of calculated terror proposed by Cleon not only offensive but ultimately self-defeating. His counterproposal was to condemn only those whom the general Paches had judged to be the guilty parties and had sent to Athens. That suggestion was less humane than it might seem, for those arrested by Paches numbered a little over a thousand, and constituted probably not less than one tenth of the entire adult male population of the rebellious towns on Lesbos.

In the end the show of hands in the assembly was almost equal, but the proposal of Diodotus won. Cleon immediately proposed the death penalty for the "guilty" thousand, and his motion passed. The Lesbians received no proper trial, either individually or en masse; the assembly simply assumed them guilty, and there is no evidence that the vote was close. This was the harshest action yet taken by the Athenians against rebellious subjects, yet however angry and callous their fear, frustration, and suffering had made them, they still shrank from the more brutal plan of Cleon.

Thucydides describes the story of the rebellion at Mytilene in the most dramatic way, first by reporting the conflicting speeches of Cleon and Diodotus, then by his exciting treatment of the denouement, focusing not on the fate of the thousand who were executed but on the rescue of the majority. The entire story is unforgettable, and establishes a devastating picture of Cleon.

The Athenian response to the rebellion at Mytilene reflected a more aggressive spirit that began to challenge the old, moderate approach that was the legacy of Pericles. New generals and political leaders were now emerging, some with ideas very different from those of the deceased leader. The election of Demosthenes in 427 was a clear signal that many Athenians wanted a change, and he soon proved himself the most aggressive and imaginative Athenian general in the Archidamian War. The next few years would see sharp departures in policy, as the Athenians searched for some way to survive and win.

But the shift to a reconceived strategy was gradual and came only as circumstances forced it upon the Athenians. The old policy had already

produced a crisis in 428 with the rebellion of Mytilene. Four years of defensive warfare had worn down Athenian resources to the point where
the Spartans were willing to risk a naval expedition in the Aegean, and
greater Peloponnesian effort coupled with more effective leadership at
this moment could have proven deadly for Athens. The fact was, by summer 427, most of the conditions that would make possible an Athenian
defeat more than twenty years later were already at hand: Athens was
short of money, part of its empire was in revolt, the undefended coastal
cities of Asia Minor were ready to rebel, and Persia stood poised to join
the war against Athens.

That same year a civil war in Corcyra threatened Athenian control of
another important ally. Athens' failure to act in response to such crises
was leading to dangerous defections and threats of collapse, a realization
that may help explain why the Athenians became more adventurous in
427. They sent the general Eurymedon with a fleet to help the friends of
Athens at Corcyra and then to sail on to Sicily in answer to a request for
assistance from Athenian allies there. Syracuse, the island's chief city,
was a colony of Corinth and friendly to the Peloponnesian cause. Athens'
allies feared a Syracusan attempt to gain control of the entire island, and
the Athenians worried that their Peloponnesian enemies would benefit
from access to Sicily's wealth and power.

In 426 Nicias carried out punitive raids against the island of Melos, a
Spartan colony that may have helped the parent city financially, and Boeotia, whose forces had joined in the ravaging of Attica. In the same year,
Demosthenes took a small fleet around the Peloponnesus on what the
Athenians must have intended as a similar mission: to assist the friends
of Athens in western Greece and do as much damage to the enemy as was
possible without risk. The allies northwest of the Gulf of Corinth urged
an attack on the island of Leucas, a Corinthian colony strategically located on the route to Corcyra, Italy, and Sicily. Leucas was a sensible and
obvious target, but Demosthenes decided instead to defend Naupactus
by attacking the barbaric Aetolian tribes that threatened it.

The Messenians of Naupactus were also allies, and their city was a valuable port on the gulf, but Demosthenes made his decision for other reasons. His bold imagination conceived an ambitious plan that might give Athens a decisive advantage. He would land on the north shore of the gulf, move rapidly eastward through Aetolia, gather allies in central Greece, and attack Boeotia from the rear. At the same time, an Athenian army would attack Boeotia's east coast. A variety of mishaps caused the plan to go awry, however, and Demosthenes found himself fighting a campaign in mountains and forests against natives who knew the territory. The Athenians lost 120 men in the fiasco, and Demosthenes chose to stay in Naupactus rather than face his angry countrymen at home.

The locals still held him in high regard despite his failure, and so did Athens' other allies north of the gulf. When the Spartans led a Peloponnesian army into their territory, Athens' Ambracian allies sent for Demosthenes to lead them, even though now he was a private citizen. Using a joint force of heavy infantry and lightly armed men and the tricks of fighting in wooded and mountainous country that he had learned, he laid a trap for the Peloponnesians, ambushed and routed them, and destroyed Spartan influence in the region.

Rehabilitated and elected general again in the spring of 425, Demosthenes launched a campaign that changed the course of the war. He joined an Athenian fleet headed west to Corcyra and Sicily and with great difficulty persuaded its commanding generals to place him with a small force of soldiers and only five ships at Pylos in Messenia, at the southwestern tip of the Peloponnesus. The site was naturally suited to his plan, which was to build a permanent base on the coast from which the Messenian enemies of Sparta could ravage Messenia and Laconia, receive their escaped helot countrymen, and even, perhaps, stir up a helot rebellion. His proposal was such a striking departure from previous Athenian strategy that the commanders of the fleet greeted it with scorn. They only agreed to put in to Pylos when a storm forced them; at the first opportunity they hurried on to Corcyra. Demosthenes built his little fort and waited.

When the news of his handiwork reached the Spartans, they immediately recalled the army from its annual invasion of Attica, brought back their fleet from Corcyra, and sent an army to attack the fort. Without a blow being struck, Demosthenes' novel action had forced Sparta onto the defensive.

The Spartans soon found that the Athenian fort was strong and well located. To help with the assault, they landed a force on the island of Sphacteria, just south of Pylos, stretching across the mouth of the Bay of Navarino. The deployment proved to be a serious mistake, for the Athenian fleet, returning from Corcyra at Demosthenes' request, sailed into the harbor and defeated the Peloponnesian navy, imprisoning the Spartan force on Sphacteria. The Spartans immediately asked for peace to recover the 420 prisoners, who represented at least one tenth of the Spartan army, and 180 of whom were of the best Spartan families.

Demosthenes conceived and executed the entire campaign with a keen eye for the special opportunities offered at Pylos and Sphacteria. He could not, of course, have known for certain that the Spartans would occupy Sphacteria and run the risk of encirclement. If, however, the Athenians could occupy Pylos and damage and embarrass the Spartans by launching raids from it and receiving escaped helots, that would still distract them from their offensive operations, damage their prestige, and cause them concern. Beyond that, it was easy to believe that they would find the Athenian occupation of a permanent base in Messenia unendurable. Initiative and daring can provoke the enemy to make mistakes; a foe is much less likely to err when unchallenged and in possession of the initiative. Credit for the victory in this case must go to the general who devised and executed the plan that forced the enemy to make a mistake.

While Demosthenes' plan was to prove a brilliant one, the generals Sophocles and Eurymedon dismissed it as a reckless diversion and told him sarcastically that "there were many deserted promontories in the Peloponnese that they could occupy if they wanted to waste the state's money" (4.3.3). Although he was not able to persuade his colleagues, at that point fortune took a hand.

In his description of the affair of Pylos and Sphacteria, Thucydides allows the element of chance (*tychê*) an inordinate degree of importance,[11] and chance was indeed crucial in making the occupation of Pylos possible. Demosthenes failed to persuade the generals to put in at Pylos, but a storm came up and carried them there. Once there he could not convince them or the soldiers or their divisional officers to begin building the fortifications. As the storm continued, however, the soldiers did decide to do what Demosthenes asked—though less, Thucydides suggests, from conviction than from boredom. Gradually the spirit of the venture took hold of them, and they hurried to fortify the most vulnerable places before the Spartans arrived; within six days they completed the needed defenses. Both fortune and determination had permitted Demosthenes to set his plan in motion.

The Spartan king Agis, learning of the fort at Pylos, took his army in Attica home after only fifteen days, the shortest invasion in the war by far. When the news of the Athenian activities reached the Spartan navy at Corcyra the ships also headed immediately for home. Before the Peloponnesian fleet could close off the harbor at Pylos, however, Demosthenes sent word to the Athenian fleet at Zacynthus, whence it hurried back to lend support.

At Pylos the Spartans planned to attack the Athenian fort by land and sea and, if that should fail, to block the entrances to the harbor and so prevent the Athenian fleet from entering. They would place troops on the island of Sphacteria, as well as on the mainland, thus preventing the Athenian fleet from making a landing or establishing a base. The Spartans believed that "without risking a sea battle they could probably capture the place by siege because it had no grain, since it had been seized with little preparation" (4.8.8). The hoplites landed on Sphacteria, but the Spartans did not, and in fact could not, close off the channels. Because the southern channel measures about fourteen hundred yards wide and about two hundred feet deep, not even the entire Peloponnesian fleet could have blocked it. The Spartans could therefore have protected the harbor only by engaging in a naval battle in the south channel with their sixty ships pitted against the Athenian forty—a contest that would have

PYLOS AND SPHACTERIA

Hill of Agio Nikolo

Harbor (now lagoon of Osmyn Aga)

Bay of Voithio Kilia

Athenian Wall

Sandbar

PYLOS

Athenian Wall

Sikia Channel

Prehistoric Fort

Bay of Navarino

Spartan camp

Well

SPHACTERIA

0 Miles 1

0 Kilometers 1

© 2003 Jeffrey L. Ward

suited the Athenians perfectly, and one that the Spartans never intended to undertake. Their plan to stop the Athenians remains a mystery to us, but it must have been either misconceived or badly executed.

Demosthenes, meanwhile, beached and fenced in his three triremes to protect them from the enemy fleet. Unable to procure conventional hoplite arms in hostile and deserted country, he had no choice but to equip the crews of his ships, which numbered under six hundred men, with only poor wicker shields. Just then, Thucydides tells us, a Messenian privateer "happened to arrive," carrying weapons and forty hoplites. Their appearance cannot have been an accident but must have been arranged in advance by Demosthenes, who remained in close touch with the Messenians of Naupactus. Still, the Athenian force defending the fort remained outnumbered and inferior in armament.

The Spartans attacked precisely where Demosthenes expected, but the Athenians stood firm. On the third day after the attack the Athenian fleet returned to Pylos from Corcyra. The battle that followed produced a great victory for the Athenian navy and a disaster for the Spartans. The Athenians sailed freely around the Spartan hoplites, cut them off, and imprisoned them on the island of Sphacteria.

The ramifications of the naval triumph at Pylos were great. After the Spartans asked for a truce they began negotiations for a general peace and for a recovery of the force on Sphacteria. The Spartan code of honor demanded of its soldiers death rather than dishonor, and this blow to Sparta's reputation and confidence was enormous.

The truce required the Spartans to turn over all their warships as hostages. An Athenian trireme carried Spartan envoys to Athens for peace talks; the truce would last until their return, when the Athenians were to restore the Spartan ships in the same condition they received them. Any violation of these terms would end the truce, which gave the Athenians a great opportunity: if the negotiations failed, they could easily claim some breach and keep the Spartan vessels. The Spartans, however, were in no position to refuse the conditions, even with such an unfavorable loophole.

Sparta presented its terms of peace to the Athenian assembly, conceding that the Athenians had gained the upper hand for the moment but reminding them that their victory was not the result of a fundamental shift in the balance of power. They would be wise to make peace while the advantage was theirs. In exchange for the prisoners on Sphacteria the Spartans proposed both an offensive and defensive alliance with Athens.

The Athenians must have understood that, after regaining their hostages, the Spartans could resume the war at any time they pleased, and that as long as the men on Sphacteria remained in Athenian hands they had a virtual guarantee of peace. Still, it might seem that the Athenians should have accepted the Spartan offer as representing the kind of peace Pericles had sought from the beginning of the war. Thucydides makes his own attitude clear by commenting that, in rejecting the Spartan offer, "they grasped for more" (4.21.2), by which he means that greed, ambition, and the extension of empire were primary motivations. This conclusion, however, was certainly not the view of the Athenians at the time. They had, in fact, good reason to want more than merely the promise of Spartan good will in the future and an alliance that depended on the continuation of that good will. Even if the Spartans were sincere in their offer, the faction that was now proposing peace and friendship might not continue in power. It was the volatility of Spartan internal politics that had helped bring on the conflict; similarly, the advocates of war had been strong enough to reject a peace offer from Athens in 430. Why should belligerence not take the upper hand again as soon as conditions were amenable?

It is far from clear, moreover, that the Periclean goal had been attained when the Spartans came to bid for peace in 425. The aims of Pericles, recall, were largely psychological: he did not hope to render the Spartans *incapable* of making war on Athens but rather to make them *unwilling* to do so. That depended on convincing the Spartans that they had not the power to defeat Athens, but the tenor of the Spartans' speech reveals that they did not consider themselves outmatched. They believed, rather, that the current Athenian ascendancy could be reversed at any time. "This misfortune we have suffered came not from our want of power or because, having grown great, we became arrogant. On the contrary, though our resources remained the same we miscalculated, to which error all men are equally liable" (4.18.2). From the Athenian point of view, in turn, the Spartans had learned nothing useful. A peace made with an enemy continuing to hold such opinions would certainly raise the questions one historian asks about the peace Pericles had hoped for when the war began: "What guarantee would such a peace give that Sparta would not begin the war again at an opportune time? Was that a goal that would have been worth such a vast sacrifice? And would Athens, and especially, would its allies then be again in a position and be willing to make these sacrifices a second time?"[12]

The Athenians must have considered these questions, though Thucydides does not report any of the speeches that followed the Spartan proposal. To have done so would have placed the opinion of Cleon, whom Thucydides reintroduces at this point, in the context of other quite similar opinions. Instead, in the historian's account, Cleon stands alone among the Athenians as a reckless and ridiculous extremist.

Cleon led the opposition to the Spartan offer, and just as Thucydides called him "the most violent of the citizens and at that time by far the most influential with the people" (3.36.6) in advance of his speech on Mytilene in 427, he here designates him "a demagogue at that time and most influential with the people" (4.21.3).[13] With such a characterization he effectively prejudices the policies Cleon will recommend and the actions he will take. In rejecting the Spartan terms for peace Cleon made a counterproposal: that the Spartans being held on Sphacteria should surrender and be brought to Athens and held as hostages. The Spartans should also hand over Nisaea and Pegae, the ports of Megara, and Troezen and Achaea, since all these places had not been taken from Athens in the course of war but had been surrendered "by a previous agreement because of a misfortune, at a time when they were rather more eager for a treaty" (4.21.3). (He was referring to the year 445, when a superior Spartan army had stood on the plain of Attica.) Only then, he argued, should the Athenians return the prisoners and agree to a lasting peace.

The Spartans did not reject these conditions outright but requested the appointment of a commission with which they could negotiate further in private. Cleon responded by violently denouncing them for cloaking evil intentions with secrecy: if they had something honorable to say, he challenged, let them present it before the open assembly. But because the Spartans could hardly discuss the possible betrayal of their allies in a public forum, they gave up and returned home.

It is tempting to blame Cleon for the breaking off of the negotiations, on the grounds that nothing would have been lost and much might have been gained by private discussions. But what, realistically, could have been achieved? Let us suppose that the Athenians had voted to negotiate by commission in secret. Given the political balance of power in Athens, Nicias and his supporters would have dominated the talks. Eager for peace, sincere in their desire for friendship with Sparta, and inclined to believe in its good faith, these men might have come to terms very attractive to the Athenians including, perhaps, an alliance, promises of eternal friendship, the restoration of Plataea, and even the abandonment of Megara. In return the Spartans might only have asked the release of the men on Sphacteria and the evacuation of Pylos, requests that would have been hard to reject.

The suggestion that the Spartans might have been willing to give up Megara, or at least its harbors, however, was unrealistic. Sparta could have abandoned the northwest and ignored Corinth's demands in regard to Corcyra and Potidaea, but to have surrendered Megara would have placed the power of Athens directly on the isthmus and cut Sparta off from Boeotia and central Greece. With that move its credibility as leader of its alliance would have been destroyed, for to honor such a commitment Sparta would have had to abandon its major allies, and even, under the terms of the proposed alliance with Athens, to fight alongside the Athenians against them. Corinth, Thebes, and Megara would surely resist. Clearly, no such agreement was possible. The ensuing bitterness would soon lead to hostility and war, with the Spartan capacity to wage it undiminished. Cleon and the Athenians who supported him had ample reason to reject secret negotiations with Sparta.

If nothing stood to be gained by secret negotiation, however, the Athenians did have something to lose: delay might enable the men on Sphacteria to escape. The Athenian blockade of the island could not be maintained in winter, and the trapped men could then flee if no peace had been made. Each day the truce permitted food to be brought to Sphacteria was another day the island could hold out, increasing the possibility that Athens might lose its trump card. Cleon recognized that danger, and the majority supported him.

This debate marks a critical turning point in Athenian politics. Until then, to talk of reaching an agreement with Sparta was plainly treason; afterward it was a course patriots could advocate with a clear conscience. The Periclean war aims, the restoration of the prewar status quo, the preservation of the empire, and the end of the Spartan crusade against it, all now seemed to be within easy reach. Some Athenians might have argued that such a peace was insufficiently secure and that Pericles himself would have insisted on greater guarantees, but prudent men could respond that it was wise to trust Sparta and pave the way for a lasting accord. Nicias probably held these very views in 425.

Cleon, however, had quite different aims. In effect, he demanded a return to the ideal state of affairs that existed before the Thirty Years' Peace of 445, when Athens controlled Megara, Boeotia, and other parts of central Greece, as well as a number of coastal cities of the Peloponnesus. The Athenians had been compelled to abandon these territories, he believed, as the result of a treaty they had signed under duress, because of certain "misfortunes." With the leverage of the events at Pylos and Sphacteria, Cleon implied, the Athenians had to insist on a return to earlier conditions, when peace did not depend on the vagaries of Sparta's politics or on expressions of its good will, but was guaranteed by Athens' possession of strategic defensive locations.

The Spartan ambassadors' return to Pylos spelled an end to the truce, but the Athenians, alleging violations by Sparta, refused to return the ships they held as hostage. The Athenians were now committed to capturing the men on Sphacteria and sent an additional twenty ships to enforce the blockade. They expected quick success, for Sphacteria contained no food and only brackish water, and the Athenian fleet had complete control of all approaches to it. The Spartans, however, displayed surprising ingenuity to keep the men on Sphacteria alive long after the time they were expected to surrender.

Eventually the Athenians themselves began to suffer from shortages of provisions, and the onset of winter would force them to lift the blockade by preventing the regular arrival of supply ships. As time passed and the Spartans sent no further embassies, the fear grew that they were confident of recovering their men, and that Athens might ultimately emerge from the impasse without either a great strategic advantage or a negotiated peace.

When the Athenian assembly learned of the alarming state of affairs at Pylos, both Cleon and his policy came under fire. Thucydides describes this gathering in great detail in one of the most remarkable sections of his history. In spite of the dramatic nature of the debate he reports no speeches in direct discourse but instead offers brief accounts of what was said, filling them out with his interpretations of what the speakers had in mind when they spoke. His description of this important assembly deserves careful examination. When the messengers relayed to the Athenians the bad news from Pylos, Cleon accused them of not telling the truth, "knowing that their suspicion was directed against him because he had prevented the treaty" (4.27.3). The messengers invited the Athenians to appoint a commission to test the veracity of their report; they complied and elected Cleon as one of the commissioners. Cleon, however, protested that sending a commission was a waste of time, one that might forfeit the great opportunity. He urged instead that, if they believed the reports from Pylos were true, they should send an additional force to assault the island and capture the men. He did so, "knowing that," if he went to Pylos, "he would be forced to say the same thing as had the men he had slandered, or, if he said the opposite, be exposed as a liar" (4.27.4). Besides, "he saw that the Athenians were now rather more eager to make an expedition" (4.27.5). Then he turned and pointed a censorious finger at his enemy Nicias and asserted that it would be quite easy, if the generals were truly men, to take an adequate force to Pylos and seize the men on the island. "He would do so himself, if he were in command" (4.27.5).

Now, Thucydides recounts, the Athenians asked Cleon why he himself didn't sail off, if the job were so easy. Nicias, sensing the mood of the crowd and "noticing Cleon's taunt" (4.28.1), added that the generals would be glad for Cleon to take any force he liked and try. At first Cleon was ready to accept, "thinking that the offer was only a ploy," but then he drew back, affirming that Nicias, and not he, was general, "when he realized that the offer to relinquish the command was genuine" (4.28.2). But Nicias persisted in urging him to undertake the campaign, offering to resign his own command and calling the Athenian people to witness his action. Cleon continued to try to evade the proposal, but the Athenians, "as is the way with the crowd" (4.28.3), kept urging Nicias to give up the command and Cleon to take it. At last, Cleon, "not having any way to escape the consequences of his own proposal," agreed to lead the expedition. Denying fear of the Spartans, he proposed to sail without any Athenian reinforcements, taking with him only a body of Lemnian and Imbrian troops who were in Athens, some peltasts from Aenos, and four hundred archers from elsewhere. With these men and those already at Pylos, he promised that within twenty days he would "either bring back the Spartans alive or kill them on the spot!" (4.28.4).

This extravagant boast provoked a burst of laughter from the audience, but the "sensible men" (*sophrones*) among them concluded that one of two good outcomes must result: "Either they would be rid of Cleon, which they considered more likely, or, if that judgment were confounded, he would put the Spartans in their hands" (4.28.5).

Such is Thucydides' narration of the event, unique in character and style. As one student of Thucydides has put it: "The account, usually so sober, here takes on the style of comedy: boasting, improvisation, impudence, all are found here."[14] The reaction of the Athenian assembly is the only recorded laughter in Thucydides' otherwise somber history. The reason for including it in his description of the meeting is to underscore the absurdity of Cleon's promise; it will have the further advantage of undermining the greatness and significance of Cleon's achievement when that promise is fulfilled. This episode is also striking in that, while Thucydides reports no speeches, but characterizes only selected moments, the historian effectively professes to be able to see into the minds of the contestants, especially that of Cleon, claiming to know what they are perceiving, thinking, and intending. It is possible that he could have questioned Nicias about his reasoning after the fact, but surely not the despicable Cleon. If taken at face value, however, the reports of Cleon's motivations are a powerful interpretative weapon.

Apart from these matters of style, Thucydides' account bristles with interpretive difficulties. For what purpose was the Athenian assembly called together, or, if the debate took place at a regular meeting, on what question did it center? How could Nicias offer a command to Cleon on behalf of all the generals, for the *strategia* had no generalissimo, and we are told of no consultation among the generals? How could Nicias offer to resign his command, when we have not been told that it had been given him? Why were the Lemnians and Imbrians and the peltasts from Aenos so conveniently present at Athens at just the right time? Thucydides' account does not give clear or certain answers to these questions, but we must try to reconstruct the events, keeping them in mind.

The purpose of the meeting was probably to discuss a request by Demosthenes for reinforcements to attack Sphacteria. Cleon was certainly in close communication with Demosthenes and knew of his plan to assail the island. Demosthenes had already begun to make preparations for the assault, sending to the allies in the vicinity for additional reinforcements. He must also have asked for the specially trained forces he needed to capture the men on Sphacteria, as the kind of light-armed troops required for the campaign were already at Athens when the debate took place. Cleon was the natural choice to serve as Demosthenes' advocate, for he was the most outspoken proponent of rejecting the Spartan peace offer and would be held accountable if the men on Sphacteria were allowed to escape. Nicias had by now come to favor a negotiated peace and feared that the capture of the Spartans would inflame the aggressive spirits in Athens and make such a peace impossible. He may therefore have been eager to delay an attack for as long as he could in the hope of reaching an agreement before it was too late. He surely opposed the request for reinforcements to launch an assault on the island.

Cleon urged the assembly to send the additional force, a measure the assembly must have voted in favor of, and appointed Nicias its commander. Now the Athenians, caught up in the game, asked Cleon why, if he believed the task was so easy, he himself didn't make the trip. His attempts to evade the assignment only provoked the assembly to press him harder. Nicias, detecting his opponent's embarrassment, repeated the offer in the hope of thoroughly discrediting Cleon, and the crowd soon joined in, some in earnest, others out of hostility to Cleon, and still others for the sheer sport of it. Cleon now had no choice but to accept the command and chose to do so with bravado, making the promise that provoked the Athenians to laughter.

Thucydides presents Cleon's pledge to succeed within twenty days and without the use of any Athenian hoplites as a show of bravado or foolhardiness, but it was in fact neither. Since Demosthenes' plan was to attack as soon as the necessary forces of light-armed troops were at hand, a quick decision was inevitable: Cleon knew he would succeed in twenty days or not at all. Still, the attitude Thucydides attributes to the *sophrones* (prudent men) seems difficult to understand, let alone excuse. That patriotic Athenians could have agreed to deliver the command of the Athenian expedition and responsibility for the lives of allied soldiers and Athenian sailors to a man they believed to be patently foolish, to say nothing of incompetent, strikingly reveals not only how potentially dangerous were the divisions that had arisen among Athenians as a result of the events of 425, but also the contempt with which Thucydides had come to regard the post-Periclean democracy.

★   ★   ★

Cleon named Demosthenes as his fellow commander and sent word to him that help was on the way. At Pylos, Demosthenes nevertheless hesitated to attack the heavily wooded Sphacteria, on which an unknown number of Spartan hoplites were concealed when, once again, fortune seems to have favored the bold. Thucydides tells us that a contingent of Athenian soldiers accidentally started a forest fire, apparently another stroke of luck.

The careful reader, however, may wonder if this crucial event was indeed the result of chance. In his campaign in Aetolia the previous year Demosthenes' trapped troops had run into a forest, but the Aetolians had "brought fire and filled the woods with it." With the cover of the fleeing men so removed, "every kind of destruction befell the Athenian army" (3.98.2). It would be a great coincidence, indeed, if such a device produced the same result, not by deliberate emulation but by accident. Before long most of the woods had been burnt off, and Demosthenes could see that the Spartans were more numerous than he had estimated. He also noticed places at which to make a safe landing that had previously been obscured, and he realized that one of the great tactical advantages of the enemy had been removed by the fire. When Cleon arrived with the fresh special troops, Demosthenes was ready to put to use the valuable lessons he had learned in Aetolia.

Just before dawn he landed on the island and saw that most of the Spartan forces were concentrated near the center of the island, guarding the water supply, while another contingent was near its northern tip, opposite Pylos, leaving only thirty hoplites to guard the point of landing at the southern end. After watching the Athenians sail by harmlessly for so many days, this small Spartan force was caught by surprise while still in bed and swiftly wiped out. The Athenians landed the rest of their forces—hoplites, peltasts, archers, and even most of the barely armed rowers from the fleet. Almost 8,000 rowers, 800 hoplites, the same number of archers, and over 2,000 light-armed troops faced the 420 Spartans.

Demosthenes divided his troops into companies of two hundred who seized all the high places on the island, so that wherever the Spartans

fought they would find an enemy in their rear or on their flanks. The key
to the strategy was the use of light-armed troops, for they "were the most
difficult to fight, since they fought at a distance with arrows, javelins,
stones, and slings. It was not possible to attack them, for even as they fled
they held the advantage, and when their pursuers turned, they were on
them again. Such was the plan with which Demosthenes first conceived
the landing, and in practice that is how he arranged his forces" (4.32.4).

At first the Spartans lined up facing the Athenian hoplites, but the
light-armed soldiers rained their weapons on them from the side and the
rear, while the Athenian hoplites stood off and watched. The Spartan
hoplite tried to charge their tormenters, who easily retreated to safety
on high, rough ground that the hoplites could not reach. When the light-
armed troops realized that the enemy was physically worn down by repeated vain pursuits and diminished by casualties, they in turn charged at
the Spartans, shouting and firing missiles as they came. The unexpected
clamor disconcerted the Spartans and prevented them from hearing the
orders of their officers. They fled to the northern end of the island where
most of them hid behind the fortification to resist further attacks.

After a while the light-armed troops launched a major assault against
the Spartan hoplites. Confused and desperate, they closed ranks and
retreated to the northern end of the island where most of them joined
with the garrison there behind the fortification. At that moment the Messenian general Comon came to Cleon and Demosthenes with a plan for
taking the Spartans from the rear. The Spartans were stunned by the appearance of Comon and his troops. Once again surrounded and outnumbered, they were by now also weak from exertion and lack of food, and
they had no place to run. Complete destruction was imminent.

Cleon and Demosthenes realized that live prisoners would be far
more valuable than Spartan corpses, so they offered the opportunity of
surrender. The Spartans accepted a truce in which to decide what to do.
Their commander refused to make the decision himself, so a herald was
sent to bring the official word from Sparta. The Spartan authorities in
turn tried to avoid responsibility, saying, "The Lacedaemonians order

you to decide your own fate yourselves, but to do nothing dishonorable" (4.38.3), so the Spartans surrendered. Of the 420 who had come to the island, 128 were dead; the remaining 292, among them 120 Spartiates, were taken prisoner to Athens within the twenty days that Cleon had promised. The Athenian casualties were few. "The promise of Cleon, mad as it was," Thucydides says, "was fulfilled" (4.39.3).

The astonishing victory fashioned by Cleon and Demosthenes was of the greatest importance. "In the eyes of the Greeks it was the most unexpected event in the war," for no one could believe that the Spartans could be brought to surrender (4.40.1). The Athenians sent a garrison to man the fort at Pylos, and the Naupactian Messenians also sent a force, which used Pylos as a base for launching raids. The helots began to desert, and the Spartans grew uneasy at the prospect of increased revolutionary activity within the Peloponnesus. The Athenians, moreover, held a trump card in the Spartan hostages, threatening to kill them if the Spartans again invaded Attica. Being placed so unequivocally on the defensive was a totally new and frightening experience for the Spartans. They sent repeated embassies to Athens to negotiate for the return of Pylos and the prisoners, but the Athenians continued to raise their demands beyond what the Spartans were willing to grant.

The events at Pylos completely changed the outlook of the war. Athens was free of the threat of invasion, free to move anywhere at sea without danger from the enemy fleet (which Athens held), and free, therefore, to extort further funds from the allies to replenish its almost exhausted treasury. The situation had also been reversed in another way. Heretofore the Spartans had been doing damage to the Athenians without appreciably suffering in return. Now the Athenians could inflict continuing harm on their enemies, on land and by sea, without fear of retaliation.

The Athenians did not share the opinion of Thucydides and the men he called "sensible." For them Demosthenes and Cleon were great heroes who had wrought something near a miracle. They showered their gratitude on the chief hero of the hour, Cleon, for Demosthenes seems to have stayed behind at Pylos to see to its security. The assembly voted Cleon

the highest honors in the state, granting him greater rewards than they
gave to Olympic winners, meals at the state expense in the Prytaneum,
and front seats at the theater.[15] Since the death of Pericles no Athenian
politician had achieved so much public approval or so much power.

Cleon seized the opportunity to make Athens financially sound
enough to carry on the war to attain the victory he believed necessary.
Some two months after he triumphantly brought his prisoners home,
about the second week in August, he dispatched a certain Thudippus to
carry a decree ordering a new, higher, assessment of the tribute levied on
the allies of Athens and setting up the machinery to carry it out. Thudippus was "probably Kleon's son-in-law."[16] Although no positive evidence
attaches Cleon's name to this action the overwhelming majority of scholars is right to believe that he and his supporters were behind the new assessment.[17] (Leading students of Thucydides have been astonished at the
historian's failure to even mention the decree.)[18] The attitude it expresses
toward the empire accords perfectly with his views in the debate about
Lesbos, and references in the comic poets to Cleon's connection with
finance further support his association with the policy. Most telling is
his unquestioned ascent during the period of the decree's passage. From
midsummer 425 at least until the spring of 424, when he was elected
general, Cleon was supreme in Athens. No bill to which he objected was
likely to have passed through the assembly.

The purpose of the reassessment was to raise additional money with
which to fight the war, and a clause in the decree provided that the as-
sessors "shall not assess a smaller tribute for any city than it was previously paying, unless owing to the poverty of the territory they cannot
pay more."[19] At the bottom of the list of cities and their assessments the
inscription gives a total, and though scholars have disagreed whether the
figure was 960 talents or 1,460, the assessment in 425 at least doubled and
may have trebled earlier assessments. This sum was reached not only by
raising the contributions from almost every city paying tribute, but also
by listing cities that had not paid for years, and even some that had never
paid at all. "In the thirties the number of cities recorded in the annual

lists of *aparchai* [offerings, i.e., tribute payments] never exceeded 175. In 425 not less than 380 and possibly more than 400 were assessed."[20]

Clearly the Athenians meant to undertake a thorough reorganization of their empire. The decree of Thudippus also provided for the tough and efficient collection of the revenue, very much in the spirit of Cleon. It is "perhaps the strongest decree that has survived from the fifth century. The executive is threatened with penalties at every turn."[21] Cleon and his supporters also wanted to abolish the anomalies in the empire that could lead to trouble. Melos, which had never paid tribute, was now assessed at fifteen talents, a sign that the Athenians meant to bring the island under their control. The Carian cities, which had been allowed to fall away, were restored to the list. However difficult attempts to fill Athenian coffers might be to enforce, they reflect Cleon's determination to return the empire to its full size, to govern it with a tight reign, and to draw from it the greatest revenue possible. The condition of Athens made some such steps necessary, and it was Cleon's great victory that had made them possible.

Thucydides does not speak of these matters, for he does not mention the decree of Thudippus at all. While to do so might provide an opportunity to reemphasize Cleon's aggressive imperialism and his harshness towards Athens' subjects, it would also bring to the fore the significance of the victory of Cleon and Demosthenes in a campaign that departed from the original Periclean strategy. The use to which the victory was put, unavailable until the Spartan surrender at Sphacteria, enabled the Athenians to help correct the great error in that strategy: the inability to pay for a long war. Reference to the Thudippus decree, therefore, would have highlighted that error and contradicted Thucydides' endorsement of the original strategy as sure to produce victory had it been followed faithfully. In that case his readers might conclude that it was Pericles who had been mistaken and that Cleon was not a reckless and lucky madman but a daring and shrewd leader, but that was not what Thucydides believed the truth to be.

CHAPTER SEVEN

Thucydides and Cleon
at Amphipolis

Thucydides at Amphipolis

ONE OF THUCYDIDES' more interesting revisions of contemporary opinion sprang directly from his own experience. In 424, the year after the events at Pylos and Sphacteria, he was elected general and sent to the Thracian region of the empire in charge of Athens' naval forces. The main Athenian base in the region was Amphipolis, and Thucydides' primary responsibility was to guard and defend that city. In the event, Brasidas, the brilliant Spartan commander, took it by surprise, and the Athenians held Thucydides accountable. They convicted him of treason (*prodosia*) and sent him into exile for the remainder of the war. It is instructive to see how Thucydides treats these events in his *History*.

The campaign at Pylos and Sphacteria had put an end to the Periclean strategy. Cleon's and Demosthenes' definition of victory was not psychological, but tangible. Their next goal was to control Megara and Boeotia and thereby to recover the invulnerability Athens had enjoyed at the height of its power after it first secured Boeotia in 457. In 424 Demosthenes conceived daring and innovative plans to achieve these objectives. They involved collaboration between opponents of the regime in the enemy cities and Athenian forces approaching under cover of surprise, and depended on careful coordination and timing. But the effort at Megara failed, while at Delium in Boeotia the Athenians suffered a rout with heavy losses.

Even before the disastrous Athenian invasion of Boeotia however, Brasidas had begun to turn the course of the war in Sparta's favor with

a daring exploit in August of 424: he took an army northward toward
Thrace to threaten the only part of the Athenian Empire accessible by
land. By then the Athenians had taken the island of Cythera, and their
harassment of the Peloponnesus, both from Pylos and Cythera, was becoming so unbearable that the Spartans were ready to try anything to
relieve the situation. Their main goal was Amphipolis, a source of strategic materials and wealth in timber and gold and silver mines. It was
also a key location from which to control passage on both the Strymon
River and the road east to the Hellespont and the Bosporus, through
which came the ships carrying Athens' vital grain supply. Events in 424
seemed to offer a favorable opportunity: the Bottiaeans and Chalcidians,
who had been in revolt from Athens since 432, and Perdiccas, king of the
Macedonians, who, though occasionally at peace or allied with Athens,
was at heart always its enemy, invited the Spartans to send an army to
Thrace, and Brasidas was able to persuade his government to approve his
plan. He determined that Acanthus, on the Chalcidic peninsula, would
be a good base for attacking Amphipolis and took his army there late in
August. He did not try to take it by storm or treachery; instead he attempted to persuade its citizens to yield. Thucydides observes of him,
with either delicious irony or dismissive condescension, that "he was not
an incompetent speaker, though a Spartan" (4.84.2.). The Acanthians,
accordingly, voted to revolt from Athens and admit the Peloponnesians
"because of the seductive words of Brasidas and fear for their crops"
(4.88.1). Stagirus, a town nearby, joined the rebellion, a success that established momentum for the Spartan cause.

Early in December Brasidas marched to Amphipolis, whose fall would
surely lead to a general rebellion in the entire area and open the road to
the Hellespont. Lying at a sharp bend in the Strymon River, Amphipolis
was defended by water in three directions. A bridge across the river gave
access to the city from the west, and an enemy crossing there would encounter a wall that surrounded the hill on which Amphipolis was built.
An eastern wall effectively turned the city into an island. A small fleet
could easily defend it from any attack from the west.

Amphipolis contained only a few Athenians, its population consisting chiefly of what Thucydides calls "a mixed multitude" (4.106.1), among them some settlers from nearby Argilus. Because the people of Argilus were secretly hostile to Athens, the Argilians within Amphipolis would not be trustworthy allies, so that in any attack or siege Amphipolis would be endangered from within as well as without.

Brasidas marched through a dark and snowy night to Argilus, which immediately declared its rebellion from the Athenian alliance. Before dawn, he reached the bridge over the Strymon, crucial for his plan. The snowstorm was still blowing, which helped him catch the guards, some of whom were traitors, by surprise. The Peloponnesians easily seized the bridge and all the land outside the city walls, taking many prisoners from the shocked Amphipolitans caught there; inside, quarrels quickly broke out between settlers of different nationalities. Brasidas himself appears to have underestimated the shocking effect of his coup, for Thucydides reports the opinion that if he had attacked the city immediately instead of pillaging the countryside he could have taken Amphipolis. His delay is understandable, for to storm a fortified place with such a small army was a fearsome thing, sure to produce casualties and likely to result in failure. The usual way to take a walled town was by treachery, and Brasidas counted on help from within. But the Amphipolitans soon recovered their courage and were able to prevent any traitors from opening the gates. Brasidas, seeing that his first plan had failed, made camp and waited.

Inside Amphipolis, Eucles, the Athenian commander of the garrison, immediately sent word by a semaphore system to Thucydides, asking him to bring help to the threatened city. But Thucydides was not, as expected, at Eion, less than three miles away near the mouth of the Strymon, but rather at Thasos, about a half-day's sail away. The Amphipolitans had clearly counted on his being on guard at Eion, whence his fleet could come to the rescue almost immediately. Scholars have tried to explain why Thucydides was at Thasos and not Eion, but he himself offers no explanation.[1] He may have been trying to gather troops to help

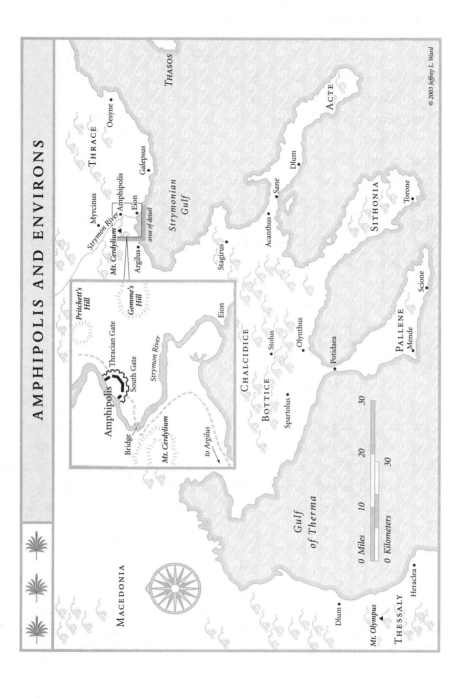

AMPHIPOLIS AND ENVIRONS

MACEDONIA

THRACE

THASOS

Oesyne

Myrcinus

Strymon River

Mt. Cerdylium

Argilus

Amphipolis

Eion

Galepsus

Strymonian Gulf

area of detail

Stagirus

Acanthus

Sane

Dlum

ACTE

Torone

SITHONIA

Pritchett's Hill

Gomme's Hill

Thracian Gate

South Gate

Amphipolis

Bridge

Strymon River

Eion

Mt. Cerdylium

to Argilus

CHALCIDICE

Stolus

Olynthus

BOTTICE

Spartolus

Potidaea

PALLENE

Mende

Scione

Gulf of Therma

Dlum

Mt. Olympus

THESSALY

Heraclea

0 Miles   10   20   30

0 Kilometers   30

© 2003 Jeffrey L. Ward

reinforce Amphipolis, though we have no evidence for such a purpose. Perhaps his trip had nothing to do with Amphipolis, and he was completely surprised, like Eucles and the others. In any case, his delay in arriving was a critical factor in subsequent events.

Brasidas certainly placed great weight on the impending arrival of Thucydides and the fleet, fearing not only its material influence, but its psychological impact. He knew that Thucydides had considerable influence in the region, and so did the men of Amphipolis. If the popular party saw Thucydides and his ships they would be encouraged and expect that he had used his personal influence to bring additional help from the neighborhood. This would guarantee their continued resistance and end the Peloponnesians' hope that the city would be betrayed. Thucydides tells us that fears of precisely this development moved Brasidas to haste and led him to offer moderate terms of surrender to the Amphipolitans. As one scholar has put it: "To Brasidas the decisive event would be Thucydides' arrival. And in the context Brasidas expected it to happen . . . . In short, he believed that he could not take Amphipolis by assault at all, and that he could not even do so on terms unless these were accepted before Thucydides arrived."[2]

Eucles and the Amphipolitans, of course, were unaware of Brasidas' intentions. The Spartan was a famous soldier and a dangerous opponent given to wily stratagems, as they had already learned to their sorrow. They knew that Thucydides had only a few ships, which might have been important in defending the city if the enemy had not already crossed the river and taken the bridge, but which would be of little value otherwise. His recruiting abilities would be of no use in the immediate crisis. An assault with or without tricks or treachery was clearly imminent. If Brasidas took the city, the fate of its citizens would be grim: the settlers who had come from Athens might expect slavery, possibly death; the others would lose their home and lands and be sent off to wander and to starve. These factors must be taken into consideration in understanding the response of the Amphipolitans to the very much gentler conditions offered by Brasidas.

His proposal was that any resident of Amphipolis, whether of Athenian origin or other, could either remain where he was in full possession of his property and with equal rights, or could leave freely within five days, taking his property with him. The price—though Thucydides takes it for granted and does not mention it—was that Amphipolis must change from the Athenian to the Spartan alliance. As the historian explains, "compared to what they had feared the proclamation seemed just" (4.106.1), and it had a powerful effect on the Amphipolitans' will to resist. The resolution shown by Eucles and the majority, which had prevented treason and led them to send for help with the evident intention of defending their city, evaporated with the news of Brasidas' offer. The Athenians in the city could no longer trust their fellow Amphipolitans, and the friends of Brasidas used the growing sense of doubt to their advantage. Though Thucydides does not report the very important speeches delivered during the debate in the city, his account does tell that Eucles argued against capitulation. At first, apparently, few dared to oppose him, but gradually the sentiment in favor of accepting Brasidas' terms found expression; at that point Brasidas' collaborators found it safe to justify them quite openly, and at last the city gave way and accepted the terms.

Not many hours after Brasidas had entered the city, on the evening of the day he had arrived at the bridge over the Strymon, Thucydides appeared at Eion with his seven ships. He had come remarkably quickly, traveling almost fifty miles in about twelve hours, if we assume that he had received word to come to Amphipolis by signal about dawn. What message did he receive? We know too little about the capacities of Greek signaling systems, but surely they could transmit such basic information as "bridge fallen, enemy here."[3] Such a message would explain the reaction of Thucydides as he himself reports it: "He wanted especially to arrive in time to save Amphipolis before it gave in, but if that were impossible to be early enough to save Eion" (4.104.5). Even if it contained no hint about treachery, Thucydides would have been well aware that Amphipolis was a divided city that might yield if an enemy army appeared at its gates. He was too late to save Amphipolis, but he did prevent the capture of Eion. We have no reason to doubt that his swift response saved Eion or that without it Brasidas would have taken the town at dawn, for the next day the Spartans sailed down the river, only to be repulsed by Thucydides.

The Athenians valued Amphipolis greatly and were very frightened by its capitulation to the Spartans. They blamed Thucydides for the loss, brought him to trial, and sent him into an exile that lasted the twenty years until the end of the war. The ancient biographers of Thucydides report that Cleon was his accuser and that the charge was treason, *prodosia*.[4] Although these sources are notoriously unreliable, we have no reason to doubt either assertion. *Prodosia*, like peculation, was an accusation often leveled against unsuccessful generals. Cleon was the leading politician in Athens, a famous prosecutor, and the likeliest candidate to introduce such a charge.[5]

Historians have long argued over the justice of the court's decision, and the problem is compounded because our only useful account is by Thucydides himself, and that account is puzzling. Thucydides never directly confronts or denies the justice of the sentence passed on him, but confines his narrative to a mere description of the events. This has led many to marvel at his objectivity and lack of self-justification,[6] but a more careful investigation suggests that the bare narrative is in fact a most effective defense.[7]

The proof is that we can so easily convert Thucydides' story into a direct response to the charge that he was to blame for the fall of Amphipolis: "The emergency arose," Thucydides might say, "when Brasidas made a surprise attack on the bridge over the Strymon. The guard at the bridge was small, partly disloyal, and unprepared, so Brasidas took it easily. Responsibility for guarding the bridge belonged to Eucles, the commander of the city. The city was unprepared, but managed to rally in time to prevent immediate treason and send to me for help. I was at Thasos at the time, and set out immediately to relieve Amphipolis if I could, but to save Eion at least. I made amazingly good time because I knew the danger of treason would be great and that my arrival could turn the tide in our favor. If Eucles had held out one more day we would have thwarted Brasidas, but he did not. My quickness and foresight saved Eion."

Although Thucydides' explanation of his actions did not convince an Athenian jury, it has had much more success among modern historians.[8] If the defense he offered in court was essentially the same as the one recounted in his history we can understand why he was convicted, for he gives no answer to the key question: Why was he at Thasos instead of at Eion? Modern historians have invented elaborate explanations for his absence,[9] but Thucydides does not provide the evidence for them. Just as it is wrong to argue that the historian's silence on this point is evidence of his guilt, so it is wrong to use it as a license to fabricate evidence of his innocence.

We may assume that Thucydides was at Thasos on some legitimate mission, but that does not acquit him of the charge of failing to anticipate the expedition of Brasidas and of being at the wrong place at the wrong time. The error does not seem to be deserving of so severe a penalty, however, particularly when we consider Brasidas' daring and unusual tactics and the fact that Eucles, who allowed the bridge to be captured and the Amphipolitans to surrender, seems not to have been brought to trial or condemned.[10] If the "irrational" demos was seeking scapegoats for the failure of its overly ambitious plans and its negligence in failing to provide for the defense of the northeast, why did it hold only Thucydides responsible and spare Eucles? We know no reason why the Athenian jury would make any distinctions between them on political or any other grounds. The Athenians, in fact, seem to have been rather discriminating in their treatment of generals. They did not punish Demosthenes, in spite of his failures in Aetolia or at Megara or in Boeotia. Even when the court condemned Pythodorus, Sophocles, and Eurymedon for their failure in Sicily in the same year as the fall of Amphipolis, it distinguished among them as to their degree of guilt: the former two were exiled, but Eurymedon was only fined. Athenian juries may have based such decisions on the facts of the case, among other considerations. The only facts we have in the case of Thucydides are provided by the defendant; if we had all the evidence the jury did, we might decide as they had.

For our purposes the question of Thucydides' guilt or innocence at Amphipolis is less important than the manner in which he tells the tale. Unless he misrepresented the facts—and that he was determined not to do—he would have had to focus attention on the great and decisive weakness in his defense: namely, his absence from Eion on the fateful day. For this, apparently, he had no satisfactory excuse. In the *History* he might have reported his trial in Athens and reproduced the speech with which he defended himself there. But that speech had not convinced the jury. In that case, moreover, he might have felt the need also to report his accuser's speech. But doing so would only underscore the failure of his own defense; because that argument had convinced the jury of his guilt, it might well have the same effect on the reader. Even if he reported only his own speech, if he reported it honestly it was likely to raise the question of his guilt, to which the jury would surely want an answer.

Instead, he chose the device of making no apparent defense, but merely of telling the story in the most impersonal way, without focusing on the crucial question. This would permit most readers to conclude that Thucydides was not at fault but was improperly condemned by an enraged and irrational post-Periclean democracy, as almost all of them have done over the millennia. The Athenians of his day found him guilty; his *History* offers an effective revision of that verdict.

Cleon at Amphipolis

Whoever was to blame for it, the fall of Amphipolis encouraged rebellions throughout the Thracian area, as factions in various regions sent secret messengers inviting Brasidas to bring their own cities over to Sparta. Immediately after the capture of Amphipolis, Myrcinus, situated just up the Strymon, and then Galepsus and Oesyme on the Aegean coast defected from Athens, followed by most of the cities of the Acte peninsula.

The Athenians immediately sent garrisons to strengthen their hold on the Thracian district, and although Brasidas requested reinforcements while he began to build ships on the Strymon, the Spartan government refused, "because of jealousy toward him by the leading men and also because they preferred to recover the men from the island and put an end to the war" (4.108.7). Ever since the capture of the men on Sphacteria a faction favoring negotiated peace had dominated the state, persuading the Spartans to send mission after mission offering terms, only to be rejected by the Athenians. They now saw the victories of Brasidas as a powerful inducement for the peace they had vainly sought, for the capture of Amphipolis and other towns placed them in a powerful bargaining position from which to trade for the prisoners, Pylos, and Cythera.

One can easily sympathize with these conservatives. Perdiccas, king of Macedon, had shown himself to be an unreliable ally. It would also be dangerous to move another army through Thessaly, and few Spartans wanted to send armed forces away from home while the enemy was still at Pylos and Cythera and the helots were restless. At the same time the run of defeats after Megara, Boeotia, and Amphipolis had discredited the advocates of aggressive war in Athens. They had begun the year inflated by hopes of a complete triumph but ended it in a chastened mood, ready to consider a negotiated peace.

The Athenians did agree to a one-year truce in the spring of 423, but troubles soon arose. The Boeotians and the Phocians rejected the pact, and the Corinthians and Megarians also objected to the terms that allowed the Athenians to keep the territory they had taken from them. By far the greatest barrier to peace, however, was the willful genius who commanded Sparta's armies in Thrace. As the truce was being concluded, the town of Scione in the Chalcidice revolted from Athens. Brasidas won over even those who had not initially favored the rebellion, and he soon stationed forces in the town, intending to use it as a base for attacks on Mende and Potidaea on the same peninsula.

Brasidas must have taken news of the truce hard, especially when he learned that Scione was excluded from Spartan control, since it had revolted after the truce was signed. To protect Scione from Athenian vengeance, Brasidas falsely insisted that its rebellion had taken place before the truce. The Spartans believed him and claimed control of Scione, but he could only expect trouble when his deception was revealed.

The Athenians, however, already knew the truth about the chronology of the events in Scione and refused to arbitrate its status. In their anger they agreed to Cleon's proposal to destroy the city and put its citizens to death; this time, there would be no second thoughts or reprieve. The dangerous defections of Amphipolis, Acanthus, Torone, and other towns in the northeast had further discredited Pericles' moderate imperial policy, and the Athenians were now willing to support Cleon's approach of deterrence through terror.

Brasidas, meanwhile, embarked on his own course, aimed at victory, not peace, contrary to the wishes of the Spartan regime. When the town of Mende revolted, clearly during the period of truce, he nevertheless accepted the rebels. The angry Athenians at once prepared a force to move against both Mende and Scione, and Brasidas sent a garrison to defend them.

Nicias and Nicostratus assumed leadership of the Athenian expedition that moved north to regain the two upstart cities, but not Torone, which had revolted earlier and therefore under the terms of the truce belonged to Sparta. They were determined not to violate the pact, whatever Brasidas had done, for they truly sought peace. They were, however, eager to recover Scione and Mende, for Brasidas' violations had angered the Athenians. If Nicias and the peace faction were not to be completely discredited they would have to recover the rebellious towns and restore the conditions in which the truce had been made.

As spring and the end of the truce approached, confusion reigned. Outside the Thracian region the armistice held, but Brasidas' violations bred suspicion and anger in Athens and prevented progress toward a stable peace. Still, neither Athens nor Sparta was willing to break the truce, which continued past its original expiration date in March well into the summer of 422. By August, however, the Athenians finally lost patience. The Spartans refused to disown Brasidas and punish him but instead tried to reinforce his army and sent a governor to rule the cities he had taken in violation of the truce. It was easy to conclude that Sparta had entered into the armistice in bad faith simply to win time for Brasidas to gain even more successes and foment further rebellions, and thus to have the leverage to make greater demands in the bargaining for peace.

The Athenians therefore sent thirty ships, twelve hundred hoplites, three hundred cavalry, and a larger force of excellent Lemnian and Imbrian light-armed specialists to recover Amphipolis and the other lost cities. Cleon was their general. Although he was inexperienced in military tactics, the need for Greek commanders of hoplite phalanxes to be experienced professionals should not be exaggerated. Standard tactics were generally well known and depended less on military experience than is true in modern wars. Still, skill and experience were important, and the Athenians were not likely to entrust such an important army and campaign to a single amateur and unskilled general, though we should remember that Athenians gave Cleon most of the credit for winning the incredible victory on Sphacteria. We should expect, at least, that they would send an experienced soldier with him, such as he had in Demosthenes at Sphacteria. Although Thucydides mentions no colleague, if we examine only the campaigns in the Thracian district throughout the war, we find that none was commanded by a single general. In 432, Archestratus sailed against Potidaea accompanied by four other generals. In 430, Hagnon and Cleopompus were sent to put an end to the siege and take the city. In the winter of 430/29 we hear of three generals operating in the region. In 423, Nicias and Nicostratus were sent out to restore the Athenian position threatened by Brasidas. We cannot believe that the Athenians deliberately made an exception in this case and entrusted the command of so many of their men to only one general, especially one who was considered inexperienced and suspect by many of his fellow citizens. Nor should we believe that Thucydides' failure to mention his colleague or colleagues is an accidental omission. The campaign ended in disaster, which has ever since been blamed on the only man we know to be connected with it; that could not have been unintended.

The force under Cleon and his anonymous associates was not strong enough to guarantee success. In addition to the men doing garrison duty in Scione and Torone, Brasidas had about the same number of troops, as well as the great advantage of defending walled towns. Athens must have counted on help from Perdiccas and from some of its allies in Thrace, while Brasidas was effectively cut off and could expect no further assistance from Sparta. With reasonable luck Cleon might have won another important victory and restored the security of the Thracian district, which would have given the Athenians favoring peace a much stronger bargaining position or, as Cleon hoped, would have encouraged the Athenians to resume the offensive in the Peloponnesus and central Greece on the way to a peace based on victory.

The first part of Cleon's campaign in the north, though treated as insignificant in the account of Thucydides, in fact achieved important and remarkable successes. The obvious tactic would have been to attack Scione immediately since it was the most annoying defector and was already under siege. Brasidas probably expected the attack there, since he was inexplicably away from Torone, his main base in the Chalcidice, when Cleon launched a surprise assault on that city. The Athenians touched at Scione only to pick up additional soldiers from the garrison there, and, perhaps, as a feint to mislead Brasidas. From there Cleon sailed across to the little port of Cophus, just south of Torone, where he learned that Brasidas was away and the forces left in the city were no match for the Athenians.

Brasidas had built a new wall around Torone, which also encompassed the suburbs, giving the inhabitants more room and some safe land to farm. Cleon brought up his main army against this new wall and drew the Spartan governor Pasitelidas and his garrison out of the city to defend the outer fortification. Brasidas seems to have given no thought to the defense of the inner city, which was vulnerable to an attack by sea—which was precisely what the Athenians had planned in concert with an inland assault on the wall. While Cleon was engaging the Peloponnesian force at the wall, the ships, under the command of one of Cleon's unnamed colleagues, sailed against the undefended city. When Pasitelidas saw what was happening he realized that a trap had been set and that he had stepped into it. Even without the diversion the Athenians were already pressing him hard, and the sight of the ships sailing to Torone completed his discomfort. He abandoned the outer wall and ran to Torone, but he found the Athenian fleet had arrived first and taken the city. Meanwhile the forces under Cleon, now unopposed, breached the wall and broke into the city without further difficulty. Pursuing his hard policy toward rebels, though in a somewhat moderated form, Cleon sent the seven hundred adult males to Athens as prisoners, while the women and children were sold as slaves. Cleon set up two trophies of victory, one at the harbor and the other at the new wall; the significance of the victory and the brilliance of the strategy amply justified them. Soon after the fall of the city Brasidas arrived with a relieving army; he had been less than four miles away when it fell.

The details of the capture of Torone have rarely been given much attention, so its strategic interest and the light it sheds on the generalship of Cleon and Brasidas have not been sufficiently appreciated.[11] Gomme's excellent evaluation of the campaign is useful: "The victory was decisive and the strategy—the decision to leave Skione to the slow siege and to attempt to carry Torone by storm—both intelligent and bold; the action was as brilliant as that of Brasidas at Amphipolis. Pasitelidas seems to have been no more competent than Eukles (we are not even told that he was hindered by discontent within the city); and Brasidas must bear at least as much blame for the defeat as Thucydides bears for Amphipolis, for Kleon was already near at hand."[12]

From Torone Cleon sailed to Eion to establish a base for the attack on Amphipolis. Once again he took advantage of his sea power and the limited mobility of the Peloponnesians to attack weak points and win back ground. His attack on Stagirus in the Chalcidice failed, but he was successful in storming Galepsus.

Thucydides tells us no more of this particular campaign, but the evidence of inscriptions indicates strongly that Cleon's activities in Thrace

were very successful. The assessment list of the Athenian Empire for the
year 422/1 includes the names of many cities in the region that must have
been recovered by Athens, and there is every reason to conclude that this
was the accomplishment of Cleon.[13] At the same time, in the realm of
diplomacy, he was doing everything possible to bring Perdiccas and his
Macedonians as well as the Thracian Polles, king of the Odomantians, to
the side of Athens. Pinned down all this time by the threat to Amphipolis, Brasidas could do nothing to prevent these losses or the encirclement
that threatened his position. As Woodhead has put it, "The war in fact
came to be focussed on Amphipolis: the net was skilfully laid and tightened round Brasidas until the moment came for the coup de grâce, and
political strategy was allied to generalship in the field in bringing this
about."[14]

Cleon planned to wait at Eion until the arrival of his Macedonian and
Thracian allies permitted him to encircle Brasidas and reduce the place
by storm or siege. He and his army accoridngly returned to Eion after his
several attacks on rebellious cities and settled there. Brasidas must have
realized that an attack on Amphipolis impended and, leaving Clearidas
in charge of the city proper, he moved his army to the hill called Cerdylium to the southwest. From here he had a good view in all directions
and could watch Cleon's every move.

It is here that Thucydides' narrative becomes very puzzling. He says
that Brasidas had taken up his position expecting Cleon to attack with
only his own army, in contempt for the small number of men under Brasidas. But Brasidas announced to his troops that their numbers were ap-
proximately equal to those of the enemy, and Cleon could not have been
grossly deceived in this matter. If Brasidas expected Cleon to misjudge
the situation so badly, however, he was disappointed, for Cleon continued to wait for reinforcements.

The account of Thucydides now presents difficulties. After a short
period of waiting Cleon marched his army northwest from Eion to a
strong position on a hill northeast of Amphipolis, but the purpose of this
maneuver is far from clear. Thucydides tells us that it was not inspired

by military considerations but by the grumbling of the Athenian troops, who were annoyed at their inactivity and distrusted the leadership of their general, contrasting his incompetence and cowardice (*malakia*) with the experience and boldness of Brasidas (5.7.1–2).[15] That the Athenian soldiers should have had this opinion of Cleon is surprising. Cowardice and lack of daring are not qualities indicated by Thucydides' earlier accounts of him. Everywhere he reveals a spirit that is, if anything, too bold and optimistic. His support of Demosthenes' plan to take Sphacteria was the boldest idea put forward, and his promise to do so within twenty days was mocked by the Athenian assembly because of its optimism, raising the not unwelcome prospect of his failure and demise in the minds of those Athenians whom Thucydides calls "the sensible men." Cleon had likewise urged the present expedition to track down Brasidas and recover Amphipolis. Brasidas, according to Thucydides, did not consider Cleon cowardly or reluctant to fight, but expected him to be rash enough to attack without waiting for his allies to help make such an attack safe.

Nor is it easy to understand the grounds for the opinion that Cleon was incompetent. Since his first appearance as a general in 425 his record of achievement had been amazing. He had carried out his promise at Sphacteria. The very men who are alleged to have doubted him were with him at Torone, where his strategy was masterful and successful. They had been with him when he stormed Galepsus and recovered the other towns in the region. It is hard to deny the truth of Gomme's observation that "the whole sentence shows the strongest bias against Kleon, a hatred and contempt for him."[16]

If we reject the first motive proposed by Thucydides, the rest of his account makes it clear that Cleon's plan was to wait until the arrival of the Thracians, encircle the city, and then take it by storm. A general intention to lay siege to a town will naturally require a good picture of its size, shape, the height and strength of its walls, the disposition of the forces and population in it, and the lay of the land outside it. To obtain that information demands a reconnaissance expedition of exactly the kind Thucydides describes Cleon as undertaking: "He came and estab-

lished his army on a strong hill in front of Amphipolis and himself examined the marshy portion of the Strymon and how the city was situated in
respect to Thrace" (5.7.4). Waiting for the Thracians may have made the
soldiers restless, and persuaded Cleon that they needed something to occupy them, but such a march would have been necessary in any case. He
did not expect to fight, but he did need to take a sizable force with him to
deter any attack that might be lauched when he got close to the city.

When Cleon reached his observation post on the hill he saw no one
posted on the wall of Amphipolis and no one coming out of the gates to
confront him. Thucydides tells us that Cleon then thought he had made
a mistake in not bringing siege equipment with him, for he believed the
city was undefended and that he could take it with the force he had at
hand. Though Thucydides often tells us what was in the minds of generals during battles, in this case we must wonder how good his information was. Cleon died in the subsequent battle and could therefore not
be a direct source, and the Athenian soldiers who might have informed
Thucydides almost two decades later were not likely to be unbiased,
even if they were privy to Cleon's private thoughts. We have no reason to
believe, in any case, that Cleon underestimated the Peloponnesian force
and so foolishly endangered his army. Even when Brasidas, who must
have begun to move his army to Amphipolis when he saw Cleon marching north from Eion, united his force with the troops of Clearidas in the
city, he did not dare risk an attack, believing his force inferior in quality
if not in numbers. Cleon had every reason to believe that, having completed his reconnaissance, he could withdraw safely to Eion.

Brasidas, however, was desperately anxious to prevent such a withdrawal. His position had been growing weaker and more dangerous by
the day. No help was to be expected from Sparta; the Macedonians had
deserted him; money and provisions were in short supply. The arrival of
the Thracians would complete the Athenian encirclement of his forces.
Time was on their side, and Brasidas could not afford to lose the chance
of attacking the Athenian army in the field, whatever the danger. He left
the main body of troops under the command of Clearidas, selecting 150

men for himself. "He planned to make an immediate attack before the Athenians could get away, thinking that he would not again find them so isolated if their reinforcements should arrive" (5.8.4).

Brasidas' plan seems to have been something like this: after arriving in the city he ostentatiously made the sacrifices that precede battle and gathered with the forces of Clearidas near the northernmost, or Thracian gate of the city. Threatening to attack Cleon from that gate would force him to move southward, past the eastern wall of Amphipolis, toward Eion. As the Athenian army filed past the city, descending from the heights so that it could no longer observe movements within, Brasidas would place his chosen men at the southern gate. There he could wait for a favorable moment to make a sudden and unexpected attack, for the Athenians would think they were out of danger once they had safely gotten by the Thracian gate. The surprised Athenians would be forced to engage and would probably concentrate all their attention on their attackers, not knowing how many they were and assuming that the whole army had moved from the northern to the southern gates to make the attack. While the Athenians were occupied by Brasidas, Clearidas could then come out of the Thracian gate, take the Athenians in the flank, and rout them.

To be sure, the plan contained an element of risk. If the Athenians were alert and kept their heads, they might destroy the small attacking force under Brasidas before Clearidas could come to its rescue. But speed and surprise were in Brasidas' favor, and he had no satisfactory alternative. In the circumstances it was a brilliant device, and it worked to perfection. Cleon appears to have gone forward to conduct his reconnaissance ahead of the main body of his army, somewhere to the north or northeast. He received word that the whole of Brasidas' army was visible in the city, most of it massed at the Thracian gate. Since the bulk of his own forces must have been south of that position, he judged it wise and safe to order a withdrawal to Eion, for he had never planned to fight a pitched battle without reinforcements. This was a sensible response, and, as Thucydides tells us, the march south to Eion and the left turn it required was "the only way possible" (5.10.3–4). Success depended on two things: an accurate judgment of the time available for the withdrawal and the proper use of military techniques to guarantee the safety of the maneuver.

As Thucydides recounts the story, Cleon, judging that there was time to get away, gave orders to signal the retreat and at the same time passed the word verbally. It appears that some complicated maneuver by the left wing was necessary to guarantee the safety of the retreating column. This movement took some time, however, and Cleon, fearing the process was going too slowly, posted himself at the most dangerous position on the right wing, and wheeled it around to march left, leaving its unshielded right side exposed to attack. Apparently this movement, or the failure to coordinate it with the movement of the left, caused confusion and a breach of order. Brasidas, who had allowed the Athenian left wing to go by, took this as a signal to attack. He burst from the southern gates on the run and struck the Athenian center, which was taken wholly by surprise. The Athenians, "amazed by his daring and terrified by their own disorder, turned and ran" (5.10.6).

At just the right moment Clearidas emerged out from the Thracian gate, catching the Athenians on the flank and throwing them into further confusion. The men on the left wing, instead of rallying to the aid of their comrades, fled to Eion. The right wing, where Cleon was in command, stood its ground bravely. Thucydides tells us that Cleon, since he had never intended to stand and fight, "fled immediately" (5.10.9) and was killed by the spear of a Myrcinian peltast. His men were not routed until attacked by javelin throwers and cavalry. The Athenian cavalry, apparently, had been left at Eion, since no battle had been intended or expected. About six hundred Athenians were killed; the rest escaped to Eion. Of the Spartans only seven men fell; among them, however, was Brasidas, who died soon after his first assault. He was carried from the field still breathing and lived long enough to learn he had won his last battle.

The picture that emerges from Thucydides' narrative is that Brasidas was heroic and brilliant while Cleon was cowardly and incompetent. The historian's report of the grumbling of the Athenian soldiers and, in the story of the battle, his emphasis on Cleon's error and flight close the case. Yet some have challenged his account. The Athenians certainly made some critical error, but what it was Thucydides does not make clear. Perhaps Cleon misjudged the time available for a safe withdrawal; he may have ordered the right to wheel too early; he may have been insufficiently acquainted with the proper techniques for conducting a withdrawal in the face of an enemy; or he may have been inexperienced in giving military signals and caused confusion in that way. All these explanations are plausible, though none is certain; Cleon may simply have been surprised by an extremely clever stratagem and could not recover from that initial disadvantage. None of these explanations would be evidence of general incompetence, especially in light of the great ability he had already displayed at Torone and Galepsus. At worst they would suggest that a talented amateur soldier had made a mistake caused by inexperience; at best that a good general had been beaten by a brilliant one.

Although Thucydides does not himself accuse Cleon of cowardice, he reports such a charge on the lips of Athenian soldiers before the battle, and it is implicit in his account of Cleon's death: "As for Cleon, since from the first he had not intended to stand and fight, he fled immediately and was overtaken by a Myrcinian peltast and was killed" (5.10.9). Modern scholars have used this passage as a basis for concluding that Cleon was "stabbed in the back as he fled,"[17] or "as better soldiers have done, he ran away, and was killed."[18] Busolt was right to detect "a cutting irony" in the account of Thucydides, but irony in this case is not justified.[19] Cleon did not run off with the left wing, "but stayed in the rear, as Greek commanders did when an army was in retreat; for he was killed by one of Klearidas' force."[20] He was killed by a peltast, moreover, and so "by a javelin, i.e., something thrown from a safe distance, and, for all that we know, he was struck in the chest."[21] As the Spartans had said in respect to their men at Sphacteria, "It would be quite a shaft that could distinguish the brave" (4.40.2).

Thucydides, to be sure, contrasts the flight of Cleon with the behavior of his soldiers on the right wing, who held their ground and resisted until their position became impossible. But since the plan was not to remain and fight, Cleon was right to flee and the hoplites of the right wing wrong to make a stand if there were any way to avoid it. We cannot determine what their options were from the account of Thucydides, but even his staunch defender, Gomme, admits that "with the evidence of Thucydides' bias before us, and considering the uncertainty of any report of this kind from the middle of a confused battle which ended in a humiliating defeat, I would not be certain that he was, on this occasion, sufficiently awake to his own principles of work, I.22.3."[22] An ancient tradition clearly shows Cleon fighting bravely at Amphipolis.[23] Pausanias tells us that in the Cerameicus in Athens, where the state's honored war dead were buried, Nicias' name was excluded from the stone commemorating those who died fighting in Sicily because he surrendered to the enemy, while his colleague Demosthenes made a truce for his men but not for himself and tried to commit suicide. Nicias, therefore, was excluded as "a voluntary prisoner and an unworthy soldier." The Athenians did, however, place the name of Cleon at the head of those who fought at Amphipolis. We should not doubt his courage any more than his countrymen did.

Thucydides' final words on Cleon make a fitting conclusion to the damning portrait he had to that point painted: Cleon opposed peace because "its coming would make the exposure of his evil deeds more likely and his slanders less capable of belief" (5.16.1). Such motives would be treated as incredible if they were suggested by Diodorus instead of Thucydides, yet they are very similar to the motives Diodorus attributes to Pericles for starting the war, which are generally and rightly dismissed as absurd. Like Brasidas, Cleon pursued an aggressive policy out of sincere conviction that it was best for his city. No doubt, his vulgar style lowered the tone of Athenian political life, and we need not approve his harshness toward rebellious allies. We must, however, recognize that in the formation and conduct of Athenian foreign policy Cleon represented a broad spectrum of opinion and that he always carried his intentions forward energetically and bravely. There is a powerful case that he was right to urge rejection of the Spartan peace offers in and after 425, to insist on the support of Demosthenes at Sphacteria, and to propose an expedition to Thrace after the expiration of the truce in 422.

Whether or not those judgments are correct, we must understand that in each case Cleon won the support of the Athenians, and that he spoke to them honestly and directly, without deception or deviousness. Though he is often referred to as the first of the Athenian demagogues, he did not flatter the masses but addressed them in the severe, challenging, realistic language sometimes used by Pericles himself. Moreover, he put his own life on the line, serving on the expeditions he recommended and dying on the last one. Whatever Thucydides' "sensible men" might think, Athens was not better off after his death. The views he represented did not disappear but were put forward by other and worse men, some of whom lacked his capacity, some his patriotism, others his honesty, still others his courage. Thucydides is correct, however, when he says that Cleon's death, like that of Brasidas, cleared the way for peace. For the moment there was no one in Athens with the stature to oppose the movement for peace, powerfully led by Nicias. If it turned out to be a false peace that led Athens to disaster and final defeat, that was an outcome in which Cleon played no part.

It is important to remember that the judgment of the mass of Cleon's contemporaries was almost always in his favor. They usually followed his policies freely and gladly, and they accorded him extraordinary honors beyond all others while he was alive and, even after a serious defeat, awarded him those honors due a respected and successful general upon his death. Thucydides' account of his career represents a radical revision of contemporary opinion.

CHAPTER EIGHT

The Decision for a Sicilian Expedition

ARLY IN JUNE OF 415 a large and magnificent Athenian force sailed
out of Piraeus bound for Sicily. Some two years later this and a second, reinforcing armament were wiped out; almost all the men were
killed, and a great fleet was destroyed. Athens was never able fully to
replace the losses, material and human, or to recover the prestige and
confidence that she had enjoyed before the disaster. Thucydides names
the Sicilian expedition alone among "the many blunders" (2.65.11) the
Athenians committed after the death of Pericles that helped bring on
Athens' final defeat, thus giving it special significance. Modern historians
are more than usually prone in this case to follow Thucydides' narrative
and to accept his interpretation of events without much question.[1] This
attitude is understandable, for the portion of the history describing the
Sicilian expedition is the most polished section of all Thucydides' work,
the most carefully constructed for dramatic effect, the most hauntingly
convincing.

But Thucydides' account of this turning point of the war inescapably provokes questions. We cannot even be sure what he thought of
the expedition's prospects for success, for though he called the move a
blunder he qualified that description in the same sentence, explaining
that it was "not so much an error of judgment with regard to the enemy
against whom they sailed as a failure on the part of those who sent them
out to support the first expedition" (2.65.11). This assessment is not only
unclear in itself, but the second part of the statement seems to contradict Thucydides' own narrative of the campaign.[2] There is also doubt
as to what he thought was the correct strategy for the Athenians' attack

and how he assessed their leaders. Perhaps the most important questions, however, for discovering Thucydides' general interpretation of the war, as well as his intentions and motives, are those that involve assigning responsibility for the disaster, first for the decision to undertake it and then for its inadequate execution.

One of the most powerful and recurrent themes in the *History* of Thucydides is the destructive foolishness of the post-Periclean democracy. Few contemporaries would have challenged the assertion that the expedition produced a terrible disaster, but not all would have agreed that the error lay in the decision to undertake the campaign rather than in its execution, or that the chief blame rested with the Athenian people at large rather than with particular leaders. These issues call for an examination of both matters.

By the spring of 421 the Athenians had grown weary of war, while the Spartans had been making peace offers ever since 425. With Cleon gone and the aggressive strategy discredited, Nicias negotiated a peace for fifty years on the basis of the status quo ante bellum, with a few exceptions. To many the pact seemed to fulfill Pericles' goals after ten long years of fighting, although it had required a sharp departure from his strategy to reach that point.

In fact, the peace was a delusion from the first. Its terms were far from satisfying even Periclean requirements, for the Spartans never acknowledged their inability to defeat Athens. To the contrary, when the Athenians hesitated in the negotiations, the Spartans made it clear that they would invade Attica, regardless of the fate of the Spartan prisoners. The Athenians had in effect yielded in the face of threats.

The Spartans, moreover, in their desperation to achieve peace, had betrayed their allies. The treaty terms left Megara's port and Corinthian territories in Athenian hands and required the Boeotians to return the Athenian fort of Panactum, which lay on their border. Not surprisingly the disgruntled allies of Sparta worked to renew the fighting and hoped to involve two other significant Peloponnesian states, Elis and Mantinea, both engaged in serious quarrels with Sparta. A major reason for the Spartans' eagerness for peace had been the expiration of their treaty with Argos in spring 421. The Argives had refused to renew it and were again making ready to challenge Spartan leadership in the Peloponnesus.

Another reason that the futility of the peace should have been immediately apparent was that the Spartans never sincerely intended to restore Amphipolis, a provision that the Athenians regarded as essential. No Athenian politician, not even Pericles at his strongest, could have compelled the Athenians to restore Pylos until Amphipolis was again in Athenian hands. Unless both conditions were met, it was only a matter of time until the accord collapsed.

Alcibiades, Pericles' charismatic and ambitious young nephew and ward, quickly emerged as the leading rival to Nicias and as the champion of those who wanted to resume the war. Since rejecting an agreement with Sparta Argos had moved ahead to form a "third force" that included Mantinea and Elis. Alcibiades wanted Athens to join them in a quadruple alliance of democratic states to destroy Sparta's position in the Peloponnesus and thus eliminate its power to threaten Athens. The success of the new strategy would make possible a major victory in a land battle against Sparta with little risk to the Athenians themselves, for the great majority of the soldiers would come from the three Peloponnesian democracies fighting against the Spartans and the remaining Spartan allies. The diplomatic part of Alcibiades' strategy worked perfectly. In the summer of 418, the Spartans fought their opponents without the aid of their Corinthian and Boeotian allies and with only a small numerical superiority. Alcibiades later boasted that "without great danger or expense to the Athenians, the Spartans had been compelled to stake their hegemony on a single battle" (6.16).

Incredibly, however, Alcibiades did not take part in the battle that crowned his strategy. In the volatile politics of the day, he failed to win reelection as general for the very year in which his plans came to fruition, while Nicias and his associates, who opposed the plan, shouldered the responsibility for its execution. Athens sent only a thousand infantry

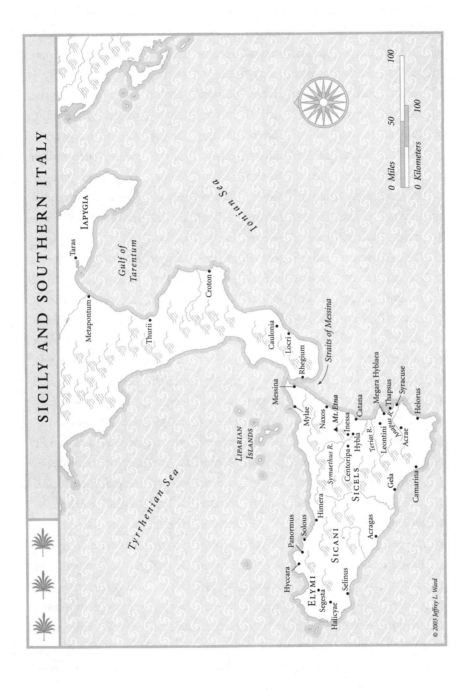

SICILY AND SOUTHERN ITALY

IAPYGIA

Taras

Gulf of
Tarentum

Metapontum

Thurii

Croton

Tyrrhenian Sea

Caulonia

Locri

Rhegium

Straits of Messina

Ionian Sea

Messina

LIPARIAN
ISLANDS

Mylae

Naxos

Mt. Etna

Catana

Inessa

Megara Hyblaea

Thapsus

Syracuse

Helorus

Hyccara

Panormus

Solous

Himera

Symaethus R.

Centoripa

Hybla

Terias R.

Anapus R.

Leontini

Acrae

SICELS

Gela

Camarina

Acragas

SICANI

ELYMI

Segesta

Selinus

Halicyae

© 2003 Jeffrey L. Ward

0 Miles   50   100

0 Kilometers   100

and a small contingent of cavalry; its navy remained idle. If the Athenians had dispatched three or four thousand more infantrymen, as they easily could have done, the odds would have swung heavily against the Spartans. If they had made naval raids on the Peloponnesus in the days before the engagement, they could have compelled the Spartans to reduce the size of their forces at Mantinea. Even so, the battle was closely fought, and the allies almost succeeded in ending the war and Spartan power.

Neither Nicias nor Alcibiades emerged from the episode with enough credit to gain the upper hand, and the nominal peace persisted uneasily as the frustrated Athenians cast about for a new policy. That was the situation when ambassadors from Athens' Sicilian allies arrived in 415 to ask for help against the menace of Syracuse and its satellites.

The Athenians had no compelling reason to go to Sicily at that time and could easily have ignored the entreaties of their small, far-off allies, had they chosen. Their appeal was the result of a dispute between Segesta and Selinus, two cities in western Sicily. When the Selinuntians won the first battle, Segesta sought help, first from nearby Acragas, then from Syracuse, and later from Carthage. They not only had no success, but Syracuse soon joined with Selinus against the Segestans. Pressed hard on land and sea, the Segestans turned to Athens. They took advantage of Syracuse's aggression against Leontini and made common cause with the other allies of Athens who were fighting against Syracuse. The Segestan ambassadors reminded the Athenians of their alliance with the Leontines and emphasized the kinship between Athens and Leontini, both Ionian states. They also put forward a practical reason for Athens to intervene in Sicily again: "If the Syracusans, who had depopulated Leontini, were not punished and, after destroying their allies who were still left, took power over all of Sicily, there was the risk that at some time in the future, as Dorians to Dorians and as kinsmen and colonists of the Peloponnesians, they might send them help with a great force and help destroy the power of Athens" (6.6.2). Finally, the Segestans offered to finance the war with their own funds.

It must be noted that the Segestan invitation was couched in the most conservative terms, emphasizing traditional ties, obligations to allies, and defensive strategy. Thucydides represents the Athenian response, however, as being of quite a different order. The Athenians, he explains, were happy to receive the request to aid their kinsmen and allies, but only as a pretext. Once again, as in his account of the outbreak of the Peloponnesian War, he maintains that there was a "truest explanation" different from the ones openly put forward, for the Athenian response: "They longed for the rule of the whole island" (6.6.1). This assertion, placed at the very beginning of the narrative, before the story is told or any facts presented, prejudices all that follows. Fundamentally, it merely repeats and underscores a statement Thucydides made at the very beginning of Book 6: "They sailed against Sicily to subject it to themselves if they could." (6.1.1).

Throughout his account the historian paints the picture of an undertaking aimed at the domination and exploitation of the entire island, an outcome demanded by an Athenian mob hungry for power and greedy for gain but ignorant of the true scope of the adventure and the difficulties and dangers it presented. "The many," he tells us, "were ignorant of the magnitude of the island and of the number of its inhabitants both Greek and barbarian and unaware that they were taking on a war not much inferior to the one against the Peloponnesians" (6.1.1). After describing the first Athenian decision to send a force to Sicily, he attributes to Nicias his own opinion that "with a slight and specious pretext they meant to conquer all Sicily, a large undertaking" (6.8.4). Later he ascribes to the "mob" the goal of securing money for the present and, for the future, additional imperial control that would provide an endless source of pay (6.24.3).[3]

Thucydides' interpretation does not in fact accord well with the Athenians' behavior as reported in his own narrative. Even if we grant what cannot be demonstrated—namely, that most Athenians did have the motives Thucydides ascribes to them at the point of sailing in the summer of 415—it is far from clear that those motives had been the same from the first. Thucydides makes a similar judgment about the motives for launching the first expedition to Sicily in 427: "The Athenians were testing the waters to see if they could bring Sicilian affairs under their control" (3.87.4–5). Yet when the reinforced expedition failed to achieve any important goal and withdrew in 424, the Athenians did not pursue the matter further. Apart from Thucydides' characterization, we have no reason to believe that the Athenians who received the Segestan request for aid in 416/15 were planning to use it as an excuse to conquer Sicily.

Thucydides' charge that the Athenian people were entirely ignorant of both Sicily's geography and its population, and therefore that they underestimated the scope of the undertaking, is even more suspect. In 424, less than nine years before the great expedition sailed, sixty Athenian triremes returned from an extended stay on Sicily. Some of their crews had been in Sicilian waters and on the island itself for three years, others for several months. At one time or another the Athenians visited Himera and Mylae on the north shore, the offshore Liparian Islands, almost every city on the eastern shore, Gela and Camarina on the southern shore, Messina on the strait dividing the island from Italy, and Rhegium and Locri in Italy itself. A small fleet under the general Phaeax revisited some of these places in 422 and traveled to Acragas, on the southern coast of Sicily, as well. Like his predecessors, he also visited the non-Greek Sicels in the interior. Segesta itself, a long-standing ally, was located almost at the western tip of the island. Since each trireme carried about two hundred men, the fleet that returned in 424 numbered about twelve thousand men. Even if only half of them were Athenians (the others being allies) and not all of them survived until 415, there still must have been no fewer than five thousand Athenian sailors and marines who knew the geography of Sicily intimately and had a rather good idea of its population. Each of them, of course, had friends and relatives, so the charge that most Athenians were ignorant of these matters is improbable.

Similarly Thucydides' account of the Athenians' response to the request from Segesta and Leontini fails to support the notion of Athenian ignorance or rashness. The assembly neither accepted nor rejected the invitation but voted to send a mission to Segesta "to see if the money was there, as the Segestans said, in the public treasury and the temples, and, at the same time, to discover how the war against the Selinuntians was going" (6.6.3). The Segestans deceived the Athenian envoys by constructing, in effect, a Potemkin village to create the impression of a fabulous prosperity. This successful imposture was persuasive, but surely more convincing was the fact that the Segestans brought to Athens sixty talents in uncoined silver, a full month's pay for sixty ships.

The Athenian envoys, with the Segestans and their money, returned home in March of 415, and the Athenians called an assembly to reconsider the appeal from Segesta. Thucydides tells us that, after hearing from both their own envoys and the Segestans that there was plenty of money to pay for the expedition and reports of other alluring things "that were also not true," the assembly voted to send sixty ships to Sicily under Alcibiades, Nicias, and Lamachus. These generals were to have full powers to help Segesta against Selinus, to join in resettling Leontini (if that were possible), and "to settle affairs in Sicily in whatever way they judged best for Athens" (6.8.2).

Thucydides offers no further detail about the first of two meetings of the Athenian assembly that decided on the expedition to Sicily. The brevity of his account—he neither reports speeches nor summarizes arguments for or against the measures finally adopted—has led some scholars to conclude that all Athenians, even Nicias, were in agreement at this first assembly.[4] But epigraphical evidence, as well as our knowledge of usual procedures, argue that there must have been some debate. There is, in fact, considerable evidence that Nicias spoke against the proposal. Thus Thucydides' silence proves nothing, for he commonly omits such important facts as the position of leading figures in significant debates.[5]

We can recover with a reasonable degree of confidence at least part of what took place at the first assembly of 415. Thucydides himself provides the first clue when he tells us that the Athenians elected Nicias general for the expedition "against his will, because he thought that the city had made a wrong decision" (6.8.4). This is an event, so far as we know, unique in Athenian history: a general accepting a command against his will. How was it known that on this occasion Nicias was unwilling to undertake the expedition just voted? Surely the likeliest source of this information was what Nicias himself had said in the assembly when the assignment was made. It would not be the first time that he had offered to step aside and surrender a command to someone else; in 425 he had done the same, however ironically, in connection with the command at Pylos and Sphacteria (4.28.3). We have good reason to believe that there was a debate in the first assembly as to who should be appointed general and that Nicias indicated his reluctance to serve.

Epigraphic evidence provides further support for this view. Eight fragments from at least two stelae found on the Acropolis in Athens contain inscriptions that epigraphers agree are connected with the Sicilian expedition of 415.[6] One of the fragments speaks of a fleet of sixty ships and, even more to the point, considers the possibility of appointing only one general to command them. This fragment must refer to the first assembly, since that meeting concluded by appointing three generals to command the sixty triremes. Plainly, the choice of generals was a subject for debate.

Later writers also provide evidence of what took place at the first assembly. Plutarch tells us that despite Nicias' opposition, he was still chosen as one of the three generals. In his account of the second assembly, Nicias again rises to try to dissuade the Athenians from the decision they had taken to go to Sicily.[7] Diodorus reports arguments made by Nicias against the expedition, one of which does not appear in Thucydides at all: the Athenians simply could not hope to conquer Sicily. "Even the Carthaginians who had a great empire had often fought wars for Sicily but had not had the power to subdue the island. . . . How could the Athenians, whose power was much less than that of the Carthaginians, do better?"[8] This report is probably an echo of the speech Nicias made at the first assembly.

Given this information, it is instructive to try to reconstruct the course of the debate at this assembly, without, of course, claiming absolute accuracy. The first motion likely to have been put forward was one authorizing a fleet of sixty ships to assist Athens' Sicilian allies at Segesta and Leontini. Presumably Alcibiades spoke in favor and Nicias against, perhaps employing the comparison with Carthage's unavailing power, as later reported by Diodorus.

Another topic for debate was the choice of commander or commanders. Some may have favored a single leader, presumably Alcibiades. As the foremost advocate of the undertaking he was the natural choice for a single command, but many Athenians who might otherwise support his policy would not trust him as the expedition's only general. The idea of adding Nicias would have appealed not only to his friends and supporters but also to those who thought it wise to balance Alcibiades' youthful, ambitious daring with the experience, caution, piety, and luck of Nicias. Nicias must have indicated his reluctance to serve as general, and perhaps even spoke directly against the motion to put him in command. But in the end, it would have been considered unpatriotic or cowardly of him to refuse. The Athenians, of course, saw the impossibility of naming to one command two generals who were political and personal enemies and who disagreed on all aspects of the projected campaign. They therefore chose a third leader, Lamachus son of Xenophanes. Lamachus was an experienced soldier, about fifty years old in 415, who had served as general as early as 425 or even before. He must have favored the expedition and could be counted on to support its general purpose while respecting the counsel of Nicias.

There must have been a lively debate over the instructions to be given to the commanders, for these would determine the precise goals of the expedition. We have seen that Thucydides portrays the Athenians as aiming from the outset at the conquest of Sicily. He also tells us that Alcibiades intended to seize not only Sicily but also Carthage, and later reports a speech made at Sparta in which Alcibiades spoke of using victories in Italy and Spain as a basis to conquer the Peloponnesus and rule over all Greeks. (6.15.2; 6.90.2–4). There surely were some Athenians at the first assembly in 415 who harbored grandiose goals and perhaps, for all we know, Alcibiades himself had already raised his sights to encompass the goals ultimately attributed to him. Thucydides' opinion supports such an assumption, although the historian was in exile from Athens at the time and could only have reached this conclusion considerably after the fact. What we can be sure of is that *nobody* advanced such ambitious goals at the assembly; Thucydides himself makes no mention of any such reference. What is more telling is that Nicias was led to reopen the question of the whole expedition at the second assembly because he "thought that the city . . . with a slight and specious pretext meant to conquer all of Sicily" (6.8.4). He *thought* it, but he did not *know* it, because no one at the assembly had spoken of such a purpose, or Nicias would have addressed and emphasized it.

At the first assembly of 415, in fact, the Athenians voted for modest goals that suited the relatively modest force they voted to accomplish them, a force and goals that were comparable to those of the 427–424 campaign: to assist Segesta against Selinus, to help restore Leontini, and "to settle affairs in Sicily" in the best interests of Athens. These did not require, and need not even imply, the conquest of the island. It may be argued that these stated goals were merely a pretext, as Thucydides claims—a screen to conceal the true nature of Athenian rapacity. The number of ships the Athenians voted for the expedition provides a satisfactory response to that contention, for it was neither the small squadron of twenty dispatched under Laches and Charoeades in 427 to prevent Syracuse from sending grain to the Peloponnese and as a "preliminary test to see if they could bring the affairs of Sicily under control" (3.86.4), nor was it the vast armada that ultimately sailed in 415. Rather it was precisely the number dispatched in 424, when Sophocles, Eurymedon, and Pythodorus brought forty triremes to reinforce the twenty already there. The force of sixty had been thought adequate to bring the war to a close, given the modest goals of that campaign (3.115.4). There could have been no question of conquering Sicily with sixty ships in 424, and the Athenians had not intended to do so. Their decision at the first assembly in 415 to send a fleet of the same size indicates that, again, their aims were limited.

This is not to say that the expedition voted by the first assembly had no aggressive intentions whatsoever. Events in Sicily since the first Athenian intervention had revealed the danger that Syracuse presented to the allies of Athens and to the freedom of the other cities on the island. Left to itself, Syracuse might develop into a power that could one day lend important assistance to the Peloponnesians, and especially to their mother city, Corinth, which was historically hostile to Athens. The Athenians who voted for the expedition may well have hoped for the conquest of Syracuse in order to forestall such possibilities; sixty ships could be enough for that purpose.

A surprise attack directly on the city from the sea might succeed, as might an attempt to recruit Sicilian allies who could bring Syracuse down by the show of considerable, if not overwhelming, force. In either event the risk to Athens would be low. In case of an assault on Syracuse by land, the Sicilian allies would do the fighting, for the Athenians were not sending an army. In case of an attack by sea, the Athenians could turn back if they found Syracuse well defended and resolute. Even if everything went wrong and the entire expedition were destroyed, that would be a misfortune but not a disaster. Many of the sailors would be allies, not Athenians, and the ships could be replaced. The one thing that surely could not result from the expedition voted by the first assembly in 415 was a major strategic defeat that might change the course of the war. Only after the second assembly did the Athenians incur such a risk, and we must ask how they came to do so.

Four days after the first, a second assembly met to consider "how the fleet could be equipped most quickly and to vote anything else the generals might need for the expedition" (6.8.3). Thucydides describes this meeting as fully as any in his *History*, directly recounting two speeches by Nicias and one by Alcibiades and recording other comments made in the assembly.

Nicias appears to have spoken first, for he meant to turn the debate away from its stated purpose toward one that was unexpected and might well be improper. He conceded that the assembly had been called to con-

sider ways and means, but said, "I believe we should consider this question
again: whether we should send the ships off at all" (6.9.1). The Athenians
do not seem to have had any law forbidding *anapsephisis*, the act of proposing the repeal or annulment of a decree just passed by the assembly. Still,
his proposal seems to have been unusual enough to be subject to a number of different legal challenges. Nicias recognized that the assembly's
presiding officer also might be criticized for allowing a doubtful motion
to be put forward, but persuaded him to do so, urging him not to fear but
"to become a physician for a state that has decided badly" (6.14).

Nicias offered an assessment of Athens' diplomatic and military situation that must have surprised both his friends and enemies and should
give pause to those who think that the Peace of Nicias was a victory for
Athens. Athens, according to Nicias, could not afford to attack Sicily and
so make new enemies, for she already had formidable enemies at home.
The Spartans had not agreed to peace willingly but were forced to it by
their misfortunes. Some of Sparta's most important allies still had not
accepted. If the Athenians should weaken their power in the homeland
by sailing to Sicily, her enemies would attack, aided by the Sicilian reinforcements they had long coveted. The Athenians had thus far prevailed,
contrary to their own expectations, but the Spartans were not convinced
that they had been beaten and were only waiting for the right moment to
erase their dishonor and recover their reputation (6.11.6). Before contemplating any Sicilian expedition, the Athenians should consolidate their
present empire by recovering the rebellious cities in the Chalcidice and
the Thraceward region. "We must not reach out for another empire until
we have made the one we have secure" (6.10.5).

This evaluation of Athens' strategic situation lay at the heart of
Nicias' policy. He must have made the same points at the first assembly, but they had not then been able to win the debate. At this second
meeting he also had to respond to the arguments advanced by the advocates of the expedition. Clearly, the wish to aid Athens' allies in Sicily
played a prominent part in the discussion, for Nicias goes far in refuting
their claim on Athenian assistance. His first reference sets the tone: "We

should not undertake a war that is not our affair, persuaded by men of an alien race" (6.9.1). Nicias calls the Segestans "a barbaric people" who require help when they are in trouble but give none when the Athenians need it (6.11.7). He dismisses the Leontines as fugitives and clever liars who supply only words while their allies take all the risks, who are ungrateful in victory and bring disaster to their friends in defeat (6.12.1). Such impolitic and harsh language, even directed against inconvenient allies, suggests that the supporters of the expedition must have put considerable weight on the appeal from Sicily and thus compelled Nicias to answer forcefully.

The threat to Athens from a Sicily dominated by Syracuse appears to have been the main argument used by his opponents at the first assembly, for Nicias confronted it with a long and sophistical rebuttal. While the ambassadors from Segesta, especially, placed emphasis on the threat from Syracuse if it were allowed to dominate the island, Nicias asserted the exact opposite: "The Sicilians . . . would be even less dangerous than they are now if ruled by the Syracusans, for now they might attack us singly out of feeling for the Spartans, but if the Syracusans were in control it is not likely that an empire would attack another empire." He argued that if Syracuse joined with the Spartans to destroy the Athenian Empire, it could expect its own empire to be destroyed by the Spartans, as well. (6.11.3). All this was such nonsense as to require no refutation, and in fact, Alcibiades made no reference to it in his own rebuttal.

Nicias' second argument may have been even weaker than the first. The Athenians, he said, could most effectively frighten the Sicilian Greeks and thus deter them from joining in an attack on Athens by staying as far from Sicily as possible. If Athens attacked Sicily and lost, the Sicilians, in contempt of Athenian power, would quickly join the Spartans in an attack. The best course of action for Athens would be not to go to Sicily at all; the next best would be to make a brief show of force and withdraw immediately: "For we all know that we marvel most at things that are the farthest away and least allow their reputation to be tested" (6.11.4). This argument, apart from its dubious psychological assumptions, ignores the possibility that the Athenians might win, thereby enhancing their reputation in a forceful enough way to discourage any attack contemplated by Sicily. Again we have a foolish argument that his opponents did not bother to answer.

In view of Thucydides' own repeated opinion, it is surprising that Nicias had nothing direct to say about the idea of conquering all of Sicily, although one or two of his remarks may be ambiguous enough to suggest a reference to such a notion.[9] The ambiguity may have been in the words of Nicias himself or may have been supplied by Thucydides, but in neither case can we find any arguments presented against a plan of general conquest. If conquering Sicily had been put forward at the first assembly as a reason for sending the expedition, Nicias could not have failed to attack such a proposal. It was the most vulnerable possible target and would not have required the tortured reasoning that he was forced to rely on to combat other arguments. It is reasonable to conclude, therefore, that no one at the first assembly openly offered the prospect of general conquest as a reason to go to Sicily, whatever private intentions they may have had.

Perhaps Nicias was frustrated by his inability to address what he would have liked to portray as the true purpose of the expedition, and perhaps that is what led him to launch not only a personal attack but also one against an entire younger generation. No one could doubt that Nicias' target was Alcibiades. The criticism of Alcibiades and of his youthful supporters may have been a device to focus attention on the most radical advocates of the expedition and on the man who was both its chief proponent and probably the most distrusted man in Athens.

After Nicias others came forth to argue each side of the case. Most of them favored the expedition, but its most ardent proponent, according to Thucydides, was Alcibiades son of Cleinias. Although Alcibiades had played an important part in Athenian affairs since the Peace of Nicias, Thucydides chose this moment to introduce and characterize him and to evaluate the role he played in the outcome of the war. He tells us that Alcibiades spoke in opposition to Nicias because of their political disagreement in general, because Nicias had attacked him personally, but chiefly because he wanted to be in command so that he might attack not only Sicily but Carthage as well, thereby winning both public glory and private wealth. In making such judgments Thucydides effectively endorses the charges that Nicias made in his speech. He also supports Nicias' accusation that Alcibiades wanted money to support the expense of raising horses and sustaining other costly activities with which he enhanced his reputation among the Athenians (6.15.1–3).

But these expenditures and the conspicuous display they financed had other, less favorable consequences, and Thucydides describes them in a remarkable passage that foreshadows the Athenian defeat not only in Sicily, but in the war as a whole. "And it was just this that later on did most to destroy the Athenian state. For the many were afraid of the extent of his lawless self-indulgence in his way of life and also of his purpose in each and every affair in which he became involved; they became hostile to him on the grounds that he was aiming at a tyranny. And so, although in public affairs he conducted his military functions in the best possible way, his activities in his private life offended everyone, so they turned the leadership of the state over to other men and before long brought the state to ruin" (6.15.3–4).

Such a dramatic summary and anticipation of future events is matched only by Thucydides' famous encomium on and evaluation of the career of Pericles, a passage that has the function of providing a framework for the reader's understanding of the entire history (2.65). The present passage has much the same function, making clear to the reader how he is to understand future events. Alcibiades' extraordinary style of living will ultimately cause trouble, although it is not he who will be responsible for the Athenian defeat but rather the offended masses who, fearing him, will award the command to other, lesser generals. There is a clear parallel to the death of Pericles and the decline of Athens under the leadership of his inferior successors.

Alcibiades defiantly defended against Nicias' attacks on his style of life and his youth, cleverly reminding the Athenians that they had voted not for a single commander but for a board of three generals. "Make use of both of us," he said, "while I am still at my peak and Nicias has the reputation of being lucky" (6.17.1). This was not the last time that Nicias' presence among the team of commanders would be used to bring about the very expedition he so vigorously opposed.

Then, challenging Nicias' depiction of Sicily, Alcibiades pictured the island as teeming with instability, its cities filled with "a mixed mob" prone to frequent relocation and constitutional overthrow. Men did not take arms to defend their cities loyally and patriotically, as in the mother country, but were prepared instead to take the wealth that they had hoarded and move elsewhere. Such people could easily be lured to the Athenian side. He claimed that the Sicilians did not have as many hoplites as was alleged, and in any case, the Athenians could balance their numbers by using the barbarian Sicels, who hated the Syracusans (6.17.2–6).

If Alcibiades' account of Sicilian affairs was one-sided and exaggerated, it was not entirely inaccurate. Early in the fifth century Sicilian tyrants had frequently transplanted populations, and the overthrow of the tyrannies caused similar upheavals. The Congress of Gela of 424 showed that the Sicilians might unite and present a formidable opposition to Athenian plans, but the subsequent period demonstrated that such unity was unlikely to last. The fate of Leontini was good evidence of internal instability in the Sicilian towns, and the war between Selinus and Segesta revealed the continuing divisions between the island's states.

In the Greek homeland Nicias had portrayed the Spartans and their allies as eager to resume the war, needing only a suitable opportunity, but Alcibiades countered that they had less hope than ever before. The Spartans' failure to take any aggressive action to recover Argos or to renounce the Peace of Nicias, in spite of Athenian provocation, suggested that Alcibiades was closer to the truth. But even if the Spartans had been strong and bold, Alcibiades argued, all they could have been capable of was to invade Attica by land, an action they could have taken at any time. They could not, however, cause harm to the Athenians where it most counted, at sea. Even with an Athenian fleet bound for Sicily, the reserve fleet at home was still a match for the enemy (6.17.7–8). Again, Alcibiades was correct in his assessment, especially when we remember that when he spoke the Athenians were contemplating sending to Sicily only the sixty ships they had already voted.

Alcibiades next turned to one of his strongest arguments, and one that was most embarrassing to Nicias—Athens' obligations to her allies. First, there was the moral case: "We must assist them, for we have given our oath" (6.18.1). Interest as well as honor dictated that the Athenians keep their commitments and send help to their allies. Athens had not made the Sicilian alliances in order to be able to summon help from that quarter to the homeland, but instead to keep its enemies in Sicily off balance so that they could not attack the Athenians. Allies like Segesta and Leontini were, in fact, a first line of defense for Athens.

Alcibiades also maintained that the very nature of the Athenian Empire required an active policy on behalf of allies. "That is how we have acquired our empire and that is how others who have had empire acquired theirs—by always coming eagerly to the aid of those who called upon us, whether Greek or barbarian" (6.18.2). To change now to a policy of restraint, to draw distinctions among allies on the basis of race, to set arbitrary limits on the extent of the empire—all these would be disastrous. Such a policy not only would prevent further growth, but would even threaten the empire's present security. Other states might pursue a course of peace and inactivity, but the Athenians could not do so without giving up their way of life and their empire, and the Athenians could not abandon their empire without running the risk of becoming the subjects of others (6.18.2–3). Alcibiades' argument is similar to that advanced by Pericles in his last recorded speech: "It is not possible for you to withdraw from this empire, if any in the present situation out of fear or from love of tranquility has decided to become honest." Pericles had put the main point more bluntly than Alcibiades dared: "By now the empire you hold is a tyranny; it may now seem wrong to have taken it, but it is surely dangerous to let it go," for "you are hated by those you have ruled" (2.63.1–2).

At that juncture, for the only time in the speech, and probably for the first time in the entire debate, Alcibiades revealed the grander purposes he had in mind for the Sicilian expedition. If the venture succeeded, "as seems likely," the Athenians might gain control of all Greece, since their power would be reinforced by the addition of Sicily. This ambitious statement was not so un-Periclean as it might seem. When Pericles was challenged by the men who in his time advocated a peaceful and passive policy, the *apragmones*, he told the Athenians: "You are the absolute masters of the entire sea, not only as much of it as you now rule but however much more you wish. And there is no one, while you have the fleet you do, who will prevent you from sailing on it, not the Great King nor any nation such as now exists" (2.62.2). Pericles, however, spoke his bold words at a time when he found the Athenians "unreasonably discouraged," and he intended not to undertake a new expedition but merely to encourage them to persevere in the war in which they were already engaged. Alcibiades, like Pericles, called his opponent's policy *apragmosyne,* but the circumstances in which he spoke were different. Athens was now at least formally at peace and could better afford a distant campaign, but the Athenians were already excessively confident and ambitious. Thucydides, no doubt, had this comparison and contrast in mind, wishing his readers to notice the distinction between Pericles, the great statesman who worked against the grain to moderate the passions of his people, and Alcibiades, the demagogue who exploited these passions for his own purposes.

But Alcibiades was prudent enough to recognize the danger of dwelling too long on the controversial question of the conquest of all Sicily. His reference to such a conquest, moreover, was made in the context of sending a force of sixty ships and no hoplites, a low-risk operation that depended more on surprise, psychology, and diplomacy than on the fortunes of battle. He was careful to bracket his suggestion of more ambitious war aims with others that were strictly defensive. The boldness of the attack on Sicily during the present uncertain peace would further reduce the confidence of the Spartans, and presumably (though Alcibiades does not spell it out) would deter them from resuming the war and at-tacking Athens. Even if the Athenians did not conquer Sicily, moreover, the expedition could at least do damage to Syracuse, and this would ben-efit both the Athenians and their Sicilian allies (6.18.4–5).

Alcibiades concluded with the subtle and unusual argument that Ath-ens must pursue an active rather than a passive policy because that was her nature. "It seems to me that a city which is not passive *(apragmon)* would quickly be destroyed by a change toward passiveness and that those men are safest who make political decisions that are least in conflict with existing habits and institutions" (6.18.7). That assertion justified, in-deed required, continued expansion of the kind Alcibiades had in mind. It conflicted directly with the policy of Pericles, which had aimed at the maintenance without further expansion of an empire. Again, Thucydides probably intended that his reader note that particular contrast.

In this second assembly of 415 Alcibiades' speech was effective, espe-cially when supported by renewed pleas from the Segestans and Leon-tines to keep Athenian oaths and send help to Sicily. The Athenians "were even more eager than before to make the expedition" (6.19.1), but Nicias did not yet give up his attempt to prevent it. This time he abandoned straightforward opposition, resorting instead to guile. Thucydides tells us that Nicias "knew he could not deter them with the same arguments but thought he might change their minds by the size of the expedition, if he proposed a large one" (6.19.2).[10] Such a tactic is a risky parliamentary maneuver at any time, and Nicias appears to have made no preliminary arrangements with his supporters regarding it.

He began with a rebuttal of Alcibiades' description of Sicily. He claimed that the Greek cities of Sicily were neither in turmoil internally, nor in conflict with one another, nor were they demoralized. They were, however, large, numerous and, except for Naxos and Catana, ill disposed to Athens. They were well equipped with hoplites, archers, javelin throw-ers, triremes, and rowers. They also had sufficient funds, some public and some private; Syracuse even collected tributes from barbarians. The Greeks of Sicily also had two important resources that the Athenians going to Sicily would lack: a rich stock of horses and grain that need not be imported.

If these cities joined together they would make up a great power against which the pitiful force that the Athenians had already voted would be inadequate. With that fleet the Athenians might make a landing, but the enemy, with its cavalry, could confine them to the beachhead and force them either to send home for supplies or to return in shame. The Athenians must realize that they would be fighting at such a distance that in winter even a messenger might take four months to arrive from home. To succeed they must send many hoplites (Athenians, allies, subjects, and mercenaries), as well as light-armed troops to harass the enemy cavalry. There must also be more warships to guarantee control of the sea and supply. The Athenians must take grain with them in merchant ships, for no force of such a size could expect to live off the land, especially since the Sicilians could not be trusted. They would also have to take plenty of money, too, for talk of funding from Segesta would turn out to be just talk (6.20–22).

Nicias, no doubt, hoped this list of necessities would daunt his audience, and he went on to paint an even darker picture. Even if the Athenians mounted an expedition that was greater than the combined forces of the Sicilian Greeks, "except, of course, for their hoplites, the force that does the real fighting, we will not find it easy to defeat them or even to guarantee the safety of our own forces" (6.23.1). The Athenians must realize that they are like colonists going out to found a new city in dangerous foreign lands where they must establish control immediately or face hostility from all the natives. Such an expedition required careful planning and, even more important, the good luck that mere mortals cannot count upon. Nicias therefore preferred to rely for safety on the best and most careful preparation. "I think that the preparations I have suggested provide the greatest security for the state and safety for those of us who go out on the expedition. But if any one thinks otherwise, I offer to give up my command to him" (6.23).

We can understand most of Nicias' speech in light of his basic aim, which was to prevent the sailing of the Sicilian expedition. But why, after trying to frighten the Athenians, did he suggest that the adoption of his proposals would make the venture safe, and why did he offer to resign his command? Both ploys suggest that he expected someone to challenge his fundamental assumption, that the mission to Sicily would be terribly difficult to accomplish, and to deny the conclusion he drew from it, that a vast and expensive force would be required if the mission were even to be attempted. He might well have anticipated that Alcibiades or some-one else would insist that Nicias was exaggerating the situation and the potential danger, and that proper use of the force already voted would insure success. If that view proved to be popular, Nicias could then hon-orably ask to be relieved on the grounds that his advice had been rejected and that he was unwilling to lead Athenians to their deaths on an impos-sible quest. Nicias may also have hoped that his resignation would sober the assembly, forcing it to realize that it was losing the experienced and lucky general it had appointed to tame the wild and ambitious youth. Failing that, there might still be further debate and, perhaps, delay, dur-ing which the excited populace might regain its composure and carefully reflect.

Although we cannot be certain of Nicias' expectations, Thucydides does make it clear that they were not realized. A certain Demostratus rose to challenge him in an unexpected and embarrassing way.[11] Though he came from a noble family, Plutarch describes him as "foremost among the demagogues in urging the Athenians to war."[12] He told Nicias "not to make or cause delays but to say at once and before them all what forces the Athenians should vote him" (6.25.1). Nicias, unprepared for such a question, answered that he would rather discuss the matter with his col-leagues at leisure, and even this he said unwillingly. But the bluntness of Demostratus would permit no delay, so Nicias put forward his estimates: at least a hundred triremes from Athens, of which some should be troop transports, and others from the allies; a combined force of Athenian and allied hoplites of no fewer than five thousand; and a proportional num-ber of light-armed troops.

Far from finding these figures daunting, the Athenians

> were not turned away from their eagerness for the expedition by the
> burdensomeness of the preparation but became more eager for it, and
> things turned out the opposite of what Nicias expected. For they thought
> he had given them good advice and that now the expedition would be
> very safe. And a passion came upon all of them equally to sail off. The
> older men thought that either they would conquer or at least that such
> a great force could not come to harm. Those who were in their prime
> longed for distant sights and spectacles, being confident that they would
> be safe. The mass of the people and the soldiers hoped to get money at
> the moment and to make an addition to their empire from which they
> would have a never-ending source of income. (6.24.3)

Here, as elsewhere, Thucydides claims to know what is in the minds of
others—in this case, of the entire Athenian populace in all its variety.
One must wonder how he could claim this, especially as he was off in
exile at the time and had been for a decade. In their name, however, he
authoritatively reaffirms his view of the reasons for the campaign: greed
and the lust for conquest, driven not by reason but by passion (*eros*). He
represents the enthusiastic, rabid majority as intimidating anyone who
might oppose the expedition by accusing him of disloyalty to the state.
In such a mood, we are to believe, the Athenians then voted to give their
generals full powers in determining the size of the expedition and "to act
in whatever way seem best to them for Athens" (6.26.2).

Nicias' maneuver had failed disastrously. His performance reminds
the reader of his similar miscalculation during the assembly in 425 that
dealt with the Spartans trapped on Sphacteria. On that occasion Nicias
had offered to relinquish his command to the inexperienced and apparently incompetent Cleon. He expected Cleon to refuse and so be discredited, but Nicias misread the mood of the assembly, which egged Cleon on
until he could not reject the offer.

At the second assembly in 415 Nicias was decisive in converting into a vast enterprise an expedition that originally had limited objectives and ran limited risks. Now actually capable of attempting the conquest of Sicily, the Athenian force was of such a size that its defeat could mean almost total disaster. Nicias had suggested an investment of men, money, and ships that no other Athenian politician would have dared to propose— and in two assemblies none had. Thucydides' portrait of the Athenian masses, greedily eager from the outset to conquer Sicily and ready to commit a vast expedition for that purpose, is not justified by any of the evidence that he provides.[13] We have no reason to doubt the accuracy of his assessment, however, after the second assembly. What convinced the Athenians to proceed from a cautious and limited venture to a bold and unlimited commitment was the assurance they had received from the pious, fortunate, and cautious Nicias. Such a guarantee from so trusted a source swept all before it, kindling new ambitions and heightening those that had already been voiced.

In their first assembly in 415 the Athenian people voted to send an expedition to Sicily to aid their allies and to check the expansion of Syracuse, a colony of Sparta's Corinthian ally. There is no evidence that anyone spoke of a conquest at that time, and while such a decision may or may not have been wise or necessary, it was reasonable and moderate, presenting no great risk. But few readers have come to the conclusion that the Athenians favored a moderate course. Because Thucydides was convinced that post-Periclean Athens, unchecked by the wisdom and skill of a great leader, was out of control, rapacious and hungry for power from the first, his account is organized so as to prevent his reader from thinking otherwise. His first reference to the expedition of 415 assumes a goal of conquest from the start: "They sailed against Sicily to subject it to themselves if they could" (6.1.1). Soon after he expands that claim: "With a slight and specious pretext they meant to conquer all Sicily, a large undertaking" (6.8.4). Before presenting an account of how the decision was made—indeed, omitting a description of the debate in the assembly— he has established his view of the motive for the action, which is unsupported by his own narrative and contradicted by the evidence as a whole. It is not surprising that most readers have been convinced of his interpretation.

Thucydides concludes his account of the preliminaries to the expedition with a lengthy and vivid description of its departure in June of 415. His account is shot through with sardonic and ironic observations that contrast the enthusiastic, hopeful mood of the Athenians with foreshadowings of the catastrophe to come. Many foreigners from allied cities were present, and they went down to Piraeus along with the Athenians to bid the expedition farewell but also to see the spectacular show. The historian describes the gathering as a *homilos* (6.30.2; 6.32.2), which may mean merely a throng or a large assemblage of people, but also indicates a mob and even an unruly mob. The reader is reminded at both the beginning and the end of the description that the departure is the work of the post-Periclean democracy, the mob and the demagogues who mislead them.

The Athenian force was not greater in numbers than the expedition Pericles had led against Epidaurus in 430, but it was "the most expensive and glorious armament coming from a single city with a purely Greek force that put to sea up to that time" (6.31.1). Not only public funds but also private expenditures by the trierarchs provided for ships that were both efficient and beautiful, and even the hoplites vied with one another in the beauty and quality of their equipment. "It looked more like a display of power and wealth before the rest of the Greeks than an expedition against enemies" (6.31.4).

On the morning of the expedition's sailing the high spirits of the Athenians were somewhat chastened by the reality of saying farewell to sons, relatives, and friends who were about to sail off on an adventure made unprecedentedly dangerous by the long distance involved. They were reassured, however, by the extraordinary power and brilliance of the force they were dispatching. At last, when all was ready, the blare of a trumpet brought silence to the vast crowd. The prayers customary before putting out to sea were offered in unison by the entire army and navy with the crowd joining from the shore. "When they had sung the paean and finished the libations they set out, at first in column, then, as they sailed off, they raced each other as far as Aegina" (6.32.2). They treated the affair as if it were an enormous regatta, the implication of which is that the expedition was vainglorious or, as the Greeks would say, an act of hubris.

The Athenians, Thucydides tells us, went off filled with hope (*elpis*). His readers could hardly fail to think of what the Athenians had contemptuously told the doomed Melians in the previous year, recounted just before the story of the Sicilian expedition. "Yes, hope is a comfort in time of danger. . . . But, since it is an expensive thing, those who risk everything on a single throw find out the cost only when they have been ruined" (5.103). The sobering Athenian observation had turned out to be correct, and the Melians who had rested their fate on hopes of Spartan assistance had paid with their lives. Thucydides' readers, who knew the terrible fate awaiting Athens' grand armada, would not have missed the irony. All this suggests that the expedition, decided upon and now cheered on by the ignorant and greedy masses, was doomed from the start, yet the historian's own account will make it clear that it took extraordinarily bad execution to bring about the ultimate catastrophe. That failure of leadership would be the responsibility not of the demagogic and wildly ambitious Alcibiades but of the man whose virtues Thucydides singles out for extraordinary praise, the same man who made the Sicilian venture possible.

CHAPTER NINE

Who Was Responsible for
the Sicilian Disaster?

A T THE END of his long, brilliant, and tragic account of the Athe-nian defeat in Sicily Thucydides delivers a rare encomium upon the death of Nicias, saying: "Of all the Greeks, in my time, at any rate, he least deserved to meet with such extreme misfortune because he had led his entire life in accordance with virtue" (7.86.5). He offers no such praise for Demosthenes, Nicias' fellow general, who was killed by the Syracusans at the same time and in the same manner. In this distinction he precisely reversed the judgment of the Athenian people, who erected a stele in the public cemetery on which they engraved the names of the generals who died fighting in Sicily. They included the name of Demos-thenes but deliberately omitted that of Nicias.[1] Whatever other reasons they had for the decision, they surely placed special blame on Nicias for the disaster, a conclusion at odds with that of Thucydides. We need to investigate his account to see how he attempted to revise the general opinion of the day.

In June 415 the great armada set off for Sicily. Led by their generals Alcibiades, Nicias, and Lamachus, they put in at Rhegium, at the toe of Italy, where things began to go wrong at once. Rhegium was criti-cal to Athenian success; it was an old ally and strategically located for attacking Messana (modern Messina) across the strait. Alcibiades had counted on Rhegium to be the main base of operations in that region and to help bring other Italian cities into the alliance. Nicias' miscon-ceived ploy in the Athenian assembly, however, destroyed the prospects for Alcibiades' plan, for the vast size of the Athenian force frightened the Italians and Sicilians more than the prospect of an aggressive Syracuse did. The Rhegians accordingly refused to allow the Athenians into their city.

The three generals now met to consider their next step. Nicias unsurprisingly proposed in essence a show of force and a swift return home. Alcibiades thought such an expedient disgraceful and suggested instead a version of his original strategy. He would use his diplomatic talents to convince the Greek cities of Sicily, and even the native Sicilians, to supply soldiers and food. With them as allies the Athenians could take Syracuse. Lamachus proposed that they sail at once and attack Syracuse directly. Later, when Demosthenes arrived in Sicily in 413 with reinforcements, he would conclude that Nicias had made a vital mistake in not following that plan and attacking immediately. Thucydides likewise endorsed that plan as the best (7.42.3),[2] and there is no reason to disagree; a swift assault might well have taken the city from the unprepared Syracusans. Lamachus, however, had no chance to execute his proposal for Nicias insisted on doing nothing significant, and the thought of an attack on Syracuse undoubtedly appalled him. Alcibiades would consider no plan other than his own. Unwilling to accept Nicias' feeble strategy, Lamachus reluctantly supported Alcibiades.

It does not seem likely that the proposal of Alcibiades would have worked in the new circumstances of a huge expedition, but it became a lost cause when a ship arrived ordering him to return to Athens to stand trial. Before the fleet had sailed, Alcibiades stood accused of involvement in a terrible religious profanation.

A strange episode brought a great scandal that terrified the Athenians. Unknown perpetrators had mutilated the statues of the god that stood at the entrance of Athenian homes, as well as at religious shrines and public spaces. They were thought to bring good luck and protection from danger; besides, Hermes was the patron god of travelers and the outrage was a terrible omen for a great naval expediton.

Many Athenians thought that this sacrilege was part of a plot to overthrow the democracy and establish an oligarchy or tyranny, and it was widely thought that Alcibiades was involved. Further suspicion arose when he was charged with participating in a mockery of the mystery rites celebrated at Eleusis. Because Alcibiades was at the height of his popularity, especially with those who were making the expedition, he demanded to be tried at once, before the fleet left. Instead, his opponents waited to bring charges until the expedition had sailed. After his departure his political enemies engineered his recall. Rather than submit, however, he fled to Sparta.

While Nicias would have liked to pursue his passive strategy, he knew that neither his troops nor the Athenians at home would have been satisfied with such a course of action, so he moved the entire armada toward Segesta and Selinus to see what could be done.

After sailing through the Straits of Messina toward northwestern Sicily, "as far as possible from the Syracusan enemy,"[3] the Athenians attacked Hyccara, a town of native Sicans hostile to Segesta, turned it over to the Segestans, and enslaved the "barbarian" inhabitants. Nicias himself went to Segesta to collect the money that had been pledged and to try to settle its quarrel with Selinus, but he left with only thirty talents, presumably all the money he could find, and rejoined his army at Catana. By now the Athenians had vainly approached almost every Greek city in Sicily for assistance. The strategy of Alcibiades, carried out with little vigor by Nicias, had now also failed.

The first campaigning season was a great disappointment; the departure of Alcibiades left the venture in the hands of a leader who did not believe in its goals and who had no strategy of his own to achieve them. Plutarch described the situation as follows: "Nicias, though theoretically one of two colleagues, held sole power. He did not stop sitting about, sailing around, and thinking things over until the vigorous hope of his men had grown feeble and the astonishment and fear that the first sight of his forces had imposed on the enemy had faded away."[4] Since he still dared not leave Sicily, Nicias and his men would now be compelled to face the main enemy at Syracuse without a clear plan of action.

The only strategy left to the Athenians was that of Lamachus, but though its author was present, the real leader of the army was Nicias.

Thucydides makes it clear how much the delay in putting Lamachus' plan into operation had already cost the Athenians. The longer they waited the more Syracusan courage revived. News that the Athenians had sailed away from Syracuse to the western end of the island and then failed to conquer it roused the Syracusans to contempt, and the excited mob demanded that their generals lead them in an attack against the Athenians at Catana. Syracusan cavalrymen rode up to the Athenians and insulted them by asking, "Have you come to settle here with us on someone else's land instead of resettling the Leontines on their own?" (6.63.3).

Unable to hesitate any longer, Nicias faced the problem of how to get his forces into position to attack Syracuse. The fleet could not land against an armed opponent who was now ready to face it, and while the hoplite army could march to the city safely, the Athenians also had many light-armed soldiers and a vast mob of bakers, masons, carpenters, and camp followers with no cavalry to protect them against the substantial force of Syracusan horsemen. The Athenians, therefore, resorted to trickery, using a double agent to deceive the Syracusan generals and lure the entire enemy army to Catana. While the Syracusans were marching the forty miles there, the Athenians landed their ships and men unopposed in Syracuse harbor on a beach south of the Anapus River, opposite the great temple of Olympian Zeus. They took up a position protected by houses and natural barriers from flank attacks by the Syracusan cavalry and built further fortifications to defend themselves from a frontal assault or an attack from the sea.

In the ensuing battle the Athenians positioned their slingers, archers, and stone throwers on the wings, where they helped fight off the enemy cavalry. In spite of the depth of the Syracusan phalanx and the individual bravery of its soldiers, the superior discipline and experience of the Athenians and their allies carried the day.

As they fought, a fierce storm with rain, thunder, and lightning terrified the Syracusans, probably helping to break their spirit, but the practiced Athenians took it in stride. Soon the enemy line broke, and the Syracusans and their allies fled. Here was the Athenians' great opportunity to score a decisive victory, for if they undertook an aggressive pursuit and inflicted many casualties they might overcome Syracusan resistance or, at least, hamper the enemy's prospects of withstanding a siege. To achieve that, however, cavalry, which could pursue faster and farther than hoplites, was essential, but the Athenians had none. The un-opposed Syracusan cavalry was able to check the pursuit, enabling their army to regroup and reach safety behind the city walls. For the Athe-nians it was a tactical victory without strategic result: Syracuse stood fast, ready and able to continue the fight, and some way had to be found to make it yield. Instead of launching a siege at once, however, the Athe-nians set up a trophy of victory and sailed back to Catana.

Thucydides attributes Nicias' withdrawal to the lateness of the season, and to the need to store up grain, to obtain more money from Athens and elsewhere, and especially to "send to Athens for cavalry and recruit some from their allies in Sicily so that they would not be completely dominated by the enemy cavalry" (6.71.2). Nicias' contemporaries blamed him for not acting more resolutely. In his *Birds*, performed soon after the battle, Aristophanes makes a joke about "Nicias-delays," and Plutarch reports the common opinion in Athens that, "by calculating too carefully and delaying and being overly cautious he destroyed the opportunity for action."⁵

Nicias' caution in response to his lack of cavalry was not unreason-able, for Athenian detachments sent to dig trenches or build encircling walls could not fight off attacks by Syracusan cavalry unless defended by horsemen of their own. But wars are often decided by issues other than material considerations. Demosthenes, a far more brilliant general, thought that had Nicias been bolder in the winter of 415, the Syracusans would have offered battle, suffered defeat, and found their city shut in by a wall before they could send for help, and consequently been forced to surrender (7.42.3). Still, it is most unlikely that the Athenians could have built a wall enclosing the city without the protection of cavalry, and so long as such a wall was not in place the Syracusans remained free to send for assistance and make good use of it. On balance, Nicias chose the correct plan and executed it with great skill, for which he deserves no blame as a tactician.

As a strategist, however, he had made an error that was the chief cause of the expedition's failure. Cavalry remained essential to the capture of Syracuse. Had it been available from the first, the Syracusans would have been forced to surrender; no outside help could have saved them. The lack of Athenian provisions for cavalry is particularly astonishing in that Nicias himself had emphasized its importance before the expedition's departure, telling the assembly: "The thing in which the Syracusans most surpass us is in their possession of many horses and their use of grain that is home-grown and not imported" (6.20.4). But in the list of forces he cited that the Athenians should vote for the expedition he omitted any mention of horsemen, and although he had plenty of time before they sailed to remedy the problem at a subsequent assembly, he never did so. Even after the council at Rhegium, when it was obvious that a siege of Syracuse would be likely, there was still time to send home for horsemen.

Perhaps the oversight was more a failure of purpose than of judgment. Nicias, as we have seen, never wanted to attack Sicily and, forced to take part in the campaign, he intended to pursue a minimal course that would avoid any committed engagement. He had probably refused to consider any step as serious as an attack on Syracuse until circumstances made it unavoidable and then found himself without the forces to carry it out. The siege of Syracuse would therefore have to be delayed a number of months until the arrival of money and cavalry from Athens.

Both sides used the intervening time to prepare for the encounter to come. On the diplomatic front the Syracusans sent to Corinth and Sparta for help. At the same time they strengthened the city's capacity to withstand a siege by extending its walls to include more territory, which would force the Athenians to build an even larger siege wall to enclose Syracuse.

On learning that the Athenians were trying to make an alliance with Camarina, the Syracusans sent their anti-Athenian leader Hermocrates there to argue that the Athenians had come not to assist their allies but to conquer Sicily. Thucydides tells us that the Camarinans felt kindly toward the Athenians, "except in so far as they thought they would enslave Sicily." Their formal response was that "since they were allied to both sides that were at war, it would be most consistent with their oaths to aid neither" (6.88.1–2). This apparent neutrality was helpful to Syracuse but not to the Athenians, who needed to gain allies in Sicily quickly or not at all. The great size of the Athenian armada probably influenced the. Camarinan decision, again working against the original strategy.

The Athenians did better with the non-Greek Sicels, some of whom came over to Athens freely, bringing food and money, while others required compulsion. Moving their base to Catana for closer contact with the Sicels, the Athenians also sought help as far away as Etruria in Italy and Carthage in Africa, both former enemies of Syracuse. A few Etruscan cities sent a small number of ships to Sicily in 413. The appeal to Carthage failed entirely, however, although the request itself undermines claims made by Alcibiades, Hermocrates, and Thucydides that the aims of the expedition included the conquest of Carthage.

The Syracusans had better luck in recruiting assistance. Corinth, the founder of Syracuse, gladly agreed to support their colonists and sent their own envoys along to help persuade the Spartans to do the same. They had a difficult assignment, for the leading Spartans were not eager to make a major commitment to Sicily, and wanted to send no tangible assistance, only an embassy to urge Syracuse to hold out against the Athenians. At Sparta, however, the Syracusans and Corinthians found help in the person of Alcibiades.

The Corinthians and Syracusans both spoke before the Spartan assembly, but Thucydides reports only the speech of Alcibiades, who was now a fugitive and an outlaw with a price on his head wherever the Athenian writ ran. His first goal was to make a name for himself among the Spartans and win influence and power by persuading them to defeat the Athenians in Sicily and then to resume the war in Greece. A skilled and trained orator, he lightly explained away or rejected his past and presented his flight from Athens as a liberation from democracy, which he described as "recognized foolishness" (6.89.6). He claimed to reveal the true motives of the Athenian expedition to the west: far from being limited to an assault on Syracuse on behalf of allies, it was an effort to conquer the entire island and more. Beyond Sicily, the Athenians meant to take control of southern Italy, Carthage and its empire, and even far-off Iberia. When all this had been accomplished the Athenians would use the vast resources of these subject states to attack the Peloponnesus itself, taking any city that resisted by siege, and "after that they would rule over the entire Hellenic people" (6.90.3). His own removal from command would make no difference to the plan, for the remaining generals would carry it out even in his absence.

But the Spartans must act quickly before the Syracusans surrendered. They must send an army to Sicily at once under a Spartiate commander. They must also resume the war on the mainland to encourage the Syracusans and to distract the Athenians. To that end they must build a permanent fort at Decelea in Attica—the one measure the Athenians feared most. From there the Spartans could cut them off entirely from their homes and crops and the silver mines of Sunium and further reduce revenues by encouraging resistance and rebellion in the empire.

There was good reason for the Spartans to be suspicious of Alcibiades, but one of his claims ought to have cast doubt on everything else he said, for it was so plainly false: "The generals who are left will carry out the same plans, if they can, without any change." We have seen that the Athenians never discussed such a plan in the assembly, much less gave orders to carry it out. In any case, Nicias was highly unlikely to ever carry out such a scheme. On that last point Alcibiades simply lied, and there is good reason to believe that he also invented the grandiose scheme he claimed to reveal to the Spartans for his own purposes: to inflate the significance of the Sicilian expedition and thereby to frighten Sparta into resuming the war against Athens. It could also help to impress the Spartans with the stature of Alcibiades and his potential value to them.

Thucydides, however, believed that the grand design was real, that

Alcibiades, at least, had had it in mind from the first, and we must wonder why. The historian was by nature skeptical, intelligent, and careful, but in 415 he was in exile himself and had been absent from Athens for almost a decade. There is good reason to think that he met Alcibiades, perhaps in the Peloponnesus, when both were in exile, or perhaps in Thrace, where Thucydides had property and Alcibiades had built a castle toward the end of the war. In that case Thucydides would surely have tried to learn as much as he could from an important and well-connected participant in political and military activities in Athens, Sparta, Argos, and elsewhere. All our sources agree that Alcibiades was brilliantly persuasive, and Thucydides in exile would not have found it easy to check his claims for his personal influence or of the motives and intentions of the Athenian people. In light of the inflated size of the ultimate expedition, its disastrous conclusion, and his own critical stance toward the excessive ambitions of post-Periclean Athens, it would have been easy for Thucydides to believe that the democracy entertained absurdly bloated goals.

It may be that Thucydides chose not to report the speeches of the Corinthians or Syracusans at Sparta but only that of Alcibiades because they would not have made any mention of the grandiose intentions the Athenian asserts. In the absence of their statements Alcibiades' claim that the Athenians aimed at the conquest of all Greece and the entire Mediterranean world stands alone and unchallenged.

We, however, need not believe that the Spartans were moved to immediate action by Alcibiades. It was only in 414, after the Athenians had taken the onus of a formal breach of the peace by attacking Laconia, that they moved to fortify Decelea, more than a year after Alcibiades' speech. The Spartans, indeed, sent a general to Sicily, but the force he commanded was negligible, made up of two Corinthian and two Laconian ships. No Spartiate soldiers went to Sicily, nor was the general, Gylippus, a true Spartiate. (He was the son of Cleandridas, an exile condemned to death for accepting bribes, and, it was said, of a helot mother; thus he was a *mothax*, a man of inferior status.) Every element of the Spartan mission to Sicily was, in other words, expendable. Reasonable Athenian precautions could have prevented this minimal force from reaching Sicily, and there was little reason to think that it could accomplish anything of note even if it got there.

If Thucydides greatly overestimated Alcibiades' impact on Spartan policy, the decision to send Gylippus, ironically, would have results far beyond any reasonable expectation.

By the spring of 414 the time had come for the Athenians to attack Syracuse. During the winter the generals had sent to Athens to ask for cavalry and money, and the Athenians quickly voted to approve what had been requested. The battle at the Anapus had proved the superiority of the Athenian phalanx over the inexperienced and ill-organized Syracusan hoplites. The arrival of cavalry would enable the Athenians to invest the city on the land side, and their fleet could close it off by sea. There was little reason to expect any help for Syracuse from the Peloponnesus, and if assistance were sent, the Athenian command of the sea should be able to prevent its arrival. Thereafter, it would be only a matter of time until Syracuse surrendered, or so Nicias and Lamachus might plausibly have reasoned as they waited for the horsemen and funds.

News of the cavalry's dispatch stirred the Syracusans to place guards at the approaches to Epipolae, the plateau overlooking their city, "for they thought that if the Athenians could not control Epipolae the Syracusans could not easily be walled in, even if they were defeated in battle" (6.96.1), but they were too late. Nicias sailed the Athenian army to Leon, not far from the northern cliffs of Epipolae, and the Athenians reached the plateau, from which they could easily repel the Syracusan attempt to dislodge them.

Soon the horses arrived, along with additional cavalrymen from their Sicilian allies. With their hoplites and their total of 650 cavalrymen the Athenians could now protect the men who would build the siege walls. At a place called Syce, to the northwest of the city and not far from the edge of the plateau, they constructed a fort that Thucydides calls "The Circle." This was to be the center of their operations in conducting the siege.

The next day the Athenians began to extend their wall northward from "The Circle." Unless the Syracusans took steps to halt it, they would soon be shut in by land, so their generals decided to build a counterwall that would cut across the line of the projected siege works. Catching the Syracusans unprepared, however, the Athenians took down the counterwall and set up another trophy of victory.

About this time Nicias became ill with the kidney ailment that would trouble him until his death. Perhaps he was already unwell when this raid was planned, for its boldness and dash suggest the touch of Lamachus. The next day the Athenians began to build the southern portion of their siege wall, from "The Circle" on Epipolae to the Great Harbor south of the city. When that was completed a key part of Syracuse would be surrounded, and the Athenians could move their fleet from Thapsus, whence they had to haul supplies overland to Epipolae, to a safe anchorage in the Great Harbor. Without the wall, protection of the Athenian fleet on the beach of the Great Harbor would have required a dangerous division of Athenian land forces.

The new construction again alarmed the Syracusans, who began to build another counterwall across the Lysimeleia marsh west of the city. The Athenians, meanwhile, completed their own wall to the edge of the cliff and prepared a new attack, this time both from land and sea. Moving their fleet into the Great Harbor, and coming down from Epipolae, they placed planks and doors on the firmest parts of the marsh, and again caught the Syracusans by surprise. The assault split the Syracusan army in two, the right wing fleeing to the city, the left running to the Anapus. The army headed for the bridge, and three hundred Athenian shock troops hurried to cut them off, but the Syracusan cavalry was at the river and, with the hoplites, routed the three hundred and turned against the right wing of the main Athenian army. The brave and bold Lamachus, though he was on the left wing, hastened to help and died fighting. The Syracusans took his body with them as they retreated across the river, toward their fortress at the Olympieum. The Athenian victory came at a high price, for it left the ailing Nicias alone in command; the skill and daring of Lamachus would be sorely missed.

The Syracusans next attacked "The Circle" up on the heights, capturing and demolishing the incomplete and undefended wall running south from the fort, within which Nicias lay. In spite of his illness he was alert enough to order the start of a fire that drove the enemy back at the same time that it told the army down in the plain that the fort was in danger. The timing was fortunate, for the Athenians near Syracuse had already driven the enemy off, just as the Athenian fleet sailed into the harbor. It was now safe to race up to Epipolae in time to save the fort and their only remaining general, as the Syracusans fled back to their city.

Nothing now prevented the Athenians from continuing their southern wall to the sea. If they extended a northern wall across the plateau of Epipolae, their fleet's control of the sea would complete the enclosure of Syracuse and, by maintaining a careful watch, they could force the enemy either to surrender or to starve. The Syracusans, who "no longer thought they could win the war, for no help had come to them from the Peloponnesus" (6.103.3), began discussing peace terms among themselves and even with Nicias, and there was talk of treason to surrender the city. As always, Nicias had excellent intelligence, and the Athenians had every reason to believe that the city might soon surrender without a fight.

At this point Nicias became careless and overconfident, ignoring the one distant cloud in the otherwise bright Athenian sky: the four ships en route from the Peloponnesus, one of them carrying the Spartan Gylippus. The right course would have been to hurry to complete the enclosure of Syracuse, send a squadron of ships to the straits or to Italy to halt the arrival of the Peloponnesians, blockade both Syracusan harbors to prevent access if even a single ship got past the forward interceptors, and guard the approaches to Epipolae, especially the entrance at the west end at Euryalus, in case any of the Peloponnesians managed to reach Sicily and came to Syracuse by land. Nicias took none of these precautions, with disastrous results.

Throughtout this time the Peace of Nicias was formally in effect, but low-level hostilities continued. Sparta and Argos continued to raid and invade each other's territory. Athens continued to make raids of its own into Messenia from Pylos and elsewhere in the Peloponnesus, but refused the Argives' requests to attack Laconia. By the odd interpretation tacitly adopted by both sides these actions did not constitute violations of the peace, but a direct Athenian assault on Laconia would certainly be construed as such. By 414, however, the Athenians could no longer deny their ally's pleas for more vigorous assistance, for Argive soldiers were serving the Athenian cause in Sicily, so the Athenians sent thirty ships to make seaborne raids against several places on the Laconian shore. In this respect the Sicilian expedition had an important effect on the war as a whole, for these actions "violated the treaty with the Spartans in the most flagrant way" (6.105.1).

Meanwhile, Gylippus and the Corinthian admiral Pythen, each in command of two ships, were making their way toward Sicily under the impression that the Athenians had completed their circumvallation of Syracuse, but at Locri in southern Italy they discovered the truth and set out to save the city, sailing to Himera to avoid the Athenian fleet. News had reached Nicias of their arrival in Italy some time before, but he took no action against such a contemptibly small force. When he learned they had left Locri he decided to send four ships to intercept them, but it was too late. The men of Himera had joined the Spartan expedition and provided arms for the Peloponnesian crew, and additional help came from Selinus and Gela and from the Sicels, who changed sides because of the death of their pro-Athenian king and the persuasive zeal of Gylippus. By the time he set out for Syracuse he commanded a force of about three thousand infantry and two hundred cavalry.

More assistance was also on the way in the shape of eleven triremes manned by the Corinthians and their allies. One of them, under the Corinthian general Gongylus, slipped through the blockade and reached the city before Gylippus could reach it overland. The Syracusans were at the point of surrender, but he persuaded them not to hold the decisive assembly, reporting that more ships were on the way and that the Spartan Gylippus had come to take command. This news changed everything, and the Syracusans sent their entire army out to greet the Spartan general.

Gylippus came onto Epipolae from the west, through the Euryalus pass, just as the Athenians had done, so it is hard to understand why they had left it unguarded. It was at a critical moment, for the Athenians had completed their double wall down to the Great Harbor, except for a short section near the sea. "The wall toward Trogilus and the other sea stones had already been laid out for the greater part of the distance, and some parts were left half-finished while others had been completed. That is how close Syracuse had come to danger" (7.2.4–5).

At the Athenian siege wall Gylippus insolently offered the Athenians a truce if they would leave Sicily within five days. With the two armies arrayed for battle the Spartan saw that his men were confused and not in proper order, ripe for a sudden Athenian attack. A defeat could discredit the new Spartan general and discourage further resistance, but Nicias was not the man to exploit the opportunity. When Gylippus withdrew toward open country, Nicias let the chance pass, staying where he was.

The next day Gylippus took the offensive, feinting an attack on the Athenian wall, while he sent another force to Epipolae, where the wall had not yet been completed, and against the Athenian fort at Labdalum. He took the fort and all its contents, and killed the Athenians within. Nicias' carelessness in failing to safeguard his fort, supply depot, and treasury was another terrible oversight, and Gylippus next exploited still another error. Nicias should have completed the walls enclosing Syracuse as quickly as possible, for a purely naval blockade would not be sufficient, yet he had chosen to build a double wall to the sea in the south before finishing the northern section on Epipolae from the round fort to Trogilus. The time and manpower used on the second wall to the south, though it might provide greater security, were luxuries the Athenians could not afford so long as the northern sector was incomplete. Gylippus built a counterwall cutting across the path of the Athenian wall as it moved north toward Trogilus.

By now Nicias was no longer thinking of conquering Syracuse. Sick and in pain, confronted for the first time by daring and aggressive enemies, he worried chiefly about the safety of his forces and their escape from Sicily. Instead of hurrying to stop Gylippus' counterwall and to complete the Athenian wall to Trogilus, Nicias decided to build three forts at Plemmyrium on the south of the entrance to the Great Harbor to make it his new naval base and storehouse to replace Labdalum. But the site had disadvantages: what little water and firewood were available were not close to the forts, so the Athenian patrols who were sent to collect these essentials were easy prey for the Syracusan cavalry, who set up a base near the Olympieum from which they could handily attack them. "For these reasons, especially, the crews began to deteriorate at that time" (7.4.6).

The move to Plemmyrium also dangerously divided Nicias' forces. The main army on the heights of Epipolae was far from its supplies, and the enemy could force it to come down to defend the forts whenever they chose to attack them. Nicias offered no persuasive defense of his new tactics, which reflected a fundamental change in goals and strategy.

At the same time, Gylippus kept building his counterwall, using the same stones the Athenians had laid out for their own wall. He regularly challenged them to fight, knowing that the ultimate decision would rest on a battle, not on a wall-building contest, and he perceived that Nicias did not want a fight. Their general's timidity hurt the morale of the Athenian soldiers as it increased the confidence of the enemy. Gylippus, however, chose a site for battle that kept his superior cavalry out of play, so he was defeated in his first fight. A new opportunity came when Gylippus' counterwall cut across the line of the Athenian wall to Trogilus, forcing Nicias to fight or abandon all hope of enclosing the city. This battle took place in the open, where the cavalry was decisive, driving the exposed Athenian left flank before it and causing a general rout. Gylippus had won a great strategic victory: the Syracusans were now able to build their counterwall across the line of the Athenian siege wall.

With all their attention on the heights of Epipolae, the Athenians could not prevent the Corinthian fleet from sailing into Syracuse harbor unharmed. The crews of these ships supplied Gylippus with well over two thousand men to help complete the counterwall and probably to carry it all the way across Epipolae, cutting Athens off from the plain and the sea to its north. All hope of enclosing Syracuse and starving it into surrender with their present forces was gone.

By the end of the summer Nicias determined that the Athenian expedition was in such danger that it must either withdraw or ask for major reinforcements. He surely preferred withdrawal, for he had never favored the campaign or believed in its prospects, and recent events were deeply discouraging. He had the power to order a retreat, and since the Athenian navy still commanded the sea, he also had the capacity to make a safe withdrawal.

Yet he did not give the order, for to have done so would bring dishonor and, perhaps, even more unwelcome consequences. Prior to the Sicilian expedition Nicias' record contained many victories and no defeats, but a retreat from Sicily with no critical goals achieved was bound to be regarded as a failure. Throughout the war the Athenians had shown themselves unforgiving toward generals who disappointed their expectations, humiliating and punishing even the great Pericles himself when the results of his policy and strategy angered them. Nicias was certain to meet severe criticism on his return, for the Athenians were unlikely to believe that he had come home because their mighty expedition was in grave danger. Many disgruntled veterans of the campaign would doubtless complain that Nicias had ordered the retreat with the fleet unbeaten and in command of the sea and the army intact. Someone would certainly recount Nicias' errors, delays, and omissions, which would become the main topic of discussion. By ordering a withdrawal without prior approval from the Athenian assembly Nicias would have risked the reputation he had spent his life building and guarding, not to speak of his property and, perhaps, his life.

He proceeded, therefore, with still another attempt at clever duplicity. With his official report that reached Athens in the fall of 414 he sent a letter to the assembly. It told of the Athenian reversals without discussing their causes and set forth the current situation: the Athenians had ceased besieging Syracuse and were on the defensive; Gylippus was recruiting reinforcements and planning an attack on the Athenians by land and sea; the Athenian position was beyond repair. He cast no blame on his own leadership, explaining that the ships and their crews had lost their quality because of the length of the campaign and requirements of the blockade, which kept them always at sea. If the Athenians relaxed their guard at all their supplies could be cut off, since everything had to be brought by sea past Syracuse.

The reversal of Athenian fortunes in Sicily brought other troubles, as well. Sailors leaving camp to collect water, wood, and forage for the horses were routinely attacked and killed by the enemy cavalry. Slaves, mercenaries, and volunteers deserted, and the resulting shortage of experienced rowers deprived the Athenian fleet of its usual tactical advantage. Soon, Nicias warned, their Italian suppliers would stop sending food, which would effectively put an end to the Athenian expedition. For none of this were the generals or the army responsible. The Athenians "must either recall the force that is here or reinforce it with another just as large, infantry and a fleet and a great deal of money" (7.15).

Nicias also asked the Athenians to relieve him from command because of his illness, and urged the assembly to make a decision quickly, before the enemy forces in Sicily grew too powerful.

The truth was that the message painted a darker picture than reality justified. The Athenians were still superior at sea, and there was no good evidence that they would soon face a shortage of supplies. Nicias' explanation for the reversal of Athenian fortunes was still less accurate, for the lion's share of the blame rested with his own lethargic, overconfident, careless, and sloppy leadership. He had allowed Syracuse swiftly to move from imminent surrender to a recovery of morale, seizure of the initiative, and the real prospect of victory. He had failed to intercept Gylippus' small squadron, and allowed Gongylus' fleet to slip through his blockade. He had failed to protect the approaches to Epipolae, and had wasted time building a double wall to the sea south of the heights and three forts at Plemmyrium while his northern wall was incomplete. He had allowed his storehouse and treasury at Labdalum to be captured, permitted the Corinthian squadron to reach Syracuse, and moved his navy to its untenable position at Plemmyrium. The deterioration of the navy was likewise not inevitable but a product of Nicias' neglect. He could have dried and repaired his ships in rotation in the months before the arrival of Gylippus. Athenian sailors died and deserted because Nicias had placed their ships in a bad location at Plemmyrium.

What Nicias really sought with his inadequate, self-serving, and less than honest account was for the assembly to order the expedition home. Failing that, he would have liked to be relieved from command with honor and replaced. If he had simply and honestly said that he judged there to be no prospect of victory, the Athenians might have agreed to withdraw. If he had only said he was too ill to do the job, they might have recalled him and sent a healthy general in his place. Instead, he offered the Athenians a choice. Fearing for his reputation and his own safety, he asked the Athenians either to do as he wished or to send a second expedition as large as the first. This seems to be another version of the ploy that had failed to deter the Athenians from making the voyage in the first place, from whose failure he had evidently learned nothing.

Once again, the Athenians confounded his expectations and voted to send another fleet and army, refusing to relieve him. To lead the reinforcements and join with Nicias in the command they chose Demosthenes, the hero of Sphacteria, and Eurymedon, who had led the Athenian forces in Sicily from 427 to 424.

Both parts of the Athenian decision evoke surprise. Most of the promises and expectations of the proponents of the expedition had turned out to be false, while most of the fears of its opponents had been justified. The Italians and Sicilians had not joined the Athenians with enthusiasm and in great numbers, the Peloponnesians were now engaged, and the Syracusans were resisting with high morale. We might expect the Athenian people to feel deceived by the optimists, to concede the wisdom of the doubters, and to recall the expedition and its pessimistic and unwell commander. Instead, they swiftly voted to grant Nicias all that he requested, sending Eurymedon to Sicily at once, with ten ships, 120 silver talents, and the encouraging news that Demosthenes would follow later with much greater forces.

Most historians agree with Thucydides in blaming these measures on the greed, ignorance, and foolishness of the direct Athenian democracy. But the behavior of the Athenians on this occasion is the opposite of the flighty indecision that is usually imputed to their democracy. They showed constancy and determination to carry through what they had begun, in spite of setbacks and disappointments. Their error, in fact, is common to powerful states, regardless of their constitutions, that are unexpectedly thwarted by an opponent expected to be weak and easily defeated. Such states are likely to see retreat as a blow to their prestige, unwelcome in itself, but also putting into question their strength and commitment and with it their security. Support for such ventures generally remains positive until the prospect of victory disappears.

But why did the Athenians insist on keeping in place the ailing and discouraged Nicias? An answer may lie in the unique regard in which they held their general. It was not the awe they felt for the brilliant imagination and rhetorical genius of Pericles. Instead, it was appreciation and respect for his character, his way of life, and the success and good fortune that had always accompanied him. He tried to behave in the same dignified manner as traditional aristocratic politicians, but without their objectionable haughtiness. "His dignity was not the austere, offensive kind but was mixed with a degree of prudence; he won over the masses because he seemed to fear them." His inadequacies as a debater, oddly, won him sympathy: "In political life his timidity . . . even made him seem a popular, democratic figure."[6]

It is not surprising, therefore, that, even less than two years after the desecration of the mysteries and the mutilation of the Hermae had insulted the gods, the Athenians refused to excuse from service the one man most beloved of the gods, the man who was their talisman of victory. If he was ill, he would surely recover; meanwhile, healthy and vigorous colleagues would help him. With the original force alone he had come close to taking Syracuse. Surely with reinforcement and able colleagues his skill and good fortune would soon gain a victory. Such thoughts and feelings must explain the decision to give Nicias once again all the forces he requested and to keep him in place. Had the Athenians recalled Nicias and sent the new generals with reinforcements and a novel strategy they might have turned the tide and achieved success.

The prospect of Athenian reinforcements' arrival in Sicily threatened all that Gylippus had accomplished, and might well have led the Syracusans once again to consider surrender. Gylippus, therefore, moved swiftly to attack the Athenians where they were vulnerable, at Plemmyrium, and took it. The strategic cost to the Athenians was great, for they could no longer bring in supplies, and "the loss of Plemmyrium brought bewilderment and discouragement to the army" (7.24). The Syracusans sent word of their victory to their Peloponnesian friends, asking them to press the war against Athens even more vigorously and sent a fleet to Italy to cut off Athenian supplies from that direction. They also reported the capture of Plemmyrium all around Sicily, using ambassadors from Corinth, Sparta, and Ambracia to lend credibility to the claims. Their effort was crowned with great success, for "almost all of Sicily . . . , the others who previously stood by and watched, now joined with and came to the aid of the Syracusans against the Athenians" (7.33.1–2).

By now the Syracusans were so confident as to risk a sea battle in the Great Harbor of Syracuse. Using tactics made possible by a new device that strengthened their ships, they won an enormous victory against the previously invincible Athenians and dominated the Great Harbor. They now believed they were superior to the Athenians at sea and would soon defeat them on land, as well, and made preparations to attack again on both fronts.

Syracusan joy was short lived, however, for soon after the battle in the harbor the Athenian reinforcements under Demosthenes and Eurymedon arrived. Demosthenes believed that an immediate assault and siege would lead the Syracusans to surrender before they could send for help to the Peloponnesus, and with characteristic clarity and boldness he sought to achieve that. "Knowing that at that moment he was most frightening to the enemy, he wanted as swiftly as possible to take advantage of their present panic" (7.42.3).

He was confident that his fleet could blockade the city by sea; the crucial assignment was to take the Syracusan counterwall on Epipolae that prevented the enclosure of Syracuse by land. But access to the heights of Epipolae was guarded by the formidable Gylippus. Demosthenes was prepared to take the gamble, for even defeat was better than wasting Athenian resources and risking the safety of his men without any plan or realistic hope of success. If he dominated Epipolae he could defeat Syracuse and hope to achieve control of Sicily; if he was unable to do so he would take the expedition home safely to fight again another day. In either case the war in Sicily would come to an end with the expedition essentially intact.

His direct attack on the Syracusan counterwall on Epipolae failed, indicating that such a maneuver by daylight would not work. Demosthenes, undaunted and ever ingenious, planned a daring assault by night. Early in August he took about ten thousand hoplites and the same number of light-armed troops through the darkness before the rising of the moon to the pass at Euryalus, at the western end of the plateau. The Athenians surprised the Syracusan garrison and took their fort, but soon the tide of the battle turned and Gylippus inflicted a terrible defeat upon them.

Athenian morale was now at its lowest. Apart from the defeat in battle, their spirits suffered from the malaria and dysentery that came with being encamped on marshy ground in a late Sicilian summer. "The situation appeared to them to be as hopeless as it could be" (7.47.2). Demosthenes argued for sailing home while Athens still had naval superiority: "He said it would be of more use to Athens to fight the war against an enemy who was building a fort against it in its own country than against Syracuse, which it was no longer easy to subdue, nor was it right, besides, to expend a great deal of money to no purpose by continuing the siege" (7.47.4). This was wise counsel, for there was no way to take the Syracusan counterwall on Epipolae, no chance of a successful siege, and there could be no more reinforcements. It was time to cut their losses before a disappointing failure became a disaster, and Demosthenes could only have been surprised that Nicias did not agree with his assessment of the situation.

Nicias knew how great a danger the Athenians faced but was still privately undecided whether to stay or to depart. His greatest hope came from a report that there was still a group in Syracuse that wanted to surrender to Athens. Nicias established communication with them, but any hopes of treason from within the city were chimerical. The arrival of Gongylus and Gylippus had ended any chance that the Syracusans would surrender. Thereafter, support from the outside and repeated success guaranteed that they would hold out to the end.

In the debate among the Athenian generals Nicias suppressed his own uncertainty and insisted on remaining in Sicily. The Syracusans, he claimed, were in even worse financial straits than the Athenians and would soon run out of funds to pay their mercenary force. The Athenians "should stay on, he said, and maintain the siege and not be defeated by money, in which they were far superior to the enemy" (7.48.6).

The Syracusans were certainly short of money, but their victories would have improved their credit and encouraged their allies and others to lend them what they needed to achieve complete success. In addition, the citizens still had wealth of their own that could be tapped by taxation in the current emergency. Here is another instance of Nicias' miscalculation. While the Athenians could choose to stay on in Sicily at great expense or to return home, the Syracusans had to resist to the end or lose their freedom along with their wealth. Selinus and other Sicilian cities supported their cause not for money but from self-interest. The Peloponnesians had already sent help and would send more if necessary.

Nicias soon revealed the true motives for his recommendation in the rest of his speech: he feared that back in Athens his soldiers would turn against him and convince the assembly that he was to blame for their failure. They would complain "that their generals had been bribed to betray them and withdraw. He himself, at any rate, knowing the character of the Athenians, did not wish to be put to death unjustly on a disgraceful charge by the Athenians but preferred, if he must, to take his chances and meet his own death himself at the hands of the enemy" (7.48.4). A distinguished scholar has made a harsh judgment of this decision: "Nikias' pride and consequent cowardice in the face of personal disgrace lead him to put forward as disgraceful a proposition as any general in history: rather than risk execution, he will throw away the fleet and many thousand of other people's lives, and put his country in mortal peril."[7]

Nicias was notorious for his timidity and for his dread of the suspicion and envy of the Athenian people, but bolder men than he had reason to fear the Athenian people's treatment of their unsuccessful generals, who could be tried and punished for a variety of alleged offenses. In 426 Demosthenes had remained in Naupactus rather than return to Athens after his defeat in Aetolia, "fearing the Athenians because of what had happened" (3.98.5), but in 413, although he had devised and conducted the fiasco on Epipolae, which had cost the lives of at least two thousand soldiers, he voted to return and face whatever charges might result.

Demosthenes and Eurymedon opposed Nicias' decision to stay, but they were outvoted when Menander and Euthydemus, the two generals elected to assist the ailing Nicias, supported their prestigious senior commander. With their backing he also rejected the compromise proposal made by Demosthenes and Eurymedon, who had urged the Athenians at least to withdraw from the swamps outside Syracuse to healthier and safer positions at Thapsus or Catana, from which they could raid the Sicilian countryside and live off the land. Outside Syracuse harbor, they could also fight in the open sea, where the new Syracusan tactics would not work and their own greater skill and experience gave them the advantage. Nicias may have opposed this plan, out of concern that, once the army boarded the ships and sailed out of Syracuse harbor, it would be impossible to keep the Athenians in Sicily for very long. So the Athenians remained in place at Syracuse.

On the night of August 27, 413, between 9:41 and 10:30 P.M., the moon was totally eclipsed. Fear overcame the superstitious Athenian army, and the men read the eclipse as a divine warning against sailing immediately. Nicias consulted a soothsayer, who recommended that the Athenians wait "thrice nine days" before departing. Even for credulous men this interpretation was not the only one possible. Philochorus, a historian who lived in the third century B.C., himself a seer, gave a different explanation: "The sign was not unfavorable to men who were fleeing but, on the contrary, very favorable; for deeds of fear require concealment, while light is an enemy to them."[8] A commander who wished to escape could easily have used such an interpretation to good effect, but Nicias accepted the omen as unfavorable without question. Now, he could insist, the gods had intervened to confirm his own judgment. He "refused to discuss further the question of their departure until they waited thrice nine days as the soothsayers recommended" (7.50.4).

Word of the debate and decision leaked to the enemy when deserters told the Syracusans that the Athenians had been planning to sail home but were delayed by the lunar eclipse. To prevent their escape the Syracusans decided to force another sea battle at once in Syracuse harbor, where they still stood the best chance, and began to practice their crews in the tactics they would use. But their first attack was by land, and in their main assault the army attacked the Athenian walls, while the Syracusan navy sent seventy-six triremes against the Athenian base.

Although neither side won decisively, the Syracusans set up trophies to mark their victories on land and sea. The Athenians also set up a trophy, as they had a right to do, to mark their rout of Gylippus at the seawall, but it was a pathetic gesture. The Athenian forces, augmented by powerful reinforcements, had suffered major defeats on land and sea. Thucydides explains the loss by arguing that the Athenian assembly had fundamentally miscalculated in two major respects: they underestimated the strength of Syracuse in both ships and cavalry, and they ignored the fact that Syracuse was a democracy, whose unity it would be difficult for Athens to undermine. It seems less than fair, however, to blame the assembly for the size of the expedition and for its reinforcement, for in both cases they followed the advice of Nicias in detail. It is even less just to attribute the second error to the Athenian people, for there is no evidence that they had ever counted on internal revolution or treason to deliver Syracuse into their hands. That was the idea of Nicias alone and, by delaying the enclosure of the city and pursuing the hope of victory through internal political unrest long after there was any chance of it, he doomed the Athenians to destruction. The Athenians in Sicily finally understood that victory was impossible; all they could hope for was escape.

The Syracusans now sought the complete destruction of the Athenian expedition and freedom for all the Greeks they ruled. If they succeeded "they would be regarded with wonder by the rest of the world and even by those who came after them" (7.56.2). The Athenians' only concern was how best to escape, by sea or land. Since they would ultimately need the ships to get back to Athens, they decided to try to break out of the harbor, however difficult that might be.

Nicias had command of the troops on land, but after he had spoken to the whole assembled force on the beach he took a boat through the Athenian fleet, stopping at each trireme and, addressing the captain by his name, his father's name, and his tribe, appealed to old ancestral and family feelings. As Pericles had done, he reminded them of the liberty their homeland provided its citizens, and, in his own way, he also spoke on a more personal level, saying, "the kind of thing that men call out in much the same language on every occasion, about wives and children and ancestral gods, but which, in the fear of the moment, they think will be useful" (7.69.1–3). Nicias lacked the aristocratic birth, the intellectual power and political skill of a Pericles, but his simple, old-fashioned manner and common touch had a powerful appeal of its own in the Athenian democracy.

In the confined waters of the harbor almost two hundred ships fought at close quarters, for ramming was impossible. All the conditions worked to strip from the Athenians the advantages of experience and skill they had gained from long years of practice and naval warfare. At last, the Syracusans routed the Athenians, who fled to shore in panic, leaving their ships behind and running to seek safety at their camp. With order and morale broken, most thought only of saving themselves. They did not even ask for a truce to allow the burial of their dead, an astonishing omission. Nothing must delay their flight, for they believed that only a miracle could save them.

One Athenian kept his wits and composure in this terrible moment. Demosthenes saw that the Athenians still had sixty viable ships against fewer than fifty for the enemy. He proposed that they collect their forces and try another breakout from the harbor at dawn, and Nicias was persuaded to make the effort. It was too late, however; the spirits of the men had collapsed entirely. They refused the generals' orders to board the ships again and insisted on seeking to escape by land.

The Athenians began their retreat, which was like a terrible nightmare from which there is no waking. They were tricked into waiting a day before starting out, by which point the enemy had had plenty of time to block the escape routes. About forty thousand men started the march, of whom about half were soldiers and the rest noncombatants. "They looked like nothing more than a city, and one of considerable size, sneaking away in flight after being reduced by a siege" (7.75.5). Tired, sick, in great pain, Nicias spoke to the men to encourage them and calm their anxieties. (Thucydides says that Demosthenes spoke in a similar way, but he reports only the speech of Nicias.) In this frightful time he achieved his finest moment. He told them not to blame themselves for their defeat and misery and held out the hope that their fortunes might soon be reversed. They were still, he pointed out, a mighty army. There was, therefore, hope of salvation if they would keep their morale and discipline and move swiftly in good order.

The first destination was northward to Catana, a city loyal to Athens that could furnish a friendly welcome and supplies, and then serve as a base for further operations. Nicias and Demosthenes each commanded a hollow rectangle of troops with the civilians inside. Almost four miles south of Syracuse, along the Anapus River, they fought through a force of Syracusans and their allies, but the Syracusan cavalry and light-armed troops stayed with them, harrying them with constant attacks and a rain of missiles. The next day they marched about two miles to the northwest, where they spent another day seeking food and water.

Barring further progress was the high barrier of what is now called Monte Climiti, a large plateau that ends with a high cliff-face eight miles northwest of Syracuse. The Athenians hoped to make their way over it to safety at Catana, but here, again, their delays betrayed them. When the Athenians started out the next morning the Syracusans and their allies attacked with cavalry and javelin throwers, forcing them back to camp. The following day they tried to force their way up Monte Climiti against a fortified position and an entrenched enemy, and got as far as the Syracusans' wall. Exposed to enemy missiles, terrified, soaking wet, and exhausted, they could not rest, for Gylippus was building a wall behind them that could cut them off and destroy them on the spot. They quickly moved the entire army back to camp on the level country away from the Syracusans and their allies.

Compelled to abandon the ordinary route to Catana, Nicias and Demosthenes decided to turn southeast toward the sea, follow one of the rivers that flowed into it to its upland source, and there either to join the Sicels or turn toward Catana by a more roundabout route. By dawn they met near the coast and marched to the Cacyparis River, planning to move inland along its banks to meet their Sicel friends. Once again the Syracusans beat them to it, but the Athenians fought their way across the river and marched southward toward the next stream in their path, the Erineus.

Nicias made camp just beyond the river, about six miles ahead of Demosthenes. The main Syracusan force from the camp at Monte Climiti arrived with cavalry and light-armed troops about noon on the sixth day of the Athenian retreat. They cut the Athenians off in an olive grove surrounded by a wall, with a road on either side, from which the Syracusans could throw and shoot missiles. When the situation became hopeless Demosthenes, at last, surrendered on these terms: if the Athenians gave up their weapons "none of them would be killed, either by violence, or by imprisonment, or by being deprived of the necessities of life" (7.82.2). The Syracusans captured the six thousand men who were left of the twenty thousand who began the retreat less than a week before and could fill four shields with the booty taken from them. Demosthenes tried to kill himself with his own sword, but his captors prevented him.

The next day the Syracusans overtook Nicias, reported the capture of Demosthenes, and ordered him to surrender, as well. Instead, he sent them an offer to have Athens pay the full cost of the war to let his army go, leaving his soldiers as hostages, one for each talent, but the Syracusans refused. They recognized this as their chance to wipe out the hated enemy in a total victory and would not trade it for any amount of money. They surrounded Nicias' men and devastated them with missiles, as they had done to the trapped army of Demosthenes. The Athenians again tried to escape in the dark, but this time the Syracusans were ready. Three hundred men, nonetheless, dared to make the effort and made their way through the Syracusan guard, but the rest gave up the attempt.

On the eighth day Nicias tried to break through the surrounding enemy to the next river, the Assinarus, some three miles south. The Athenians no longer had a plan, only a blind urgency to escape and an increasingly terrible thirst. Through the onslaught of missiles, cavalry attacks, and hoplite assaults, they managed to reach the Assinarus. There all discipline collapsed as each man rushed to get across the river first, the army becoming a mob that clogged the passage and made it easier for the enemy to prevent its crossing.

Since they were forced to go forward in a close mass they fell on top of and trampled one another; some were killed immediately, impaled on their own spears, while others got tangled in their equipment and with each other and were carried away by the stream. The Syracusans stood along the opposite bank of the river, which was steep, and threw missiles down on the Athenians below, most of them drinking greedily and heaped together in disorder in the hollow bed of the river. The Peloponnesians also came down and butchered them, especially those in the river. And the water immediately became spoiled, but it was drunk, nonetheless, though it was muddy and full of blood, and most of them even fought over it. (7.84)

All that was left of the great Athenian army was destroyed at the Assinarus. The Syracusan cavalry, which had caused the Athenians so much trouble throughout the campaign, killed the few men who did make their way across the river. Nicias gave himself up to Gylippus, "trusting him rather than the Syracusans" (7.85.1). Only then did the Spartan commander order an end to the killing. The prisoners taken with Demosthenes numbered about six thousand, but of Nicias' troops, only about a thousand were still alive.

The triumphant Syracusans took their prisoners and booty and stripped the armor from the dead enemy, hanging it from the finest and tallest trees along the river. On returning to Syracuse they held an assembly where they voted to enslave the servants of the Athenians and their imperial allies and to place Athenian citizens and their Sicilian Greek allies into the city's stone quarries for safekeeping. A proposal to put Nicias and Demosthenes to death provoked more debate. Hermocrates objected, on lofty grounds of generosity, but the assembly shouted him down. Gylippus' more practical argument was that he wanted the glory of bringing the Athenian generals home to Sparta: Demosthenes, its bitterest enemy because of his victories at Pylos and Sphacteria, and Nicias, their friend who had argued for releasing the prisoners and made first a peace and then an alliance with the Spartans. But the Syracusans would have none of it, and neither would the Corinthians, so the assembly voted to execute both generals.

The Syracusans held over seven thousand prisoners in their quarries, crowded together in inhuman conditions, burned by the sun during the day and chilled by the autumn cold at night. They were given about a half-pint of water and a pint of food each day, much less than what the Spartans had been permitted to send to the slaves on Sphacteria, and they suffered terribly from hunger and thirst. Men died from their wounds, from illness, and from exposure, and the dead bodies were thrown on top of one another, creating an unbearable stench. After seventy days all the survivors, with the exception of the Athenians and the Sicilian and Italian Greeks, were sold into slavery. Plutarch tells the tale of slaves freed for their ability to recite the verses of Euripides, for the Sicilians were mad for his poetry. Neither poetry nor anything else could help the men in the quarries, however, who were kept there for eight months; presumably no one survived any longer.

Thucydides calls the Sicilian expedition "the greatest action of all those that took place during the war and, so it seems to me, at least, the greatest of any which we know to have happened to any of the Greeks; it was the most glorious for those who won and the most disastrous for those who were defeated. For the losers were beaten in every way and completely; what they suffered was great in every respect, for they met with total destruction, as the saying goes—their army, their ships, and everything were destroyed—and only a few of many came back home" (7.87.5–6). To most Greeks it seemed the war was all but over.

As we have seen, Thucydides wrote an extraordinary eulogy of Nicias: "For this reason, or for one very much like it, he was killed; of all the Greeks, in my time, at any rate, he least deserved to meet with such extreme misfortune because he had led his entire life in accordance with virtue [aretê]" (7.86.5).[9] The people in Athens held a different opinion. The antiquarian Pausanias saw a stele in the public cemetery of Athens on which were engraved the names of the generals who died fighting in Sicily, all except that of Nicias. The reason for the omission he learned from the Sicilian historian Philistus: "Demosthenes made a truce for the rest of his men, excluding himself, and was captured while trying to commit suicide, but Nicias surrendered himself voluntarily. For this

reason Nicias' name was not written on the stele: he was condemned as
a voluntary prisoner and as an unworthy soldier."[10] Philistus need not be
trusted as to the Athenians' reasons for excluding Nicias from the role
of honored dead, but that they regarded him in some way as especially
culpable is an inescapable conclusion.

But who was ultimately responsible for this terrible disaster? Alcibiades was the author of the Sicilian expedition, but Nicias' role was more
central. Thucydides regarded the venture as a folly undertaken by the
unguided and misguided democracy. Although he places no blame on
Nicias but indeed praises him in the highest terms, Thucydides' narrative
account gives a very different impression from that of his interpretation.
It was Nicias' failed rhetorical trick that turned a modest undertaking,
offering few risks, into a massive campaign that made the conquest of
Sicily seem both feasible and safe. He also made a critically damaging
technical error in omitting cavalry from his list of requirements for the
campaign.

Once in command in Sicily, he made a series of errors of commission
and omission that brought destruction to the expedition. He failed to
complete the siege of Syracuse by delaying the construction of a single
circuit of walls before doing anything else. He wasted time talking with
dissidents in Syracuse; he did not send a squadron to cut off Gylippus'
arrival in Sicily; he did not mount a competent blockade to prevent Gongylus and the Corinthian ships from reaching Syracuse by sea; he did not
fortify and guard Epipolae to prevent a surprise attack, thereby allowing the enemy to revive and drive the Athenians from their dominant
position. He then moved the Athenian navy, the supply depot, and the
treasury to an untenable position at Plemmyrium, where the morale and
quality of the fleet deteriorated and from which Gylippus was able to
drive them, capturing their money and supplies.

Faced with a doomed campaign after the summer of 414, Nicias refused to withdraw out of fear for his reputation and safety. Instead, he
asked the Athenians to choose between withdrawal, and both sending
huge reinforcements and relieving him of the command. An objective

assessment of the dangerous situation and his own incapacity might well have led to withdrawal and avoided the great disaster. Even after the terrible defeat on Epipolae, Nicias refused to take his expedition home. To save his reputation and escape punishment he seized on the lunar eclipse as a last chance to avoid the inevitable and destroyed the Athenians' final opportunity to escape.

We cannot fail to be struck by the force of Thucydides' tribute, for he calls Nicias not only a man who did not deserve his terrible fate, but the man *in his time least worthy of it*, thereby, in some way, placing Nicias above all his contemporaries, even Pericles. That emphasis is what catches our attention and makes us ask why Thucydides chose to write one of his rare eulogies and why he cast it in the superlative form he did. His readers could be expected to regard the praise as a general commendation of Nicias' qualities yet, as a keen modern reader has observed: "No one who has read this history up to the present point is likely to have formed a favourable view of Nikias."[11] But the prevailing unfavorable view is precisely what made it necessary for Thucydides to write so effusive a eulogy of Nicias; that few readers come away from the *History* with the unfavorable opinion described above is evidence of the eulogy's effectiveness.

If we had Thucydides' account of Nicias' career without this final evaluation we might come to the very conclusion that Nicias' contemporaries seem to have reached: that a major reason for the Sicilian disaster was his incompetent statesmanship and generalship. Thucydides, it seems clear, would not deny that this was a contributing factor, but for him it is neither a sufficient explanation nor the main one. Thucydides wants his reader to understand that the primary cause of the disaster was the post-Periclean democracy, unchecked by the wise restraining leadership of a powerful and intelligent statesman, misled by thoughtless and ambitious demagogues, abandoned therefore to its own ignorance, greed, superstition, and fear. It was the mob who decided to attack Sicily and add it to the Athenian Empire so that the people could profit from the spoils. The mob had been seduced by the ambitious selfishness of Alcibiades, yet it

yielded to its own superstitious fear and chose Nicias as one of the generals in spite of his opposition to the venture. Then it refused to excuse
him from his command even when he was sick and no longer in full possession of his talents. The mob continued to throw money, equipment,
and men into the bottomless pit of Sicily long after prudence dictated an
end to the campaign. The mob was panicked into a reign of terror by the
religious scandals of 415 and manipulated by demagogues into driving
away the originator of the very expedition they were undertaking, probably the cleverest man among them, and forcing him into the camp of
the enemy, where he did great damage to his native land. That is the way
of democracies that have degenerated into mob rule, and Thucydides is
determined that his reader take away this important lesson.

The eulogy of Nicias points the reader in the right direction, in the
view of Thucydides, for it calls his attention to the other and greater eulogy in the history, the panegyric of Pericles in 2.65. There he is reminded
that after Pericles, Athens, which had really been under the rule of an
outstanding statesman, became a true democracy and that the politicians who succeeded him were a lesser breed, each of whom lacked at
least some of his gifts. Nicias, though a good man of considerable talents,
did not have in sufficient degree the intellectual qualities of intelligence
(*xynesis*), foresight (*pronoia*), and good judgment (*gnômê*). The Athenians
chose him for leadership because of his public reputation for piety and
for his history of success (*eutychia*), which the mob believed to be the
fruit of such piety. But Thucydides would have us believe that the mob
was wrong, for success, insofar as man and not chance contributes to it,
comes not from piety and the favor of the gods but from the intellectual
acuity of a Pericles. Thucydides was not, we may believe, unconscious of
the irony in the fact that the Athenians saw their hopes ruined by their
faith in a man who, like themselves, believed that piety and faith in the
gods were superior to worldly human wisdom; it was this very faith that
brought Nicias from *eutychia* to the most terrible disaster (*dystychia*)—a
disaster that he, least of all men, deserved.

In writing his eulogy Thucydides was not interested chiefly in defending the reputation of Nicias, although there is reason to believe he would have been glad to do so. Both men appear to have been admirers of Pericles; both hated Cleon and opposed his policies. The two in fact had much in common, and Thucydides could easily have seen Nicias as an undeserving victim of the irrational demos, much like himself. His main purpose in the obituary, however, was to revise what he judged to be a misinterpretation, or at least an oversimplification, of the disaster in Sicily, which fixed the blame chiefly or solely on the faults of Nicias. No fair-minded reader can deny that he was justified in resisting so simple an interpretation or fail to appreciate his broader and deeper explanation. A modern reader with a lesser knowledge and shallower understanding of the events than the great Athenian historian but, perhaps, with a greater distance from them, may take note of the lessons in the dangers of unchecked direct democracies and yet, at the same time, observe that events put the fate of the Athenians into the hands of the one man who was able to turn a mistake into a disaster.

Conclusion

I HAVE ARGUED that the efforts by Thucydides to revise common opinions held by Athenians of his day were and remain controversial. My own view is that in the important cases examined here the contemporary view was closer to the truth than his own. That this book's conclusions differ from those of Thucydides, and from those of most modern scholars, may strike the reader as presumptuous. But the revisionist historian of the Peloponnesian War himself would be the first to decry undue deference to the authority of even the greatest traditions. He was not the perfect picture of detachment his admirers thought him to be, and he was certainly not the purely literary genius, free from the trammels of historical objectivity, that too many recent scholars have claimed him to be. For all his unprecedented efforts to seek and test the evidence, and for all his originality and wisdom, he was not infallible.

That we can study his *History* and come to conclusions different from his is far less important than his achievement in inventing a kind of history and a kind of questioning that shaped and improved the quality of human thought and continues to do so today.

We have seen that Thucydides used a large array of devices to communicate his account of events to his readers. Like all historians he inevitably needed to select what events to include and which to omit. Some of his omissions are hard to understand but seem to serve his revisionist interpretations. His juxtaposition of events sometimes serves to underscore his point of view. On occasion he seems to read the minds of historical actors, attributing to them intentions and motives for which he presents no evidence. He emphasizes some episodes by treating them at length, often providing speeches to strengthen his message. Sometimes he minimizes the importance of events by the brevity of his treatment.

This is not to say that Thucydides meant to deceive. Quite the opposite is true. He is determined that the reader will not be deceived, so he selects his material in such a way as to emphasize and clarify the truth. We must remember that his immediate audience knew much more than we do, for instance, about the events that led to the Peloponnesian War. When Thucydides treated the Megarian Decree so briefly, his contemporary readers were fully aware of all the evidence on the other side, and Thucydides knew it. His peculiar emphasis was not an attempt at deception but at interpretation. We should also remember that the great majority of the evidence that permits us to reject the Thucydidean interpretation is provided by Thucydides himself. The purpose of Thucydidean interpretation is provided by Thucydides himself. The purpose of Thucydides was to set before us the truth as he saw it, but his truth need not be ours. If we are to use his history with profit, as we can and must, we must distinguish between the evidence he presents and the interpretation he puts on it. Only then can we use it, as he wished us to, as a "possession forever."

Studies of Thucydides' mind or thought, his purposes, intentions, or methods have tended to treat him almost as a disembodied mind, not as a living human being, part of his time and place and influenced by them and his own experience in them. To be sure, his was an extraordinarily powerful and original mind. He stood on the edge of philosophy. He was so much the historian as to feel compelled to establish the particulars and to present the data as accurately as he could, but he was no less concerned that he convey the general truths he had discovered.

Any satisfactory understanding of the historian, however, demands a critical look at Thucydides, the man himself in the world of action, not merely of thought. We must remember that he was a contemporary of the events he describes and an active participant in some of them. More than any historian in antiquity he put the highest value on accuracy and objectivity, but we must not forget he was a human being with human feelings and foibles. The very fact that he was a participant, moreover, influenced his judgments in ways that demand evaluation. Simply accepting his interpretations uncritically would be like accepting without question Winston Churchill's histories of his own time and his understanding of the two world wars in which he played so critical a role.

Recent scholarship has emphasized what careful readers of Thucydides have always recognized—that behind that cool, distant, analytical style there stands a passionate individual, writing about the most important events of his time, about the greatness of his city and its destruction. A generation younger than Pericles, he clearly admired him beyond all other statesmen. A blue-blooded aristocrat, he nonetheless lived comfortably in the Athenians' democracy, and flourished in its most extreme moments, for he was elected general in 424, five years into what he thought of as the degenerate post-Periclean democracy, when Cleon's power was at its height. Yet his history makes it clear that he had contempt for the democratic system.

His attitude becomes easier to understand when we remember that it was during his year in office the Athenians held him responsible for the failure to save Amphipolis and condemned him to exile. For twenty years he lived among foreigners and fellow exiles, all hostile to democracy. They must have wondered, perhaps in questions they posed directly to him, at the paradox of a man like Thucydides, a nobleman contemptuous of democracy, who had lived and prospered in the greatest of the democracies and who admired the greatest of democratic leaders. *The Peloponnesian War* may be viewed as his response to those questions, a revisionist work that was meant to show that the common opinion was wrong in all major respects. Pericles was not responsible for the war but rather deserved praise for recognizing that it was inevitable and making intelligent plans to face it accordingly. Far from being the cause of Athenian suffering and defeat, Pericles' strategy was correct and would have triumphed had he not died too soon and had his plan not been reversed by incompetent and self-seeking successors. Most importantly, Pericles was not a demagogue nor even a democrat but a remarkable statesman who ruled the people rather than being ruled by them.

Thucydides sought to explode the beliefs that Cleon and Demosthenes had won a great victory at Sphacteria, which alone made it possible for Athens to survive and achieve an acceptable peace. He would discreetly present the case that his own condemnation for the loss of Amphipolis was a miscarriage of justice, like those imposed on other generals punished by the popular courts in the course of the war. He would show that the enormously popular Cleon, lavishly honored by the Athenian democracy, was a brutal, incompetent, and cowardly demagogue who had persuaded the Athenians to reject a Spartan offer that should have brought peace in 425.

He would demonstrate that the ignorant post-Periclean democracy had foolishly and unnecessarily launched the Sicilian expedition out of greed, the lust for power, and arrogant ambition. He would make the case that the terrible disaster the Athenians suffered in Sicily was not, as they believed, the fault of Nicias and his many errors but of the folly of a democracy run riot without the moderating leadership of a man like Pericles. Such, I believe, were Thucydides' motivations for seeking to reinterpret the major events of his life. His *History*, I suggest, was both an answer and a defense—not merely a history of his own times.

Such an assertion of Thucydides' humanity, of his passionate involvement in the events he describes and analyzes, goes against the long tradition that marveled at his disengagement, his almost divine objectivity. Rousseau says that Thucydides "reports the facts without judging them,"[1] and Nietzsche, rejecting "the morality-and-ideal swindle of the Socratic schools," observed that Thucydides was "the grand summation, the last manifestation of that strong, stern, hard matter-of-factness instinctive to the older Hellenes."[2] In this they eloquently agreed with a judgment that dated back to antiquity and that the German historians of the nineteenth century would enshrine as a model for all historians.

In spite of many assaults in recent decades that view remains wide-spread. Here is a typical opinion from a respected scholar:

> Thucydides seems to embody all the qualities that Nietzsche admired and did not always manage to embody himself. It is easy to understand the admiration. Almost all historians except the very dullest have some characteristic weakness: some complicity, idealization, identification; some impulse to indignation, to right wrongs, to deliver a message. It is often the source of their most interesting writing. But Thucydides seems immune. Surely no more lucid, unillusioned intelligence has ever applied itself to the writing of history.[3]

The case studies presented here argue otherwise. No historian is immune from human motives; the burden of this book has been to argue that Thucydides labored to revise opinions that he passionately wanted to refute. At the same time that he wrote for an anonymous audience in the future, intending his *History* to teach valuable general truths, he also wrote for his contemporaries to correct their erroneous opinions of the specific issues about which he felt indignation, aiming, "to right wrongs, to deliver a message." His work was surely meant to be a possession forever but also an *apologia pro vita sua*.

Thucydides may have been a man like the rest of us—subject to prejudices and inclined to focus on those aspects of the past that seemed to him the most telling and revealing, however much others might disagree with his point of view and his conclusions—but he was also a great man. His greatness lay chiefly in his insistence that the study of history was both a serious and a useful undertaking. He saw it not as an entertainment, like Homeric poetry, and not merely the commemoration of great deeds and men and events, like the *History* of Herodotus, but as the best device available for understanding human experience in a disciplined manner.

While cognizant of the pitfalls that stand in the way of discovering the truth, he nonetheless insisted on the most rigorous effort to pursue it without fear or favor. Serious people cannot use historical writing to better comprehend human behavior and, perhaps, to make wiser decisions if they cannot trust the writer to do his very best to ascertain what is true, and simply to get the story right. In almost every instance where we have found it necessary to disagree with Thucydides and to offer a different interpretation, the evidence that raised the doubt and furnished the material for a divergent reading comes from his own account.

Thucydides does not write as a modern historian would—the canons of source citation in use today would not be invented for millennia to come—but he invented the modern idea of careful, laborious, and skeptical examination of sources, and no writer in the ancient Graeco-Roman world equaled him in this respect. Because Thucydides, moreover, was writing contemporary history, most of his sources would have been oral, and thus much harder to check and compare than the written documents modern students of contemporary history today have available. We would like him to have confronted contrary opinions directly and have made a detailed argument against them. Sometimes he did, although without naming the source with which he disagreed, but the interpretations he chose to revise were mainly not accounts written by other historians, available for dissection and contradiction. They were usually the general opinions of masses of ordinary people or the deeply held and largely unexamined prejudices of Thucydides' fellow exiles. Addressing such an audience called for powerful rhetorical skills more than careful annotation and source criticism.

Thucydides was also inventing a new kind of history, different from the *Genealogies* of Hecataeus; different from the mythography, ethnography, and local chronicles of his older contemporary Hellanicus; and different from Herodotus. Where Herodotus wrote of the recent past and delved deeply into the distant past, painted on a broad canvas the portrait of many nations and peoples, and was interested in their religious, social, and cultural practices, Thucydides focused his powerful critical eye almost entirely on the present; he fixed his gaze intently on the Greeks, and especially on his own Athenians; finally he concentrated the reader's attention on the war, its diplomacy, and its politics. In so doing he effectively invented political history. For him, as for Lord Acton, "History is past politics."

In the ancient world Thucydides' focus on politics routed the broader but shallower one of his predecessors. Herodotus, with his meandering style full of discursive side trips into the customs and habits of various cultures and his serious consideration of the causal role of the gods in human affairs, did not become the model for what was thought to be the best historical writing in antiquity. Polybius and the Romans Sallust, Livy, Tacitus, and Ammianus Marcellinus were the great historical writers of their eras, and they wrote chiefly about their own times, their own nations, and, especially, about war and politics.

During the Renaissance and the early modern period of European history Polybius, whose history of Rome's conquest of the Mediterranean world followed the Thucydidean model, and Tacitus, who examined politics in Rome, were the favored historians. In the seventeenth century Thomas Hobbes published the first complete English translation of Thucydides' *History* directly from the Greek original in 1628. "Thucydides," he wrote, "is one, who, though he never digress to read a lecture, moral or political, upon his own text, nor enter into men's hearts further than the acts themselves evidently guide him, is yet accounted the most politic historiographer that ever writ."[4] That is, he provides both an instructive account of and guide to an understanding of the subjects included in the category "politics": the internal political competition within a city-state or nation and interstate relations in time of peace and war.

The writers of the eighteenth century, with their interest in the manners and civilization of earlier periods and of the entire world, rediscovered Herodotus, although as philosophical historians themselves they also admired Thucydides' search for a useful history that sought the causes of events in the lasting elements in human nature and the human condition. The nineteenth century, however, especially in Germany, saw the triumph of political history and the eclipse of Herodotus by Thucydides.

In the first part of the twentieth century and into the cold war era the Thucydidean approach so dominated historical studies that it was necessary to remind ourselves that historiography must combine the story of politics, diplomacy, and war with that of society, culture, and civilization, and a movement away from purely Thucydidean political history grew stronger. By now the world of historical writing has changed so much as to make these remarks seem dated. In much of the American academy "extra-political history" has all but supplanted political history. The most famous and influential of the social historians, Fernand Braudel, dismissed the elements of politics, diplomacy, and war as mere *évènements,* transient and trivial in comparison with the greater and longer-lasting issues posed by geography, demography, and social and economic developments over long periods of time. In his best known work, *The Mediterranean and the Mediterranean World in the Age of Philip II,* the political decisions, events, and developments are of small moment compared to the inanimate and impersonal forces that shape societies over the very long run.

It is clear enough that such forces exist and that they have considerable impact on politics, war, and diplomacy, chiefly in establishing the limits of what is possible. Within those limits, however, individuals and groups of human beings make decisions that are of vital importance, and those decisions that are military, diplomatic, and political influence ever larger groups of people in ways that can affect the very existence of peoples, nations, and the human race. It is important that we understand the underlying conditions and forces (geographic, demographic, anthropological, psychological, etc.) that help to frame and influence the choices that people make in these decisive realms. But the historian must connect this knowledge to the specific facts, decisions, and events made in the public arena, that is, in the world of politics.

Herodotus, for all his wanderings into geographical, sociological, and anthropological descriptions and analyses, tried to connect them, however remotely, with his major aims as set forth at the beginning of his history of the Persian Wars: "This is the result of the inquiry of Herodotus of Halicarnassus, published so that time may not erase the memory of past events from the mind of mankind, so that the great and marvelous deeds of the Greeks and the barbarians should not be without fame, and especially to explain why they fought against one another." It was those "great and marvelous deeds" in the wars against Persia and the attempt to explain why they came about that justified the whole effort, including the broader inquiry into earlier societies and distant peoples. Outside the narrow purviews of professional historians in the academy these are the issues that today still spark the interest of most readers of history: the internal competition of factions and the competition between nations in war and peace—in short, political history.

In this respect they agree with the philosopher Aristotle, a man with as broad a set of interests as anyone who ever lived; of all his pursuits he held that of politics as supreme. At the end of his *Nicomachean Ethics* he sets out the issues that most urgently require study:

> let us study what sorts of influence preserve and destroy states, and what sorts preserve or destroy the particular kinds of constitution, and to what causes it is due that some are well and others ill administered. When these have been studied we shall perhaps be more likely to see with a comprehensive view, which constitution is best, and how each must be ordered, and what laws and customs it must use, if it is to be at its best.[5]

For Aristotle this work was of supreme importance. Every art and investigation aims at achieving some good, but some of these pursuits are subordinate to others, as bridle-making is to horsemanship, which is a master art, that is, architectonic. Architectonic ends are more desirable than subordinate ends, and the master end of all is the Supreme Good. That is the object of the most authoritative science, the science of politics.

Since most people live in states, and it is states that determine how they will be educated and since politics controls even the most important human faculties such as strategy, economic management, and tactics of persuasion, politics, to some degree, controls all fields of knowledge. Politics, after all, lays down what people may or must do and what they may or must not do.

> Therefore, the Good of man must be the end of the science of Politics. For even though it be the case that the Good is the same for the individual and for the state, nevertheless, the good of the state is manifestly a greater and more perfect good, both to attain and to preserve. To secure the good of one person only is better than nothing; but to secure the good of a nation or a state is a nobler and more divine achievement.[6]

Aristotle concerns himself chiefly with the politics and constitutional arrangements within a particular state, but the other elements that combine to create the fuller conception of politics are no less powerfully significant. We live in an age unparalleled in its interest in and focus on the individual, one in which many regard considerations of politics in its widest sense either as secondary or even irrelevant, on the one hand, or menacing, on the other, even as events reveal the critical nature of such considerations. Surely the twentieth century has demonstrated the decisive importance of whether we live under a totalitarian regime or under a democracy, whether we are at war or live in peace, whether we win the wars that we wage or lose them. One need not be an Aristotelian or even an ancient Greek to understand the centrality of politics to the human condition.

Herodotus deserves the title of "the father of history," but Thucydides was the father of political history. That is the chief reason why his work has deservedly won the highest praise and the most serious attention over the millennia, whatever we may think of his judgments on the events of his time. His *History* raises for the first time countless questions about the development of human societies that remain very relevant today. He looks deeply into the causes of war, drawing a distinction between those openly alleged and those more fundamental but less obvious.

His work considers the reasons why states and their citizens go to war and suggests that fear, honor, and interest are the most fundamental—categories that are still helpful and ring true to this day.

He examines the role of economics in the development of human society toward civilization, and the military and naval power economic strength makes possible. He analyzes and emphasizes the critical role of financial resources in the conflicts of his day, showing how they enable or limit different strategic approaches to war.

His famous observation that "war is a violent teacher" (3.82.2) comments on the tendency of people to abandon traditional restraints of custom, religion, even of family ties under the extreme pressures caused by war and plague. This is especially true, he tells us, in the case of revolution and civil war, where factional hatred overrides all morality, where words are forced to change their meaning to suit political purposes. Civil wars and revolutions, he points out, are more likely to break out in wartime, not merely in the states engaged in the conflict but in others, since each faction is encouraged to seek alliance with one of the combatants as a means of gaining power.

Thucydides' *History* also examines the strengths and weaknesses of alliance between states. A hegemonic state may gain power by having allies useful in war, but reliance on those states may compel the hegemonic state to go to war against its own interests in order to preserve the alliance. Bismarck observed that when the international system is riven into competing alliances a state may need allies, but in that case it is essential "to be the rider, not the horse." Thucydides' account shows how difficult an assignment that can be.

Thucydides also examines the characteristics and advantages and disadvantages of different kinds of polity. He praises the oligarchic mixed constitution of Sparta because of its unmatched stability but cites the Corinthians' critique of its slowness to react to danger and the disadvantage this incurs in the face of the threat from the quicksilver actions that characterize the Athenian democracy. His analysis of that democracy is central to his entire work. He understands the benefits provided by such a constitution and the sea power on which it rests, but he is critical of the excessive confidence and ambition to which it can give rise. His own judgment is that such a regime can be effective only when led by a strong, wise, competent, unselfish leader like Pericles. Without such guidance a true democracy is likely to go astray and follow the advice of unfit, irresponsible, and selfish demagogic leaders who will lead the state into factious disputes, grandiose and dangerous undertakings, and disaster. Since no state can rely regularly upon finding leaders like Pericles, Thucydides prefers a constitution like that of the Five Thousand, which the Athenians adopted very briefly in 411. He called it "a moderate blend of the few and the many"—what we might call a limited democracy or a broad oligarchy.

These issues, and many others like them, are the subjects Thucydides addresses in his magnificent *History*. They are questions that remain ever vital in the critically important areas that are his concern: politics, international relations, and war. They remain inescapably crucial to the understanding and conduct of human affairs, regardless of the intellectual fashions of our time. That we can study his *History* and come to conclusions different from his is far less important than his achievement in inventing a kind of history and a kind of questioning that have shaped and improved the quality of human thought and continue to do so today.

The purpose of Thucydides was to set before us the truth as he saw it, but his truth need not be ours. If we are to use his history with profit, as we can and must, we must distinguish between the evidence he presents and the interpretation he puts on it. Only then can we use it, as he wished us to, as a "possession forever."

NOTES

Translations from Thucydides are from Charles Foster Smith's in the Loeb Classical Library (Cambridge, Mass.: Harvard University Press; and London: William Heinemann Ltd., 1930), sometimes emended by me. Those from Aristophanes are by an anonymous translator, published as Aristophanes, *The Eleven Comedies* (New York: Horace Liveright, n.d.), also emended by me. All others are my own except when otherwise attributed.

Introduction

1. Unattributed references are to Thucydides' *History*.
2. Marshall's words come from a speech at Princeton University on February 22, 1947. Cited by W. R. Connor, *Thucydides* (Princeton: Princeton University Press, 1984), 1.
3. All dates are B.C.E.
4. Xenophon *Hellenica* 2.3.23.
5. H. T. Wade-Gery, "Thucydides," *Oxford Classical Dictionary*, 3rd ed., rev. (Oxford: Oxford University Press, 2003), 1517.
6. H. Diels and W. Kranz, *Die Fragmente der Vorsokratiker*, "Xenophanes," frg. 14–16 (Berlin, Weidmann, 1934–1937).
7. Ibid., "Protagoras," frg. 4.
8. The influence of the Hippocratics on Thucydides is the theme of C. N. Cochrane's *Thucydides and the Science of History* (Oxford: Oxford University Press, 1929).
9. Ibid.
10. *The Art*, chapt. 11, cited by B. Farrington, *Greek Science* (Baltimore: Penguin Books), 74–75. The italics are Farrington's.
11. Cochrane, *Science of History*, 26.
12. John H. Finley Jr., *Thucydides* (Cambridge, Mass.: Harvard University Press, 1942), 312.
13. R. G. Collingwood, *The Idea of History* (New York: Oxford University Press, 1956), 31.
14. It may be argued that there is another possibility for such speeches, i.e., that they represent what Thucydides thinks the speaker ought to have

said on the particular occasion. If this be so, such speeches would tell us as much about the mind of Thucydides as about the speaker's. For an explanation of my interpretation of the speeches see Donald Kagan, "The Speeches in Thucydides and the Mytilene Debate," *Yale Classical Studies* no. 24 (Cambridge: Cambridge University Press, 1975), 71–94.

15. Connor, *Thucydides*, 233.

16. Donald Kagan, "The First Revisionist Historian," *Commentary*, May 1988, 43–49.

17. G. E. M. de Ste. Croix, "The Character of the Athenian Empire," Historia 3 (1954), 3. In practice Ste. Croix did not always follow his own advice. In defending his unique explanation for the origins of the war he says, "the picture I have drawn is thoroughly based on the evidence of the most reliable sources, Thucydides above all, and anyone who dislikes that picture had better begin by trying to discredit Thucydides, if he can." (*The Origins of the Peloponnesian War*, Ithaca and London, 1972, 290). For a critique of his work see my review in *American Journal of Philology* 96 (1975): 90–93.

Chapter One: Thucydides the Revisionist

1. For details, see Simon Hornblower, *A Commentary on Thucydides*, 3 vols. (Oxford: Clarendon Press, 1991–2008), 1:49.

2. Ibid., 1.57–58.

3. G. E. M. de Ste. Croix, *The Origins of the Peloponnesian War* (Oxford and Ithaca: Cornell University Press, 1972), 295, cites passages in Andocides, Plato, and Aeschines to that effect.

Chapter Two: Causes of the War—Corcyra

1. The debate over an alliance with Corcyra, the first step on the road to war, carried over to a second day, a rare event. Even then, the treaty had to be softened from an offensive and defensive alliance to one purely defensive before the assembly approved it.

2. See also Plutarch *Pericles* 29.3.

3. Aristophanes *Acharnians* 515–22.

4. Ibid., 532–39.

5. Aristophanes *Peace* 601–9.

6. Ibid., 615–18.

7. Ibid., 619–27.

8. Plutarch *Pericles* 31.

9. Anaxagoras was Pericles' teacher and a famous rationalist theorizing about nature.

10. Plutarch *Pericles* 32.

11. Diodorus 12.38–39.

12. A standard translation of this vital and much debated passage is the following by Smith in the Loeb Classical Library: "The reasons why they broke it [the peace] and the grounds of their quarrel I have first set forth, that no one may ever have to inquire for what cause the Hellenes became involved in so great a war. The truest explanation, although it has been the least often advanced, I believe to have been the growth of Athens to greatness, which brought fear to the Lacedaemonians and forced them to war. But the reasons publicly alleged on either side which led them to break the truce and involved them in the war were as follows." A similar understanding may be found in the translation of Jacqueline de Romilly in the Budé edition, *La Guerre du Péloponnèse*, 5 vols. (Paris: Les Belles Lettres, 1953–72), and that of Antonio Maddalena, *Thucydidis Historiarum Liber Primus* (Florence: LaNuova Italia, 1961), 3:98. The English translation of Richard Crawley, based on the same understanding, is very free, but in my opinion closer to the real sense of the passage than any other. It deserves quotation: "The real cause I consider to be the one which was formerly most kept out of sight. The growth of the power of Athens, and the alarm which this inspired in Lacedaemon, made war inevitable. Still it is well to give the grounds alleged by either side, which led to the dissolution of the treaty and the breaking out of the war." (New York: Modern Library, 1951, 15.) For a valuable discussion of the scholarship bearing on this passage see Hornblower, *Comm.*, 1.64–66.

13. Diodorus 11.50.

14. See also Plutarch *Cimon* 17.2.

15. Diodorus 12.10.3–4.

16. Wilhelm Dittenberger, *Sylloge inscriptionum Graecarum* #6 (Leipzig: S. Hirzel, 1924).

17. Plutarch *Pericles* 29.1.

Chapter Three: Causes of the War—From Corcyra to the Megarian Decree

1. Plutarch *Pericles* 29.5.

2. Ibid., 30.3.

3. Ibid., 30.1.

Chapter Four: The Strategy of Pericles

1. *Fates*, cited by Plutarch *Pericles* 33.7.

2. Plutarch *Pericles* 33.5–6.

3. For a full discussion of Pericles' strategy see Donald Kagan, *The Archidamian War* (Ithaca: Cornell University Press, 1974), 24–42.

4. For the details of the calculations see Kagan, *Archidamian War*, 36–40.

5. Plutarch *Pericles* 35.1.

6. Ibid., 34.3–4.

7. Ibid., 38.1.

8. Ibid., 38.3.

9. Ibid., 38.4.

10. Gaetano de Sanctis, *Pericle* (Milan and Messina: G. Principato, 1944), 253–54.

11. Georg Busolt, *Griechische Geschichte*, vol. 3, pt. 2 (Gotha: F.a. Perthes, 1904), 901. In a later generation Hermann Bengtson, *Griechische Geschichte,* 3rd ed. (Munich: Beck, 1965), 221n5, holds very much the same view.

12. Busolt, *Griechische Geschichte*, 1015. A. W. Gomme, *Historical Commentary on Thucydides*, vol. 2 (Oxford: Clarendon Press, 1945), 277, suggests that not lack of money but a shortage of men explains the use of hoplites. In this case he is certainly wrong, for by this time the men who had rowed the one hundred ships around the Peloponnese, most of whom were necessarily thetes and not hoplites, were again available to row the much smaller fleet that would be necessary to bring the one thousand soldiers to Lesbos.

13. B. D. Meritt, H. T. Wade-Gery, and M. F. McGregor, *The Athenian Tribute Lists* (Cambridge, Mass.: Harvard University Press, 1939–53), 3:343, set the figure at 945.

14. Busolt, *Griechische Geschichte*, 1016.

15. Meritt, Wade-Gery, and McGregor, *ATL*, 1:196–99.

16. Plato *Gorgias* 516a.

17. For an excellent discussion of the entire process see Gregory F. Viggiano, "Unreported Speeches and Selection in Thucydides," (Ph.D diss., Yale University, 2005), 71–119.

18. Plutarch *Pericles* 11–12; see also Donald Kagan, *The Outbreak of the Peloponnesian War* (Ithaca: Cornell University Press, 1969), 142–45. Jacqueline Romilly, *Thucydides and Athenian Imperialism*, trans. Philip Thody (Oxford: Blackwell, 1963), 127, correctly identifies the *apragmones* as "the people hostile to the empire, who, through fear, would have liked to act in a virtuous manner," and connects them with the opposition to the empire going back to its origin. In her translation of Thucydides, in the Budé edition, vol. 2. pt. 1 book 2 (1962), 100, she rightly says that Pericles' argument seems to be directed against "a very determined group of adversaries."

19. On the question of the speech's authenticity see Kagan, *Archidamian War*, Appendix B, 365–67.

Chapter Five: Was Periclean Athens a Democracy?

1. Busolt, *Griechische Geschichte*, 470.
2. Ibid., 497–99.
3. He conceded that Pericles "would nevertheless be held within bounds by the fact that the people, by means of the *epicheirotonia* that took place each prytany, could suspend him from office and place him before a court" and that "as the official power of Pericles was dependent on popular election and the mood of the people, he could only steer the entire ship of state in the direction he set if he could hold the leadership of the popular assembly in his hand" (ibid., 499).
4. Plutarch *Pericles*. 3.1–2.
5. Ibid., 5.1–3.
6. Ibid., 15.2–3.
7. Ibid., 3.3; 24.6.
8. Ibid., 13.6.
9. Ibid., 31.2.
10. Ibid., 31.4.
11. Ibid., 32.
12. Ibid., 32.1.
13. F. J. Frost, "Pericles, Thucydides son of Melesias, and Athenian Politics Before the War," *Historia* 13 (1964): 396.
14. Plutarch *Pericles* 32.3.
15. F. J. Frost, "Pericles and Dracontides," *Journal of Hellenic Studies* 84 (1964): 72.
16. Aristotle *Constitution of the Athenians* 16.8.
17. For accounts of the trial see J. F. Roberts, *Accountability in Athenian Government* (Madison: University of Wisconsin Press, 1982), 30–34; Viggiano, "Unreported Speeches," 71–119.
18. Aristotle *Constitution of the Athenians* 48.4
19. Ibid., 61.2
20. Ibid., 50.2.
21. Pseudo-Xenophon *Constitution of the Athenians* 1.1.
22. Plato *Gorgias* 515.
23. Aristotle *Politics* 1274a.
24. Malcolm F. McGregor, "The Politics of the Historian Thucydides," *Phoenix* 10 (1956): 102.

Chapter Six: Cleon's Lucky Victory at Pylos

1. See chapter 4 of this book.
2. Aristophanes *Acharnians* 299–302; *Knights* 136–37.

3. Aristophanes *Acharnians* 664.
4. Aristophanes *Knights* 40–44.
5. Aristotle *Constitution of Athens* 28.3.
6. Plutarch *Nicias* 8.3.
7. W. R. Connor, *The New Politicians of Fifth-Century Athens* (Princeton: Princeton University Press, 1971), 162.
8. See chapter 4.
9. A. Andrewes, "The Mytilene Debate: Thucydides 3.36–49," *Phoenix* 16 (1962): 75.
10. Ibid., 76.
11. F. M. Cornford, *Thucydides Mythistoricus* (London: E. Arnold, 1907), 88ff., and J de Romilly, *Thucydides and Athenian Imperialism*, 173ff., have elaborated this point. Gomme, *HCT*, 3:488–89, however, argues that *tychê* does not necessarily imply chance or accident, but often merely contemporaneity. Even he admits that the word is employed frequently, and we must add that the frequency is unique in Thucydides. It seems inescapable that Thucydides portrays the victory at Pylos and Sphacteria as the result of extraordinary luck.
12. K. J. Beloch, *Die Attische Politik seit Perikles* (Leipzig: Teubner, 1884), 23.
13. A. G. Woodhead, "Thucydides' Portrait of Cleon," *Mnemosyne* 13 (1960): 311, points out that "We are again told that he was *pithanotatos* [most influential] with the *plethos* [people], and this lends to the description, *demagogos* [demagogue] a sinister flavour, even if the word was not yet the 'smear word' it later became."
14. De Romilly, *Guerre du Péloponnèse*, 3:xiii.
15. Aristophanes *Knights* 280, 702, 709, 766, 1404.
16. Hornblower, *Comm.*, 2:94. He points out that "Thoudippos is an exceedingly rare name at Athens."
17. Among those arguing in favor of Cleon's predominant role in the reassessment decree are Beloch, *Attische Politik*, 40, and *Griechische Geschichte*, 2nd ed. (Strassburg, Berlin, and Leipzig: K. J. Trübner, 1912–1927), vol. 2, pt. 1, 330–31; Eduard Meyer, *Geschichte des Altertums*, 5th ed. (Stuttgart and Berlin: J. G. Cotta, 1884; reprinted 1954 and 1956), 4:107–8; Busolt, *Griechische Geschichte*, vol. 3, pt. 2, 1117; F. E. Adcock "The Archidamian War," *Cambridge Ancient History*, vol. 5 (Cambridge: Cambridge University Press, 1940), 236; Bengtson, *Griechische Geschichte*, 226; Woodhead "Portrait of Cleon," 301–2; and R. Meiggs and D. Lewis, eds., *A Selection of Greek Historical Inscriptions to the End of the Fifth Century B.C.* (Oxford: Oxford University Press, 1969), 196–97.
18. Hornblower, *Comm.*, 2:94, gives a few examples: "Gomme described

this as 'the strangest of all omissions in Thucydides', Andrewes called it 'the most spectacular omission of all', and M. I. Finley listed it among the 'astonishing gaps and silences' in Thucydides, 'whole chunks of history that are left out altogether'." This consensus has been challenged by L. Kallet-Marx in *Money, Expense, and Naval Power in Thucydides' History 1–5.24* (Berkeley: University of California Press, 1993), 164–70. She argues that Thucydides' failure to mention the decree should not be surprising, even though her main purpose is to show that, contrary to the common opinion, he had a serious interest in financial resources. One keen-eyed reviewer points to some difficulties in her argument: "There are two main contentions in this work: firstly, that the importance of financial resources is not neglected in Thucydides; and secondly, that Thucydides understood well that *dynamis* requires *chremata*, because the latter provides (in the form of *dapanes,* when *chremata* yields *periousia*) sea power, which is the basis of *arche.* These contentions are very convincingly supported with clear and lucid arguments, and particularly with refreshingly skillful handling of epigraphical evidence. The irony is, however, that the success of the attempt itself seems to strengthen the very view that the author originally sets out to dislodge. For her work irrefutably demonstrates that Thucydides' interest in finance is strictly limited to a very closely confined area in which *chremata* was essential to sea power, and that he completely neglected or ignored financial matters that fell outside this narrowly defined scope. Thucydides' paramount interest is in *dynamis,* and he pays attention to *chremata* only because it forms an indispensable component of *dynamis.* In other words, he would not have treated any aspect *of chremata,* had he not recognized its fundamental relationship with *dynamis.* In this sense, therefore, a conventional view that he neglected financial matters *per se* seems to remain valid." Haruo Konishi, review of Kallet-Marx, *Phoenix* 50 (1996): 82. Simon Hornblower is more sympathetic with some of her views, but I agree with Konishi's judgment in *Classical Review* 44 (1994): 333–34, that "Th. stresses finances when he wants to, and that he often does; but that his coverage of financial matters, as of some others, is a touch more episodic, uneven and oblique than K.-M allows." I have argued above that his understanding of the importance of money for success in the war was keen from the beginning, but that he refrains from giving the subject its due when that would detract from the message he wishes to convey. That seems to me clearly at work here and leads me to continue to accept the traditional view that finds the omission remarkable.

19. Translated by Meiggs and Lewis in *Greek Historical Inscriptions*, 193.

20. Ibid., 194.
21. Ibid., 196–97.

Chapter Seven: Thucydides and Cleon at Amphipolis

1. For a discussion of some of the explanations see A. W. Gomme, *Historical Commentary on Thucydides*, vol. 3 (Oxford: Clarendon Press, 1956), 585–88; and H. D. Westlake, *Essays on the Greek Historians and Greek History* (Manchester: University of Manchester Press, 1969), 135–36.
2. R. A. Bauman, "A Message from Amphipolis," *Acta Classica* 11 (1968): 171n9.
3. Ibid., 179.
4. Ammianus Marcellinus *Life of Thucydides* A 23, B 46; Anonymous *Life of Thucydides* 3; see Busolt, *Griechische Geschichte*, 625n1.
5. See Gomme, *HCT*, 3:585. Thucydides' notorious hostility toward Cleon in his history makes the case even more plausible.
6. E.g., G. B. Grundy, *Thucydides and the History of His Age*, 2nd ed., vol. 1, *Thucydides and the History of his Age* (Oxford: Blackwell, 1948), 30; E. Meyer, *Forschungen zur alten Geschichte*, vol. 2 (Halle: Niemeyer, 1899), 343, says he tells the story "without losing even one word in his defense."
7. Westlake, *Essays*, 123–37, has shown in detail how Thucydides has put forward a most effective defense of his action by his choice and omission of evidence. Bauman, "Message from Amphipolis," assumes that the Thucydidean account is an apologia.
8. For the fullest and most vigorous defense of Thucydides see Hans Delbrück, *Die Strategie des Perikles* (Berlin: G. Reimer, 1890), 178–88. He is followed by Meyer, *Geschichte des Altertums*, 4:120n1. The judgment of Finley, *Thucydides*, 200, is typical: "It was for this failure—a failure which, given the forces then and previously at his command, would seem to have been unavoidable—that Thucydides was exiled. . . . He seems to have been a victim of the people's exorbitant hopes. Indeed, after Delium, there must have been a still greater demand for scapegoats."
9. For an account of these, see Westlake, *Essays*, 135ff.
10. Thucydides tells us nothing of the fate of Eucles, nor is he mentioned elsewhere. The silence of all the sources gives us no reason to believe that he was accused when he got home.
11. Honorable exceptions are Woodhead, "Thucydides' Portrait of Cleon," 304; B. Baldwin, "Cleon's Strategy at Amphipolis," *Proceedings of the African Classical Association* 11 (1968): 211–12; and, especially, Gomme, *HCT*, 3: 631–32.
12. Gomme, *HCT*, 3:632.

13. The fundamental study is by A. B. West and B. D. Meritt in "Cleon's Amphipolitan Campaign and the Assessment List of 421," *American Journal of Archaeology* 29 (1925): 54–69. See also Meritt, Wade-Gery, and McGregor, *ATL*, 3:347–48. Some have resisted giving Cleon credit for this achievement, either by denying that the assessment was realistic and that Athens necessarily controlled all the cities listed, or by giving Nicias credit for their capture. These arguments are satisfactorily answered by Woodhead, "Thucydides Portrait of Cleon," 304–6.

14. Woodhead, "Thucydides' Portrait of Cleon," 305.

15. The word *malakia* may mean "softness," "weakness," or "lack of energy," but here, where it is contrasted with *tolma*, "courage," "boldness," "daring," I agree with Gomme, *HCT*, 3:637, that here it must mean "cowardice."

16. Gomme, *HCT*, 3:637.

17. J. G. Frazer on Pausanias 1.29.13, cited by Gomme, *HCT*, 3:652.

18. Adcock, *CAH*, 5:248.

19. Busolt, *Griechische Geschichte*, 3:2, 1.181, n. 2.

19. A. W. Gomme, "Thucydides and Cleon, the Second Battle of Amphipolis," *Hellenika* 13 (1954): 7.

20. Ibid.

21. Gomme, *HCT*, 3:652.

22. Diodorus 12.74.2. While his account of the battle itself is worthless, there was no good reason why Diodorus, or his probable source, Ephorus, neither of whom is particularly friendly to demagogues, democrats, or Cleon, should have abandoned the account of Thucydides to invent Cleon's bravery. Most likely, they are merely reporting an alternate account, although Diodorus is fond of describing heroic deaths of generals. As Baldwin, "Cleon's Strategy at Amphipolis," 214, points out, moreover, there is support for the idea of a pro-Cleon tradition in Pseudo-Demosthenes *Second Speech against Boeotus* 25, where Cleon is spoken of as a great general because of Pylos.

23. Pausanias 1.29.11–13.

Chapter Eight: The Decision for a Sicilian Expedition

1. One distinguished scholar has gone so far as to say of Books 6 and 7 of Thucydides, "We can do little but paraphrase his famous narrative." W. S. Ferguson, "The Athenian Expedition to Sicily," *Cambridge Ancient History*, 5:282n.

2. Among the many who have seen the apparent contradiction is Gomme, *HCT*, 2:195–96, and "Four Passages in Thucydides," *Journal of Hellenic Studies* 71 (1951): 70–72.

3. The words I have translated as "mob" are *ho de polys homilos.*

4. For a discussion of the controversy see Doanld Kagan, *The Peace of Nicias and the Sicilian Expedition* (Ithaca: Cornell University Press, 1981), 167.

5. He does not tell us what Pericles said or thought about the Corcyraean request for an alliance in 433, and we must rely on Plutarch (*Pericles* 29.1) to know that "[Pericles] persuaded the people to send aid" to Corcyra. Thucydides does not even mention the meeting of the assembly and the debate that must have preceded the dispatch of a second fleet to reinforce the ten ships first sent to Corcyra. Again, it is Plutarch who supplies the arguments that his opponents used to force his hand. Another example, the debate on the fate of Mytilene, presents an almost perfect parallel to Thucydides' account of the assemblies in 415. On that occasion, too, there was a first assembly in which important decisions were reached that were subsequently changed by a second assembly. There, too, Thucydides gives only a brief account, reporting no speeches but only the actions taken and the general mood that led the people to vote as they did. Only in writing about the second assembly does he mention that Cleon and Diodotus had been the chief opponents in the first assembly as they were in the second. He gives no account of what they said on the earlier occasion, though it is evident that Diodotus, at least, used different arguments each time. Again, in his account of the Athenian expedition to Sicily in 427, he gives no account whatever of the assembly that must have voted it. There are no speeches, no arguments offered by proponents or opponents, no names of partisans of either position, only Thucydides' own statement of what were the pretended and real purposes of the expedition (3.86).

6. Meiggs and Lewis, *Greek Historical Inscriptions*, 78. See also A. W. Gomme, A. Andrews, and K. J. Dover, *Historical Commentary on Thucydides*, vol. 4, (Oxford: Clarendon Press, 1970), 223–27.

7. Plutarch *Nicias,* 12.

8. Diodorus 12.83.6.

9. See Kagan, *Peace of Nicias*, 178n68.

10. Thucydides repeats the same attribution of motive to Nicias in 6.24.1. We have no reason to doubt that he understood Nicias' intention.

11. Thucydides (6.25.1) does not mention Demostratus but speaks only of "a certain Athenian." Plutarch *Nicias* 12.4 and *Alcibiades* 18.2 provides the name.

12. Plutarch *Nicias* 12.4.

13. A striking sample of the contradiction between his interpretation and his narrative is this: at the very beginning of Book 6 he tells us that the Athenians "wanted to sail against Sicily again with a force bigger than the one led by Laches and Eurymedon." The force brought back by Eurymedon and

his colleagues in 424 consisted of sixty triremes, exactly the number the Athenians voted to send to Sicily in the first assembly of 415. Dover, *HCT*, 4:197, noting that the number of ships on both occasions is identical, suggests that the bigger force mentioned by Thucydides "must therefore refer to the greater scale of land forces now envisaged." But there is no reason to believe that the assembly that voted to send sixty ships to Sicily in 415 voted to send greater land forces than accompanied the earlier expedition.

Chapter Nine: Who Was Responsible for the Sicilian Disaster?

1. Pausanias 1.11–12
2. See Kagan, *Peace of Nicias*, 215n19.
3. Plutarch *Nicias* 15.3.
4. Ibid.
5. Aristophanes *Birds* 640; Plutarch *Nicias* 16.8.
6. Plutarch *Nicias* 2.4, 6.
7. Dover, *HCT*, 4:426.
8. Plutarch *Nicias* 23.5.
9. There has been some debate about this passage. Part of the problem is how to understand the word *aretê*, which we translate "virtue." Some want to modify it with another word in the sentence to produce a translation like Jowett's: "No one of the Hellenes in my time was less deserving of so miserable an end; for he lived in the practice of every customary virtue." Good and sufficient arguments against this version are provided by Dover in *HCT*, 4:463.
10. Pausanias 1.29.11–12.
11. Dover, *HCT*, 4:461.

Conclusion

1. Jean-Jacques Rousseau, *Emile: or, On Education*, trans. Allan Bloom (New York: Basic Books, 1979), 239.
2. Friedrich Nietzsche, "What I Owe to the Ancients," in *Twilight of the Gods*, trans. John Burrows, *A History of Histories*. (New York: Alfred A. Knopf, 2008), p. 50.
3. John Burrows, *A History of Histories*. (New York: Knopf, 2008), p. 50.
4. Thomas Hobbes, "To the Readers," *The History of the Grecian War by Thucydides*, in *English Works*, 11 vols., ed. Sir William Molesworth (London, 1843), 8:viii.
5. Aristotle *Nicomachean Ethics* 109467–8. Slightly amended translation by H. Rackham, Loeb Classical Library (Cambridge, Mass.: Harvard University Press, 1926).
6. Ibid, 1.2.1094b.8.

INDEX